MACROECONOMIC THEORY

Keynesian and Neo-Walrasian Models

MACROECONOMIC THEORY

Keynesian and Neo-Walrasian Models

John A. Sawyer

Professor of Economics
University of Toronto

upp

University of Pennsylvania Press

Philadelphia

First published 1989 by
Harvester Wheatsheaf
66 Wood Lane End, Hemel Hempstead,
Hertfordshire, HP2 4RG
A division of
Simon & Schuster International Group

First published in North America 1989
by University of Pennsylvania Press,
418 Service Drive, Philadelphia,
Pennsylvania 19104-6097

Printed and bound in Great Britain by
BPCC Wheatons Ltd, Exeter

Library of Congress Cataloging-in-Publication Data

ISBN 0-8122-1296-7
Library of Congress Catalog Card Number: 89-050195

CONTENTS

Chapter 3 A model from Keynes's *General Theory*   62

PREFACE

This book is basically a review of the literature on macroeconomic theory written for senior undergraduates or beginning graduate students. Hopefully it will also be of use to economists who are interested in the evolution of modern macroeconomic theory. It assumes that readers have had an introduction to both micro- and macroeconomics and are familiar with basic statistical and mathematical concepts. Although the advanced student of economics should know calculus and matrix algebra, all algebra involving such knowledge has been placed in appendices so that the reader who prefers to do so may omit them without loss of continuity.

The book grew out of my experiences in teaching macroeconomic theory. It has, however, its roots in a project started in the mid-1960s at the Institute for Policy Analysis of the University of Toronto which led to the development of the TRACE econometric model of the Canadian Economy and my participation in the 1970s in Project LINK. I became increasingly convinced that econometric models must be solidly based on microeconomic theoretical foundations. Moreover, I began to feel that a synthesis of mainstream macroeconomic theory was not feasible and that the model builder should select a view of the world before building his model: a neo-Walrasian or Keynesian view.

In the classroom, I also became convinced that students could only understand modern theory if they knew something about its historical origins. Moreover, students should be made aware that theory is continually evolving as researchers work within the boundaries of specified scientific research programmes.

Appreciation is expressed to the students in Economics 325H at the University of Toronto on whom various drafts of the book were used as a text and from whom many useful suggestions for improvement were received. To my colleague James Pesando, I express my thanks for his comments on drafts of Chapters 5–7 which resulted in substantial rewriting. Martin Timbrell of Exeter University made some useful suggestions. An anonymous reader's comments on my interpretation of Keynes's *General Theory* and on the policies advocated by A.C. Pigou were also most helpful in clarifying my thinking. I am indebted to my colleague Yehuda Kotowitz who provided much of the theoretical under-pinnings for the TRACE model and to Sir James Ball of the London Business School for raising many theoretical issues at Project LINK meetings. Errors in the final version are entirely my responsibility.

The writing of the book was enabled by leaves granted by the University of Toronto and the writing was begun while the author was a visitor in the Depart-ment of Economics of the University of Arizona during the winter semester of 1981. The hospitality of that university is gratefully acknowledged.

Bristol Harbour Village

ACKNOWLEDGEMENTS

Permission to quote from the writings of Arthur Cecil Pigou has been granted by The Macmillan Press Ltd of London and Basingstoke. Permission to quote from the *The Collected Writings of John Maynard Keynes* has been granted by The Macmillan Press Ltd and by the Cambridge University Press. Franco Modigliani kindly gave his permission for the lengthy quotation from his *The Debate over Stabilization Policy*. Frank Hahn, Robert Lucas, Jr., and Joseph Stiglitz were also very cooperative in giving permission to quote from their writings. Cambridge University Press gave permission to quote from the writings of Mark Blaug, S.J. Latsis, Michio Morishima, David Ricardo, and E.R. Weintraub. Oxford University Press gave permission to quote from the writings of Sir John Hicks. Unwin Hyman gave permission to quote from Leon Walras's *Elements of Pure Economics*. Permissions to quote were freely given by members of the Association of American University Presses and this was used for quotations from the *Canadian Journal of Economics*, the *Journal of Money, Credit and Banking*, and the MIT Press. All other quotations were deemed to be 'fair use'.

1·INTRODUCTION

The formulation of laws and theories that permit the prediction of future occurrences are among the proudest achievements of empirical science.

Carl Hempel (1965, p. 333)

1.1 OVERVIEW OF THE BOOK

This book presents economic theory as a body of thought that is continually evolving over time. This evolution seems to take place within the context of 'scientific research programmes'. The book takes the position that what is sometimes regarded as mainstream macroeconomic theory should be regarded as two distinct research programmes: the neo-Walrasian programme and the Keynesian programme. With this approach the traditional distinction between micro- and macroeconomic theory disappears at the level of the basic assumptions of the theory – the 'hard core' of the research programme.

The term 'neo-Walrasian' is used to group together those theories that stem from Leon Walras's view of the economy as one in which economic decisions in a competitive economy tend, in the absence of interferences with the functioning of markets, to be pre-coordinated through the price system and in which markets tend to clear. Although there are a variety of interpretations of Keynes's *General Theory* in the literature, this book takes the view that the keys to understanding Keynes's theory are his emphasis on the role of uncertainty and the resulting inability to make long-run forecasts as an explanation of why the level of investment may be inadequate to produce full employment, his explanation of why the decisions of individual economic agents may fail to be coordinated by the price system, and his notion that equilibrium may exist at less than full employment.

The models arising out of the two research programmes are placed in a context of the history of economic thought so that the reader can appreciate that they have evolved as researchers turned their attention to specific problems in economic theory (sometimes in response to the needs to develop economic policies). Moreover, the theories will continue to evolve as attempts are made to resolve the incompleteness or inconsistencies in current theories.

Since this book is primarily concerned with economic theory, the distinguishing features of Keynesian economics emphasized here are those relating to the foundations of economic theory. An alternative demarcation between Keynesians and the neo-Walrasians that is often made is to associate Keynesians with 'activist' monetary and fiscal policies and neo-Walrasians with rules or non-discretionary policies. In situations where rigidities or 'stickiness' associated with interferences with the market-clearing mechanism result in short-term unemployment, however, many neo-Walrasians also support activist policies.

The book avoids discussion of econometric evidence with respect to the different models because the task of evaluating it would, in itself, be a major project. Frank Hahn (1984, p. 287) has pointed out that if the difference of opinion between Keynesians, who argue that there is a role for government intervention in the economy through fiscal and monetary policy, and neo-Walrasians, who argue that, under certain conditions, intervention may be ineffective and unnecessary, 'is really empirical it is so on a grand scale concerned with what is the most appropriate model of the *whole* economy'. (Italics added.)

The first chapter presents some background which may be useful in understanding the various models presented in subsequent chapters. It begins with a brief summary of the characteristics of macroeconomic models followed by a brief historical sketch of the evolution of modern economic theory. As a preface to the presentation of the models, there is a brief summary of the contributions of some philosophers of science which is relevant to the notion of a scientific research programme and the corroboration of economic theories. The relation of laws to theories is then discussed. This is followed by an explanation of some basic model-building concepts. The chapter concludes with a set of questions in macroeconomics which are relevant to subsequent chapters.

1.2 THE CHARACTERISTICS OF MACROECONOMIC MODELS

The characteristics of macroeconomic models are:

1. They are concerned with national aggregates of production, income, expenditure, employment, and inflation rates.
2. They assume a fairly large degree of homogeneity among economic agents, products, and assets so that aggregation requires only the specification of the behaviour of a very small number of groups of economic agents – households, business firms, and government – and the analysis of a very small number of aggregate markets – labour, product, asset, and foreign exchange markets – in order to model the total economic activity of the economy.

3. They follow a general equilibrium approach in that they explain the effect on *all* markets of a change which initially may affect only one market.
4. They are concerned with the coordination, or the failure of coordination, of the outcomes of the decisions of individual economic agents.
5. Money and other financial assets exist and may serve as a store of value over time.
6. Government fiscal and monetary policies may play an important explanatory role in the model.

Macroeconomic models may be of three types:

1. *Static models:* Models in which the economy is initially assumed to be in equilibrium and where the model is used to derive the effect on the equilibrium position of a disturbance (a shift of a demand or a supply curve) in one of its markets. Equilibrium positions before and after the disturbance are compared to see the effect of the disturbance. This type of analysis is referred to as 'comparative statics' and is used in Chapters 2 and 3. Static models consider only one period of time and all the adjustment takes place within that period. No explanation is given of the path by which the economy moves to the new equilibrium position. The assumption of a 'stationary state' – an economy in which the stocks of various economic variables (for example, capital) settle down at new levels which, in the absence of another disturbance, remain constant – is frequently made.
2. *Dynamic models:* Models in which current values of economic variables depend on the values of economic variables in previous periods of time so that the time paths of economic variables are explained. One example of a dynamic process is the path of adjustment of an economy from one position of equilibrium to another after a shock has disturbed the initial equilibrium. Business cycles are another example of dynamic processes in economics. Dynamic models are discussed in Chapters 5 and 6.
3. *Growth models:* Models which are constructed to explain the long-run path of real output of an economy attributable to the growth of labour and capital over time because of demographic factors and net investment or technological change. Growth models are not discussed in this book.

1.3 A SKETCH OF THE EVOLUTION OF ECONOMIC THEORY

1.3.1 Classical economics

Classical economics developed from the mid-1700s to the mid-1800s. In some respects, classical economics may be best understood if one thinks of a world of small farmers or master craftsmen in which private economic agents do not have significant market power. Adam Smith, Professor of Moral Philosophy at Glasgow University from 1752 to 1762, produced the seminal work of the classical economists, *An Inquiry into the Nature and Causes of the Wealth of Nations* published in 1776. This was followed by two major works: Jean-Baptiste Say's *A Treatise on Political Economy* (first edition, Paris, 1803) and David Ricardo's *On the Principles of Political Economy and Taxation* (first edition, London, 1817). Ricardo (1951, pp. 5–6)[1] referred to the 'science of Political Economy' and asserted that its principal problem was to determine the laws which regulate the distribution of the total product to rent, profits and wages.

Two of the major concepts of classical economics which are relevant to the understanding of the models discussed in this book are the notion of 'natural price' (and the related concept of 'equilibrium') and the development of 'laws of markets'.

With respect to natural price, Adam Smith (1937, pp. 55–8) wrote:

> When the price of any commodity is neither more nor less than what is sufficient to pay the rent of the land, the wages of the labour, and the profits of the stock employed in raising, preparing, and bringing it to market, according to their natural rates, the commodity is then sold for what may be called its natural price. . . . When the quantity brought to market is just sufficient to supply the effectual demand and no more, the market price naturally comes to be either exactly, or as nearly as can be judged of, the same with the natural price. . . . The natural price, therefore, is, as it were, the central price, to which the prices of all commodities are continually gravitating. Different accidents may sometimes keep them suspended a good deal above it, and sometimes force them down even somewhat below it. But whatever may be the obstacles which hinder them from settling in this center of repose and continuance, they are constantly tending towards it.

The notion of natural price is a 'long-period' concept and the classical method of analysis was one which considered divergences between market and natural prices. Implicit in this method of analysis is the presence of an adjustment mechanism which moves market prices towards natural prices for each commodity so that, as long as this mechanism is functioning, there is a 'tendency' to long-run equilibrium at natural prices.

The development of the laws of markets was an attempt to explain the way in which market demand and supply were equated and the mechanism of adjustment by which market equilibrium is restored when a disturbance creates excess demand or excess supply in a market. Say's 'Law of Markets' (which he did not refer to as a law) is the classic statement, although he was vague about the mechanism of adjustment. The essence of his 'law' was that an increase in the production of goods will generate sufficient demand so that overproduction will not occur. As he expressed it (1964, pp. 134–5):

A product is no sooner created, than it, from that instant, affords a market for other products to the full extent of its own value . . . the mere circumstances of the creation of one product immediately opens a vent for other products.

He recognized that saving must be transformed into consumption for his view of the functioning of markets to hold (p. 110 and cited by Spiegel, 1983, p. 263):

No act of saving subtracts in the least from consumption, provided the thing saved be re-invested or restored to productive employment.[2]

For Say's Law to function, there must be a mechanism of adjustment which ensures that there is no leakage of the income that is generated by the production of goods so that the resulting demand fully absorbs all the additional product. In the event that saving occurs and that saving is not immediately translated into real investment, there must be a mechanism which equates saving and investment while aggregate demand for goods remains at the level necessary to purchase the total supply. That is, in an economy in which money is a store of value, in contrast to a barter economy in which money is no more than a unit of account and a facilitator of transactions, what is it that ensures that aggregate demand is not diminished if there is an increase in the holding of real money balances? The classical answer was that the rate of interest changed in such a way as to adjust the quantity invested and the quantity saved in opposite directions so that their equality was achieved at full employment. In one way or another, this classical view that there is a long-run tendency for markets to adjust so that, in the absence of interference with the market mechanisms, aggregate demand is always sufficient to purchase the total supply seems to have been the view of mainstream economics from Ricardo until it was challenged by Keynes.[3]

An essential feature of the classical view of the tendency of the economy to return to a full employment position after a disturbance was the assumption of perfectly competitive markets in which labour and capital moved freely from less advantageous to more advantageous employments. As Ricardo (1951, pp. 90–1) expressed it:

Let us suppose that all commodities are at their natural price. . . . Suppose now that a change in fashion should increase the demand for silks, and lessen that for woollens; their natural price, the quantity of labour necessary to their production, would continue unaltered, but the market price of silks would rise, and that of woollens would fall. . . . This increased demand for silks would however soon be supplied, by the transference of capital and labour from the woollen to the silk manufacture; when the market prices of silks and woollens would again approach their natural price.

A separate component of economic thought is the relation between the supply of money and the price level. One particular form of this relationship – the Quantity Theory of Money, which may be attributed to John Locke in the 1690s and which was restated by David Hume in the 1740s – applies to an inconvertible paper currency (fiat money) and asserts that the average level of prices is always in proportion to the supply of money, other things remaining the same. Hence, money is merely a medium of exchange and its quantity has no effect on real economic activity – money is 'neutral'.

1.3.2 Neoclassical economics

Around 1870 two major changes occurred: one in economic theory and one in economic policy.[4] Economists began to apply optimizing principles to the explanation of the behaviour of firms and households by introducing profit- and utility-maximizing behaviour and marginal concepts. This was the beginning of neoclassical economics and two of its pioneers were William Stanley Jevons in Britain and Carl Menger in Austria. Jevons had been educated in mathematics, biology, chemistry, and metallurgy and began to apply scientific methodology to economics. His principal work in economics was his *The Theory of Political Economy*, first published in 1871. It was partly at Jevons's urging that in Britain the name of the subject changed from 'political economy' to 'economics', reflecting the new emphasis on the behaviour of the individual household or firm.

Leon Walras of the University of Lausanne developed a general equilibrium model of a multi-market economy in his *Elements of Pure Economics*, first published in Lausanne in 1874. Although microeconomic in the sense that his model dealt with individual markets, Walras's model was macroeconomic in that it dealt with the total economic activity of an economy and was a general equilibrium model in which the equilibrium positions of all markets were solved simultaneously. One important missing piece of classical economics was a description of the process by which market prices are set. Walras used the fiction of an invisible auctioneer to explain how market-clearing prices could be arrived at. The auctioneer initially communicates to all economic agents a starting price chosen at random, obtains quantity demanded and quantity supplied at that price, and computes the excess demand. If excess demand is zero, he announces that price as the market price and all trades take place. If excess demand is positive, he raises the price, and repeats the process until he finds the market-clearing price. Similarly, if excess demand is negative, he lowers the price until the market-clearing price is found. Trades take place only at market-clearing prices; there is no false trading. Walras referred to this as a '*tâtonnement* process'. This continuous market clearing implies that prices in all product, labour, and asset markets are flexible. Economists sometimes refer to markets which function as if a Walrasian auctioneer was present as 'auction markets'.

An implication of Say's Law of Markets that was demonstrated by Walras was that the market identity implicit in Say's proposition was equivalent to the statement that the sum of excess demands (treating excess supply as negative excess demand) in an economy must be zero. Hence, in an economy in which there are n markets, if $n-1$ of the markets are in equilibrium, the nth market must also be in equilibrium. The proposition has come to be known as Walras's Law.[5]

Walras's successor at the University of Lausanne was Vilfredo Pareto, who developed important theorems in welfare economics. When an economy's resources are allocated so that no reallocation can make anyone better off without making at least one person worse off, the allocation is said to be 'Pareto optimal'.

Alfred Marshall, Professor of Political Economy at the University of Cambridge, was a major figure of neoclassical economics, whose *Principles of Economics* was first published in 1890. Marshall frequently analysed individual markets, assuming that the interactions with markets other than those for close substitutes or complements, were negligible; that is, he concentrated much of his analysis on *partial*, rather than general, equilibrium analysis. Marshall's model, unlike Walras's model, was not a perfect competition model with a Walrasian auctioneer who precluded any false trading. Marshall's firms experienced both internal and external economies, but his firms were not price-setters. Prices were determined by supply and demand as goods moved through the manufacturer–wholesaler–retailer channels of distribution. He recognized that there would be a substantial amount of ignorance in the market place and that trades at non-equilibrium prices would occur, but argued that the last price at which goods were traded would approximate the market-clearing price. Economic agents optimize, given their knowledge, but false trading occurs until finally the equilibrium price is reached. It is not the Walrasian world of perfectly competitive markets with prices automatically adjusting to produce equilibrium states with full employment of resources.

Marshall's successor at Cambridge in 1908 was Arthur Cecil Pigou, who published a number of major works on economics over the life span of his career which ended with his death in 1959. Marshall and Pigou also reformulated the Quantity Theory of Money so that it became a theory of the demand for money.

Neoclassical economists had both a theory of long-run tendencies of the economy which explained the establishment of the long-run equilibrium position of the economy and a theory of the business cycle (trade cycle or industrial fluctuations) which explained fluctuations around the long-run tendency. Frederick Lavington's *The Trade Cycle* (1922) and Pigou's *Industrial Fluctuations* (1929) are examples of their business-cycle theory. Pigou (1929, pp. 207–8) summarized the initiating causes of industrial fluctuations as including harvest variations, industrial disputes, inventions, and changes in fashion. These were amplified by errors of optimism and of pessimism on the part of businessmen and by autonomous monetary movements. The observed business cycles were a result of these causes coming into play with economic institutions. To Pigou, the most significant of these were monetary and banking arrangements, the policy of firms regarding markets, and the policy of workers as regards the 'rigidity of wage-rates'.[6] Pigou remarked (p. 202) that 'rigidity in the system of wage-rates in any community has a more important bearing on industrial fluctuations than popular arguments . . . suggest.' He also pointed out (p. 206) that 'imperfections of mobility [of labour] . . . in times of booms render unemployment distinctly larger than it would have been with perfect mobility.' In his analysis of business cycles, Pigou clearly departed from the Ricardian world of labour mobility and full employment.

Simultaneously with the 'marginal revolution' of the 1870s had come in Britain a change in the view of economic policy, which partly reflected the change from an agricultural and trading economy to an industrial society with poverty and unemployment. The Second Reform Act of 1867 and the trade union legislation of 1871 are examples of the legislative retreat from the classical individualistic approach to the problems of an industrial economy. Marshall (in 1886) and Pigou (in 1908) both recognized the existence of mass unemployment and advocated public works as a means of countering the problem. Pigou had written a small book entitled *Unemployment* which was published in 1913, followed twenty years later by his *The Theory of Unemployment*. Pigou expressed the view that by the end of the First World War the power of trade unions had grown and wage flexibility had markedly decreased. Hence, price rigidities could result in substantial unemployment for periods of time and wage cuts might not be a practicable solution to the problem of attaining full employment. He suggested that government expenditures might play a role in reducing unemployment. This was in contradiction to the doctrine that had come down from Ricardo that an increase in government expenditure intended to stimulate aggregate demand and increase employment would only crowd out private expenditure and not decrease unemployment.

Chapter 2 presents in modern language a version of a closed-economy static neoclassical model in which markets are highly aggregated into a single labour market, a single product market, and aggregate markets for financial assets.

The model is designed to set out the basic characteristics of a model in which Say's Law operates and in which the Quantity Theory of Money holds. This model implicitly incorporates the view that if the economic system were subjected to a disturbance which created unemployment, it would, if left to itself, in the long run automatically adjust and return to a position of full employment. If it fails to do so, it is because of interferences with the market mechanisms preventing prices and wages from adjusting to market-clearing levels.

1.3.3 Keynes's *General Theory*

John Maynard Keynes was a University of Cambridge graduate, trained in mathematics, who had written a dissertation on probability[7] which earned him a fellowship at King's College to which he was appointed in 1908. He subsequently turned to economics and attended lectures by Marshall and Pigou. Keynes's father, John Neville Keynes, had been registrar of the University of Cambridge and had authored a book on *The Scope and Method of Political Economy*, a book which is still regarded as a classic.

In 1923, Maynard Keynes published *A Tract on Monetary Reform* which contained a detailed statement of the Cambridge version of the Quantity Theory of Money originally expounded by Marshall and Pigou. He continued to work on monetary theory and in 1930 published a two-volume work *A Treatise on Money*. The model in this book was still, however, within the framework of the Quantity Theory of Money and was designed to analyse changes in the price level, assuming real output and employment remained constant.

In the late 1920s and early 1930s, Keynes wrote newspaper articles and political pamphlets in which he addressed the current unemployment problem in Britain and put forth policy recommendations that were markedly different from those in the Ricardian tradition which were generally accepted by most policy makers.[8] Pigou (1945, p. 20) summed up the classical view of the workings of the economy:

> The architects of [classical political economy] never had any doubt that, provided only thorough-going competition exists among wage-earners, there must be a tendency towards full employment, and, apart from changes and frictions, there must actually be full employment. This implies that in stable conditions, apart from friction, imperfect mobility and so on, the establishment of a sufficiently low rate of money wages would carry with it full employment in *all* circumstances.

Keynes challenged this view, but saw that the approach in his *Treatise* could not provide an explanation of the mass unemployment in Britain in the 1920s and 1930s. He took a completely different approach in which real output and employment were variables while prices might remain unchanged, at least, in the short run. This culminated in the publication of his *General Theory of Employment, Interest and Money* in 1936 and his rejection of the relevance of both Say's Law and the Quantity Theory of Money to a situation in which an economy was at less than full employment and likely to remain in that position for a considerable period of time.

In part, the model of Keynes's *General Theory* was developed to provide an answer to the question whether full employment could be restored by cuts in money wage rates. An important part of his argument against wage cuts was the recognition that, while wages are an element of costs to business firms, wages are also a source of income which provides demand for the products of industry. Moreover, in contrast to the certainty which economic agents have about the future in the neoclassical model and which enables economic decisions to be coordinated, the world of Keynes's model is characterized by uncertainty about the future so that expectations of the future values of key economic variables cannot be quantified. In this respect Keynes's early work on probability theory had an important impact on his thinking about economic problems. In constructing his model, Keynes placed great emphasis on the psychological factors influencing the behaviour of households and business firms. These psychological factors were summarized in three behavioural relations: the propensity to consume, the marginal efficiency of capital, and liquidity preference – terms invented by Keynes to emphasize the newness of his theory and its essential difference from the earlier neoclassical theory.

An essential distinguishing feature of Keynes's model was an asymmetry of behaviour between the adjustment mechanisms in the economy in situations of full employment and in situations of less than full employment. Keynes argued that effective demand would frequently for long periods of time be at a level below that required to maintain full employment. In his opinion, the self-adjusting mechanism that would return the economy to full employment, the mechanism implied by Say's Law, would not function except possibly in the very long run. Keynes had earlier expressed impatience with the view that the long run is relevant to the analysis of current economic affairs. In his *A Tract on Monetary Reform* (1923, p. 65) he had said:

> But this *long run* is a misleading guide to current affairs. *In the long run* we are all dead. Economists set themselves too easy, too useless a task if in tempestuous seasons they can only tell us that when the storm is long past the ocean is flat again.

Although Keynes was concerned with showing that the long-run tendencies of the classical model to a full-employment equilibrium only existed under very special conditions which, in general, did not exist, his emphasis was on the short run, not the long run. Hence, the theory that he developed was also a theory that was useful in explaining the business cycle. Indeed, from this time onward the division of macroeconomics into long-term tendencies and business-cycle theory began to disappear, apart from growth theory.

Keynes's model of the *General Theory* was, however, incomplete in a number of ways and to some extent inconsistent in that he tried to keep as much as possible of Marshall's neoclassical theory while at the same time trying to show that the conclusions of classical economics for economic policy were wrong. It is unfortunate that the Second World War diverted Keynes's attention from economic theory so that he never had the opportunity to re-examine the *General Theory*. During the war Keynes was an advisor to the British government and developed the blueprint for what became the International Monetary Fund. In recognition of his services he was granted a peerage in 1942 and took the title Baron Keynes of Tilton (Lord Keynes). He died in 1946.

Keynes's *General Theory* marked the beginning of a new research programme as an alternative to the neo-Walrasian research programme and the beginning of long debates on the relative merits of the two programmes which are still being carried on. Prominent interpreters of Keynes's model include Richard (Lord) Kahn, Nicholas (Lord) Kaldor, and the late Joan Robinson of the University of Cambridge, Sir John Hicks of Oxford University, Terence Hutchison of the University of Manchester, the late Alvin Hansen of Harvard University, Robert Clower and Axel Leijonhufvud of the University of California at Los Angeles, James Tobin of Yale University, Franco Modigliani and Robert Solow of the Massachusetts Institute of Technology, Richard Lipsey of Queen's University (Canada), John Fender of the University of Lancaster, the late Alan Coddington of Queen Mary College of the University of London, and Victoria Chick of University College of the University of London. Chapter 3 presents a version of Keynes's model which is based closely on the static model in Keynes's *General Theory*, but modified by adding a price equation which is not explicit in Keynes's writing. Chapter 4 discusses some further aspects of Keynes's economics.

1.3.4 Neo-Walrasian economics

Neo-Walrasian economics may be thought of as beginning with the work of Sir John Hicks of Oxford University whose *Value and Capital* was first published in 1939. Hicks was concerned with developing dynamic models in which expectations about future prices and quantities were incorporated within the model and not regarded as determined outside the model as had been done by Keynes. In this respect, he was influenced by the work of the Swedish economists, particularly Erik Lindahl. Hicks introduced the notion of 'temporary equilibrium' or 'flexprice' models to indicate models in which prices adjusted within each period of time so that market clearing occurred in each market, and the term 'fixprice' models to indicate economic environments in which prices are set by firms and only change irregularly in response to changes in market demand or supply conditions.

Neo-Walrasian economics was also concerned with the fact that Walras had assumed, without providing a proof, that there was a solution to his general equilibrium model and that the solution was stable so that, in the event of a disturbance which moved market price away from equilibrium, the law of supply and demand operated to restore equilibrium. It was not until the 1950s that mathematical economics had developed to the point where the existence of a stable competitive equilibrium could be proved and the conditions under which the model had these properties could be stated. This work was done by Kenneth Arrow, Gerard Debreu, and Lionel Mackenzie.

In the late 1960s and 1970s, a resurgence of inflation in the Western world led to a revival of the Quantity Theory of Money and a debate between neo-Walrasians and some Keynesians who had argued that there was a stable relation between the rate of inflation and the unemployment rate – the Phillips curve trade-off debate. Those who argued that there was no long-run relation between the unemployment rate and the inflation rate and who supported the Quantity Theory of Money were called 'Monetarists'. The leading Monetarists were Milton Friedman of the University of Chicago, Edmund Phelps and Phillip Cagan of Columbia University, Karl Brunner, now of the University of Rochester, Allan Meltzer of Carnegie-Mellon University, and David Laidler and Michael Parkin, now of the University of Western Ontario.

The successors to the Monetarists as champions of Walrasian economics and opponents of Keynesian economics are the 'New Classical Economists', principally Robert Lucas, Jr. of the University of Chicago, Robert Barro of Harvard University, Bennett McCallum of Carnegie-Mellon University, and Thomas Sargent and Neil Wallace of the University of Minnesota. An important part of the contribution of the New Classical Economists was their extension of the Walrasian model to include the implications of the 'rational expectations hypothesis' formulated by John Muth in 1961. The rational expectations hypothesis stated that the expectations of rational economic firms and households should be same as the solution values of the relevant economic models, thereby implying that all the relevant information is used in forming expectations. Two hypotheses relevant to macroeconomic policy-making were developed from the rational expectations hypothesis by the New Classical Economists: the 'policy ineffectiveness proposition' and the 'financing equivalence proposition'. A second strand of their contributions has been to business cycle theory where they have been developing models based on the rational behaviour (in the Muth sense) of individuals. Lucas (1987, pp. 107–8) has remarked:

The most interesting recent developments in macroeconomic theory seem to me describable as the reincorporation of aggregative problems such as inflation and the business cycle within the general framework of 'microeconomic' theory. If these developments succeed, the term 'macroeconomic' will simply disappear from use and the modifier 'micro' will become superfluous. We shall simply speak, as did Smith, Ricardo, Marshall and Walras of *economic* theory.

Chapters 5, 6 and 8 present some of the economic theory relevant to the positions of the neo-Walrasians (Monetarists and New Classical Economists) and contrast their results with those of a Keynesian model.

1.3.5 Keynesian economics

From the 1940s onward there were attempts to develop a synthesis between Keynesian economics and the neoclassical approach. Keynes had contributed to an encouragement of this approach when he said (1936, p. 3):

> I shall argue that the postulates of the classical theory are applicable to a special case only and not to the general case, the situation which it assumes being a limiting point of the possible positions of equilibrium.

Some of those who adopted the synthesis approach placed great emphasis on the 'stickiness' or 'rigidity' of prices and/or wages as being responsible for the existence of unemployment. As indicated above, however, and as will be developed more fully in Chapter 2, wage stickiness or rigidity was recognized by the neoclassical economists (especially Pigou) and is not a distinctive part of Keynesian theory. Another direction that the synthesis approach took was to attribute the difference in results from the neoclassical and Keynesian models not to basic differences in underlying theory, but to numerical values of critical parameters determining the elasticities of the demand for money or investment. Modigliani (1986) summarizes the debate over stabilization policy and presents econometric evidence which is summarized in Chapter 4.

There is a 'Post Keynesian' view of Keynesian economics that centres around the University of Cambridge and to which the late Joan Robinson was a leading contributor. The Post Keynesians relate Keynes's theories to the classical economic theory of production and distribution and place great emphasis on the role of institutions. They also draw on the writings of the Polish economist Michal Kalecki. Post Keynesians advocate a role for government in influencing the nature of investment and thereby the balance between consumption and capital accumulation. Their theory is briefly summarized in Chapter 4.

The distinctive Keynesian research programme that developed in the 1970s and 1980s has moved in the direction of trying to develop theories that are consistent with the rational (or near-rational) behaviour of individuals and which will lead to prices and/or wages being set at non-market-clearing levels so that unemployment will exist in an equilibrium situation. An early contributor to an explanation of equilibrium wage and price setting was the late Arthur Okun of The Bookings Institution. Some of the contributors to the 'New Keynesian Economics' are Joseph Stiglitz and Alan Blinder of Princeton University, Bruce Greenwald of Bell Communications Research, and Janet Yellen of the University of California at Berkeley. Greenwald and Stiglitz (1987a) set out the ingredients of a model which preserves Keynes's emphasis on market imperfections while developing theories of why wage rates may be set at non-market-clearing levels, the role of restrictions on the availability of credit in determining fluctuations in real investment and inventories, and, more generally, the effects of imperfections in information. Blinder (1987b) has introduced the concept of a failure of 'effective supply' to complement Keynes's emphasis on deficiencies of 'effective demand'. The New Keynesian Economics, which is summarized in Chapter 7, supports Keynes's contention that involuntary unemployment may persist for long periods of time.

1.4   SCIENTIFIC RESEARCH PROGRAMMES

Since economics began to evolve into a branch of science in the nineteenth century, economists, like other scientists, have been concerned with methodology and have drawn on the philosophy of science and scientific practice as a guide to their approach. Stanley Jevons, the first of the British neoclassical economists, had come to economics from a science background and published in 1874 his *The Principles of Science: A Treatise on Logic and Scientific Method*. His view of scientific method was:

> As we deduce more and more conclusions from a theory, and find them verified by trial, the probability of the theory increases in a rapid manner; but we can never escape the risk of error altogether. Absolute certainty is beyond the powers of inductive investigation, and the most plausible supposition may ultimately be proved false. . . . We sometimes find ourselves therefore in possession of two or more hypotheses which both agree with so many experimental facts as to have a great appearance of truth. Under such circumstances we have need of some new experiment, which shall give results agreeing with one hypothesis but not with the other. (1892, pp. 518–19).

> . . . The successive verification of an hypothesis by distinct methods of experiment yields conclusions approximating to but never attaining certainty. (p. x).

One can proceed directly from Jevons to the contributions of Sir Karl Popper, born in Vienna, who became Professor of Logic and Scientific Method at the London School of Economics. Popper set as his principal objective the finding of a demarcation principle which would distinguish science from non-science. The two major books which set out his views are his *The Logic of Scientific Discovery* and *Conjectures and Refutations: The Growth of Scientific Knowledge*. He rejected the notion of 'verification' of theories and replaced it with the principle of 'falsifiability' as the test of a scientific hypothesis. This resulted from Popper's rejection of the notion that it is possible to prove that a theory is always true. How do you prove that the sun will rise tomorrow? He argued that scientific statements are statements which have the potential of being false. A major discovery to him was the discovery of a new theory. To Popper, the agenda for a scientist is: 'Create bold hypotheses and weed them out ruthlessly . . .' (Weintraub, 1985, p. 30).

Thomas Kuhn, Professor of Philosophy and History of Science at Harvard University, in his *The Structure of Scientific Revolutions* argued that the progress of science is associated, not with a sequence of conjectures and refutations as Popper claimed, but with revolutionary episodes in which a 'paradigm' changes. Kuhn (1970, p. 175) used the term paradigm to stand for the 'entire constellation of beliefs, values, techniques, and so on shared by members of a given [scientific] community'. He also used 'paradigm' in a more narrow sense to refer to a set of axioms of the model that is used for problem-solving activity followed in 'normal' science. The vagueness of Kuhn's concepts together with the notion that there are abrupt changes (revolutions) which lead to changes in the paradigm has resulted, however, in Kuhn's approach not receiving wide acceptance although it stimulated others to improve on his description of the way in which science progresses.

Imre Lakatos began his work in Hungary and migrated to London where he was Professor of Logic at the London School of Economics until his death in 1974. One of his principal papers was on 'Falsification and the methodology of scientific research programmes'. He argued that knowledge is advanced by scientists working within scientific research programmes. A scientific research programme has a 'hard core', a 'positive' and a 'negative heuristic', and a 'protective belt'. The hard core consists of a group of propositions accepted as true and irrefutable by all adherents to the programme – for example, maintained hypotheses about the foundations of economic behaviour which are not directly put to test, such as rational behaviour, the ordering of preferences, and so forth. The hard core is the scientist's view of the world out of which his theories will develop. The positive heuristic is a set of instructions concerning the methodology to be used in developing the theories. The positive heuristic tells the scientist the questions to be investigated and how to proceed – for example, construct a model based upon optimizing behaviour by economic agents and then use the model to make predictions about the effect on the equilibrium position of the system of a change in an economic variable. Associated with and protecting the hard core is the negative heuristic which tells the scientist that certain paths of research are ruled out – for example, the core is not to be subjected to direct testing. The protective belt consists of specific theories derived from the core following the positive heuristic – for example, the 'law of demand' which states that an increase in the price of a commodity, other things remaining the same, is associated with a decrease in the quantity demanded.

At the level of the protective belt and the theories contained in it, Popperian falsifiability becomes relevant and Lakatos developed further Popper's notions.[9] Popper's falsificationist approach went through two stages: naive and sophisticated falsification. For a naive falsificationist, an individual theory is the object of a crucial experiment upon whose results the fate of the theory depends. If observed data contradict the theory, the theory is then rejected. Sophisticated falsificationism (sometimes termed methodological falsificationism) applies, not to an isolated theory, but to a series of theories and no experiment or set of observations alone can lead to the rejection of the series of theories. Falsification only occurs when a better set of theories emerges.

To illustrate, consider a situation where current knowledge consists of a theory T_1 and a new challenging theory T_2. The 'empirical content' of T_1 is defined as its set of potential falsifiers. The new theory T_2 would be 'bold' if it has 'excess empirical content'; that is, if it predicts new facts – facts improbable in the light of, or even prohibited by, T_1 – so that it has a larger set of potential falsifiers. A theory is regarded as being 'corroborated' if it has defeated some falsifying hypothesis. Theory T_2 would be corroborated if some of its excess content over T_1 is corroborated. The supreme challenge is when a bold new theory not only claims that the old one is false but that the new theory can explain all the truth-content of the challenged theory. The growth of a science is measured, according to Popper and Lakatos, by its success at producing theories with excess corroboration.

A corroborated theory should be regarded as a challenge to the critical ingenuity of a scientist to come up with a new theory which has excess content and which can be subjected to a severe test. A bold theory should be accepted into a science even if it has been refuted. It will provide subject matter for further criticism, testing, and so forth until a new bold theory supersedes it. If a prediction from a theory is accurate, corroboration for the theory is provided. Since prediction implies that a corroborating 'fact' has been discovered after the theory was put forth, it can be argued that it should be given more weight than an existing fact explained by the theory. If the prediction is wrong, the experiment is carefully examined to ensure that the result is valid. If so, the degree of corroboration of the theory is reduced. Theories which repeatedly fail to be corroborated are modified, classed as anomalies, or discarded. The hard core and positive heuristic of a research programme are retained, however, until an alternative research programme emerges which has a core which is capable of providing a richer protective belt in that it produces theories which are more successful – have a higher degree of corroboration – in explaining economic events. Indeed, within this approach, the form of a theory can only be chosen rationally on the basis of an appraisal of the research programme within whose protective belt it resides.

An illustration of the replacement of one theory by another that is used by Lakatos (1978a, p. 39) is the replacement of Newton's theory by Einstein's. Einsteinian theory contains many known anomalies, but it explains everything that Newtonian theory (as of 1916) successfully explained, it explained some Newtonian anomalies, and it forbade some events about which Newtonian theory had nothing to say. Moreover, some of the excess content of Einsteinian theory has been corroborated by experiments.

The hard core and heuristics of a scientific research programme and their interpretation are, however, being continually refined as the programme develops and the hardening of the core occurs slowly by a long process of trial and error. Alternative economic research programmes exist side by side as different schools of economists develop alternative theories from different hard cores in order to explain current and/or historical events. It may take many years for a full set of theories to be developed from a core and for these theories to be tested. Much of the macroeconomic literature of the past half-century has been devoted to the research of the two major competing research programmes which try to explain macroeconomic phenomena – the neo-Walrasian and Keynesian research programmes. The notion of a scientific research programme will be used as an organizing concept to examine some of the models which have emerged from these two programmes.

There has been a tendency for economists to attach themselves in a very partisan way to particular research programmes and to debate fiercely with members of competing research programmes (as do other scientists). An exception to this is Frank Hahn of the University of Cambridge who has been one of the most effective critics of some of the neo-Walrasian economics. Hahn (1984, p. 18) describes himself:

> On the final truths of economics I am completely agnostic. Until such final truth is unequivocably revealed I hold all coherent theorising as worthy of attention and respect.

1.5 LAWS IN ECONOMICS

Economists refer to laws: the law of supply and demand, the law of demand,

Say's Law, Walras's Law, the law of diminishing returns. Frequently, however, they give little explanation of what is meant by a 'law' and what distinguishes a law from an hypothesis or a theory. Moreover, sometimes different writers state a particular law with a different set of 'other things remaining the same'.

According to Carl Hempel (1965, pp. 334–79), Professor of Philosophy at Princeton University, the explanation of an event may be conceived of as a deductive argument based on the particular facts involved and the general laws on which the explanation rests. The laws involved in such an explanation are referred to as 'covering laws'. To qualify as a covering law, the statement should be of the form that 'whenever A occurs, B also occurs'. A law should be universally true. It must be recognized, however, that there is always the possibility that a particular law is not true. Hence, what are usually referred to as laws should be regarded as 'lawlike statements' which almost always gave accurate predictions in the past and are expected to do so in the future. Lawlike statements, because they can be shown to be false, fit into Popper's scheme and may be regarded as theories which have a very high degree of corroboration.

An example is the 'law of demand'. It can be stated as follows[10]: If a good is normal (the income effect is positive), then when its price increases, the quantity demanded of it will not increase. In this form, the 'law' is incapable of being falsified. Given Popper's criteria, does it qualify as a law? A bolder statement would be: When the price of a good increases, the quantity demanded of it will decrease. In the latter form, the prediction from the law will be wrong if the good is an inferior good and if the income effect outweighs the substitution effect. Is the occurrence of the circumstances that would give rise to an incorrect prediction of the market price of the good sufficiently rare that the bolder form of the law will almost always give an accurate prediction? If so, the latter form is preferable since it is a richer law. Another example is the 'law of supply and demand'.[11] Generally economists predict that if, in a competitive market, at the current price there is an excess demand for a good, the price of that good will rise and equality between supply and demand will be restored. If, however, the slope of the supply curve is algebraically less than the slope of the demand curve, a rise in price will increase the excess demand. Such cases are, however, so rare that they are generally ignored and economists regularly make predictions concerning the behaviour of prices in a competitive market based on the law of supply and demand – a lawlike statement.

1.6 ECONOMIC MODELS AND ECONOMIC FORECASTING

A model is a formalized expression of a theory or hypothesis by which an explanation of real-world observations can be made. A model abstracts from the reality of the real world in order to focus attention on the key interrelationships and to keep the analysis manageable.[12] Models represent a major part of the protective belt of a scientific research programme. An economic model uses the hard core and the positive heuristic of the programme to express the behaviour of economic variables (such as market prices and quantities) in such a way as to capture the interrelationships among the different variables.

The variables whose values are explained by a model are referred to as *endogenous* variables. The variables whose values are determined outside the model and whose values are not affected by changes in endogenous variables are *exogenous* variables. The effect of a change in one variable upon another may be expressed quantitatively by a coefficient. If the coefficient is constant over time, it is called a *parameter*. When the sign (positive or negative) of a parameter is specified on the basis of economic theory, the model can, in many cases, determine unambiguously whether an increase in the value of an exogenous variable, the value of other exogenous variables and parameters remaining constant, increases or decreases the value of a specific endogenous variable. Most economic theory is of this form and this type of analysis is referred to as 'qualitative' economic analysis. Econometrics is the application of statistical inference to the estimation of the numerical values of parameters of economic models and the use of econometrics may permit the actual magnitude of a change in an endogenous variable to be predicted.

Where the model explains all the change in an endogenous variable in terms of changes in exogenous variables or the previous (lagged) values of endogenous variables, the model is said to be 'deterministic'. Most endogenous variables cannot be completely explained by deterministic models, however, because they respond, in addition to explicit changes in exogenous variables, to unforeseen changes in economic information which occur randomly. Hence, econometric models contain random (stochastic) disturbance (or error) terms which have certain specified statistical properties. Hence, the time path of an economy may be regarded as the outcome of a 'stochastic process'. The amount of the variance of an endogenous variable which is explained by the deterministic component of the model may be regarded as a measure of the economist's success in developing a theory of how the economy behaves, conditional upon the values of the exogenous variables and the stability of the parameters. The unexplained variance attributable to the random error term is a measure of the economist's inability to explain and, therefore, to make forecasts of the future. It is important to recognize, however, that, since the exogenous variables are not explained by the model, and the economist by that fact admits an inability to explain their values, all economic forecasts are 'conditional forecasts' – forecasts conditional upon the future values of the exogenous variables and the stability of the values of the parameters of the model.

1.7 MATHEMATICS IN ECONOMICS

Most scientific models are expressed mathematically because most scientists believe that the best way to understand real structures is through mathematical structures. The notion of the effect of a change in one variable upon another, other things remaining the same – the economist's concept of a *marginal* quantity (marginal cost, marginal revenue, and so forth) – is expressed mathematically as the partial derivative of the first variable with respect to the second. Calculus is also a powerful tool for finding the maximum or minimum of a function of variables. Matrix algebra is a convenient way of solving a system of linear equations which may comprise a model expressing the interrelationships between variables. While geometry (for example, IS–LM diagrams) may be very helpful, the number of variables that can be managed in geometric models is restricted.

The knowledge of mathematics and the ability to express economic models in mathematical form and to solve them is a technical factor which limits the economist's ability to incorporate theories into models. As economists' knowledge of mathematics has grown and as new mathematical tools have been developed, economic models have become capable of handling more complex problems. For example, the Arrow–Debreu–Mackenzie solution of the Walrasian model was facilitated by mathematical developments arising out of John von Neumann's 1936 paper which used explicit duality arguments, explicit fixed-point techniques for an existence proof, and convexity arguments.[13]

1.8 A SET OF QUESTIONS IN MACROECONOMICS

The contents of the remaining chapters of this book may be regarded, in part, as an attempt to provide readers with a background with which to answer a number of questions in macroeconomics:

1. What are the underlying assumptions – the hard cores – of (a) the neoclassical macroeconomic model and (b) Keynes's model of the *General Theory*?
2. In each of these two models, is there an automatic adjustment mechanism which always returns the system to full employment after a shock?
3. If the automatic adjustment mechanism is missing, what government policies can be used to compensate for its lack?
4. How are the rate of interest, the price level, and the real wage rate determined in each of these models?
5. Does the Quantity Theory of Money hold in each of these models?

6. What are the implications of the models for the cyclical behaviour of real wages and employment?
7. How do imperfections in the labour, product, and asset markets affect the outcomes from the models?
8. Does the Phillips curve, which relates the rate of inflation to the rate of unemployment, fill a gap in Keynes's model?
9. What are the implications, with respect to the two models, of the Phillips curve literature for reducing the rate of inflation through the control of the rate of growth of the money supply?
10. How can the formation of expectations (the making of forecasts by economic agents) be modelled?
11. What are the implications of the rational expectations hypothesis for the conduct of monetary and fiscal policy?
12. Are business cycles attributable to *real* or *monetary* factors?
13. What are the strengths and weaknesses of Keynes's *General Theory* as perceived by the New Keynesian Economists?
14. What rationale can be provided for equilibrium wage and interest rates existing at non-market-clearing levels?
15. Does an increase in government spending on goods and services crowd out private spending?
16. With respect to the effect of an increase in government spending on goods on real variables (output and employment), does it matter whether government spending is financed by selling bonds to the general public, selling bonds to the central bank, or increasing tax revenues?
17. What is the open-economy version of the Quantity Theory of Money and how does it relate to (a) the law of one price and (b) interest rate parity?
18. In a flexible foreign exchange-rate system, what determines the exchange rate (a) in the short run and (b) in the long run?
19. In a pegged foreign exchange-rate system, what determines the change in official reserves of foreign exchange in (a) the short run and (b) the long run?
20. Are the answers to the previous two questions affected (a) by whether or not domestic and foreign securities are perfect substitutes and (b) by the way in which economic agents form expectations?
21. What are the conditions under which intervention in the foreign exchange market by the central bank is appropriate?
22. Should central bank intervention in the foreign exchange market be 'sterilized'?
23. Does a government budget deficit affect the exchange rate?
24. Is inflation in a particular country more appropriately explained by the

behaviour of that country's money supply or by the behaviour of the world money supply?

1.9 FURTHER READING

Histories of economic thought which the reader may find helpful are Blaug (1985), Deane (1978), Schumpeter (1954), and Spiegel (1983). Spiegel's book contains an excellent annotated bibliography. On Say's Law the reader should read Spiegel, Leijonhufvud (1981, Ch. 5) and Sowell (1972). Hegeland (1951) gives a history of the Quantity Theory of Money and its interpretation.

Further reading on methodology in economics and the notion of scientific research programmes may be found in Blaug (1980), Weintraub (1979, 1985), and in the volumes edited by Hacking (1981a) and Latsis (1976a). Hutchison (1978) is an interesting and instructive history of revolutions in economics with particular attention to the marginal (Jevonian) and Keynesian revolutions in contrast to classical (Ricardian) economics.

Sheila Dow's *Macroeconomic Thought: A Methodological Approach* (1985) is an excellent presentation of the methodology of the various schools of economic thought, including Post Keynesian, neo-Austrian, and Marxian, and their implications for macroeconomics. She, however, treats the neo-Walrasian and Keynesian programmes as a single mainstream school in contrast to the approach taken in this book. The neo-Austrian school stems principally from the work of Carl Menger, Friedrich von Hayek, Ludwig von Mises, and Ludwig Lachmann. To them, economics is the science of human action and should concentrate on the subjective motivation for action. Theory is to be derived by deductive logic from an unchanging essence of human nature. Some of the Austrian thinking on expectations and the integrating role played by market prices is similar to that of the New Classical Economists. Marxian economics focuses on the changing structure of social relations resulting from the historical unfolding of capitalism.

NOTES

1. References to year of publication refer to the edition cited in the References (see page 206), not to the year of first publication.
2. Smith (1937, p. 16) had earlier expressed a similar notion: 'What is annually saved is as regularly consumed as what is annually spent, and nearly in the same time too.' Brems (1986, pp. 64–7) discusses saving and the other possible sources of leakage: imports and taxes.
3. The first major challenge to Classical Economics was made by Karl Marx; the first volume of his *Das Kapital* was published in 1867. Thomas Malthus, a contemporary

of Ricardo, had earlier expressed concerns about aggregate demand which in some ways anticipated Keynes's rejection of the classical view and his development of the concept of effective demand. Cliffe Leslie in the 1870s was another who argued against classical (Ricardian) theory.

4. Hutchison (1978) documents these changes.
5. Oscar Lange (1942) put this name on what is sometimes termed Say's Identity.
6. Pigou (1935, p. 91) later also used the term 'sticky' to refer to wage rates that were slow to move in response to changes in market conditions.
7. This was subsequently published as *A Treatise on Probability* (1921).
8. See Keynes (1972) for a reprint of some of these.
9. Lakatos (1978a, pp. 30–7, and 1978b, pp. 170–6) sets out Popper's approach and his own extensions to it.
10. See Hicks (1959, pp. 59–68) for a discussion of the law of demand.
11. See Walras (1954, pp. 180–1) for a statement of this law and Samuelson (1947, p. 263) for a restatement.
12. Lucas (1987, pp. 6–19) gives a description of the properties of economic models and their usefulness for policy discussions.
13. See Weintraub (1985, pp. 59–107) for a survey of the development of mathematical economics and of the proof of the existence of a competitive equilibrium.

2 · A STATIC NEOCLASSICAL MODEL

What then *is* the classical view? It is, in its most rigorous form, that full employment does, indeed, not always exist, but always *tends* to be established.

A.C. Pigou (1949, p. 86)

The static neoclassical macroeconomic model is essentially the static perfect competition model of microeconomics presented in the form of a macroeconomic model. Thus, in this sense, there is no distinction between micro- and macroeconomic theory. It is the problems which are addressed that are different. The resulting macromodel is used in Chapter 3 as if it were the model which is criticized by Keynes in his *General Theory*, although it does not correspond exactly to any version that may be found in the writings of a neoclassical economist. It should be interpreted as a 'vintage 1930s neoclassical model' presented in modern dress and not as a modern neo-Walrasian model. Chapters 5 and 6 will present some of the theory of the modern neo-Walrasians.

The distinguishing characteristic of this neoclassical macroeconomic model is that the assumptions embedded in the hard core of the research programme from which the model is derived are such that Say's Law holds. Hence, the solution, in the absence of interferences with the market mechanisms, will be a full-employment solution. Explicit assumptions are made in defining the model so that an increase in the supply of money affects only the values of nominal variables (for example, the price level) while the values of real variables (such as the level of real output) remain unchanged in the new equilibrium position. This preserves the classical dichotomy between explaining the behaviour of real variables and the price level. The dichotomy, as will be seen, is possible only when product market equilibrium is defined only in terms of relations among real variables and when expectations are such that money is not required as a store of value. In this model the Quantity Theory of Money holds: an increase in the supply of money leads to a proportionate increase in the price level.

2.1 THE HARD CORE AND HEURISTICS

The following propositions specify the assumptions relating to the behaviour of individual economic agents which comprise the hard core of the research programme out of which the neoclassical model developed[1]:

1. Economic agents have a consistent set of preferences (a complete preordering of alternatives and a choice which is not dominated, in terms of their preferences, by another available one) about the outcomes of economic decisions.
2. Economic agents independently optimize subject to economic constraints. The endowment of economic resources and the technology available to firms are given. Private economic agents act as individuals only and independently of all other economic agents. That is, agents do not cooperate. The rationality of economic agents implies that they make all decisions in terms of the real, not nominal, values of variables whose values can be expressed in monetary terms.
3. Economic agents have full information on current and future market prices and on other relevant economic matters such as the money supply.
4. Choices are made in interrelated markets and observable economic outcomes are coordinated. The interrelationship of markets and the interaction of the decisions of individual economic agents means that the ultimate outcome of an economic event is not completed until the system has reached an equilibrium position. Hence, economic outcomes must be discussed with reference to equilibrium states and the stability of the equilibrium.

The positive heuristics of the programme are:

1. Specify the nature of markets and of economic agents. The specification of the nature of markets and of economic agents includes the following propositions:
   (a) The private sector of the economy consists of a very large number of private economic agents. In the tradition of neoclassical economics, these may be classified as workers, capitalists, landlords, and entrepreneurs. Government is also an economic agent.
   (b) There are markets in which all goods and services may be freely bought and sold and the exchange of goods and services takes place without significant costs.
   (c) The existence of very large numbers of very small private economic agents in each market implies that no private economic agent has market power and that competition prevails in all markets.

(d)   There is perfect mobility of factors of production between alternative uses.

(e)   All goods and factors of production are infinitely divisible. Hence, each worker can have the appropriate amount of capital to work with and there are constant returns to scale.

(f)   Entrepreneurs form business firms, hire workers, and make decisions about production and investment in new capital, but their business firms have no set-up costs and no explicit form of organization. Hence, anyone can choose to become an entrepreneur and form a firm.

2. Construct theories in which economic agents optimize and in which psychological and other non-economic content is eliminated.

3. Make predictions of the effect of changes in economic variables on equilibrium states.

The negative heuristics are:

1. Do not construct theories in which economic agents behave irrationally.
2. Do not construct theories in which equilibrium has no meaning.
3. Do not test the hard core of the programme.

The University of Chicago has long been a home for economists who hold very strongly to the hard core and heuristics of the neo-Walrasian programme. Melvin Reder (1982, p. 13) describes their attitude towards the programme as having very strong prior beliefs that the outcome of any empirical research relevant to price theory will be in accordance with neoclassical price theory:

> Any apparent inconsistency of empirical findings with implications of the theory, or report of behavior not implied by the theory, is interpreted as anomalous and requiring one of the following actions: (i) re-examination of the data to reverse the anomalous finding; (ii) redefinition and/or augmentation of the variables in the model, particularly the permissible objects of choice and the resource constraints; (iii) alteration of the theory to accommodate behavior inconsistent with the postulates of rationality (constrained optimization) by one or more decision makers (resource owners); (iv) placing the finding on the research agenda as a researchable anomaly.

Reder points out that the Chicago approach implies shunning (iii). Attention is focused upon (i) and (ii), and failing a quick resolution of the anomaly, (iv) is adopted. With respect to monopoly, Chicago economics says 'it is of infrequent occurrence and limited impact'. Moreover, 'market failure or more generally failure of individual decision makers to achieve a Pareto-optimum, is treated like monopoly: an unusual situation, to be analysed *ad hoc* but not requiring a shift of emphasis away from the basic competitive model'. (Reder, pp. 15–16.)

Some further comments on some aspects of the hard core and heuristics are in order. The full information on prices possessed by all economic agents could be achieved by assuming that there is a complete set of spot and forward markets so that all transactions relating to future output, incomes, and so forth, can be carried out now at known prices. This implies that complete price information is all that is required for economic agents to make decisions on purchases and sales. An alternative to assuming that there is a complete set of forward prices, which implies that the future consists of a number of different periods of time, is to regard the model as a single-period model in which there is *perfect foresight* and expectations are certain and static; that is, current prices are expected to continue indefinitely until some event shifts a demand or a supply curve. The latter assumption is used in this chapter.

Certainty about the future enables economic agents to allocate resources to take advantage of any profitable opportunities. In the competitive economy, such actions eliminate such profitable opportunities and equalize returns on all assets.

Given the lack of market power by private economic agents and their possession of full information, the prices of products and factors of production (labour and capital) are determined in the market place as if a Walrasian auctioneer existed and all trades take place only at market-clearing prices. This does not, however, explain the process by which prices are actually set in the real world.

In the model presented here, land is not a factor of production and there are no landlords. Individual persons may be both workers and capitalists in that workers may save, accumulate wealth, and lend their accumulated capital to entrepreneurs who may use it in the production of goods within business firms. The term 'household' will be used to describe a unit which may provide labour services, consume goods, save, and provide capital. The term 'firm' will be used to designate the production unit formed by an entrepreneur. Hence, there will only be two types of economic agents in the private sector: households and firms. If labour and capital are perfectly divisible and if there is a complete set of spot and forward markets, anyone can decide to become an entrepreneur, form a firm, sell the output that will be produced in a forward market, obtain funds in financial markets to obtain the services of capital, and begin production. Because of the existence of constant returns to scale, there is no distinction between the size of firms and the number of firms.

The concept of equilibrium plays a very important role in the neoclassical research programme and has several dimensions which require explanation: the period of time which is required to reach equilibrium, the clearing of markets, the holding of assets, and the stability of the equilibrium. Equilibrium in a neoclassical model may be said to exist when a set of non-negative prices comes into existence in all markets for goods, services, and financial assets such that, if households and firms were each individually to optimize taking those prices as given, the resulting market demand and supply quantities would be equated – all markets would clear – and the market prices would be identical to the prices that the economic agents had taken as given.[2] Moreover, all agents would be holding the quantities of the various assets that, given the budget constraints, they desire to hold so that equilibrium would exist for both flows (incomes and expenditures) and stocks (balance sheets).

Equilibrium also implies, given the optimizing behaviour of economic agents, that the rates of return on all resources will be equal in alternative uses. Such an equilibrium in a perfectly competitive economy will be such that no opportunities exist for the economic position of any economic agent to be improved without the position of other agents being worsened. That is, the equilibrium will be Pareto optimal.

The existence of equilibrium implies that it is logically possible for the choices (decisions) of all economic agents to be reconciled. That is, a decentralized, individualistic system, operated on principles of self-interest, does tend to produce coordinated and coherent outcomes. The important distinction in economics is between models in which coordination is successful and those in which coordination fails.[3] As will be seen in Chapter 3, Keynes's model is of the latter type.

It is also important that the equilibrium be stable so that if a disturbance moves the system away from an equilibrium position, an adjustment process automatically goes to work, in the absence of interference with the functioning of markets, to restore equilibrium. The neoclassical adjustment mechanism is the law of supply and demand.

Obeying these heuristics and deducing theories from the hard core of the research programme, a neoclassical macroeconomic model will be constructed to explain the comparative statics of the economic system. Solution of the model defines an equilibrium position without reference to the length of time that it takes the system to reach equilibrium. If perfect price flexibility exists and the law of supply and demand holds, the equilibrium may be reached very quickly. In keeping with the writings of the classical and neoclassical economists, however, the equilibrium should be regarded as a long-period equilibrium.

2.2 THE COMPONENTS OF THE STATIC NEOCLASSICAL MODEL

2.2.1 Simplifying assumptions

To keep the model simple for mathematical analysis and to avoid aggregation problems, the following simplifying assumptions are made:

1. There is only a single good produced in this economy. This good may be used either as a consumption good by households or as a capital good by business firms.[4]
2. There are a very large number of very small firms, each of which has the same production function.
3. Firms pay out all profits to shareholders in the form of dividends and hold no assets other than the real capital used as an input in the production process. Firms finance the acquisition of all new capital goods by selling equities (common shares) to households.
4. There is a single government which purchases goods for its own use and collects lump-sum taxes. There is no income tax. A government budget deficit is financed by the sale of government bonds to households or to the central bank. The government operates a central bank which issues fiat (paper) money and conducts open-market operations in the bond market.
5. There are no commercial banks. Hence, the fiat money issued by the central bank is the only money and it does not earn interest.
6. All money and the equities of firms are held by households. Government bonds may be held by households or by the central bank, but not by firms.
7. Households purchase goods for consumption and sell labour services to firms. In addition to wages, households receive income in the form of interest from the government bonds and dividends from the equities.
8. There are no transactions costs.
9. Given the assumption of perfect markets, there is no unemployment due to frictional causes.
10. To avoid dealing with the problems of defining an equilibrium position for a stationary economy, it will be assumed that the stock of capital remains constant within the period even though positive net investment may be occurring. Since the analysis refers to that of equilibrium within a single period of time, the increased stock of capital does not enter the analysis. One could rationalize the holding of the stock of capital constant by assuming that the initial stock is so large that the addition through net investment has a negligible effect on it. (Chapter 9 will contain some discussion of equilibrium conditions for an open-economy stationary state.)
11. The economy is closed in the sense that there is no international trade in either goods or financial assets. (This assumption will be relaxed in Chapter 9.)

2.2.2 Production function

The production function of a representative firm at a moment of time is[5]

$$y = f(n, k) \tag{2.1}$$

where y is the number of units of the good produced per period of time

f the production function

n input of labour services in hours per period of time

k input of the services of capital per period of time (assumed to be proportional to the stock of capital accumulated by the firm)

The time and firm subscripts of the variables have been suppressed.

Production is assumed to be subject to diminishing returns with respect to both labour and capital. Hence, using a shorthand notation, the properties of production function can be described as

$$f_n > 0, f_{nn} < 0, f_k > 0, f_{kk} < 0$$

In this notation, when the name of a function is written with a subscript, it stands for the change in the value of the function (the value of the left-hand-side variable) which will occur when there is a very small increase in the value of the subscripted variable, the values of all other arguments of the function remaining constant.[6] Hence, the marginal product of labour – the rate of change in output with respect to a very small increment in the input of labour, the input of capital being held constant – will be written in this shorthand as f_n. The change in the marginal product of labour with respect to a very small change in the input of labour will be written f_{nn}. The change in the marginal product of labour with respect to a very small change in the input of capital will be written f_{nk}.[7]

Such a production function is shown in Fig. 2.1 for a given stock of capital, k_1. The slope of a tangent to the curve at a specific point gives the marginal product of labour for the given input of labour. Since the slope decreases as n increases, there are diminishing returns with respect to the input of labour.

Labour and capital are assumed to be complements so that $f_{nk} > 0$. That is,

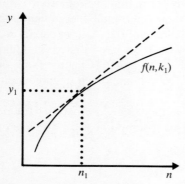

Fig. 2.1 Production function

an increase in the input of one factor of production increases the marginal product of the other. If no change occurs, the factors are said to be neutral with respect to each other. Presumably, a firm would not adopt a change which reduced the marginal product of a factor. In Fig. 2.1, an increase in the stock of capital would, if labour and capital are complements, shift the production function upward in such a way that the slope increases at each level of n for the higher stock of capital.

Constant returns to scale are assumed. That is, a proportionate increase in the input of both factors increases total output in the same proportion:

$$f(\mu n, \mu k) = \mu f(n, k)$$

where μ is a positive real number.

It can be shown that, under the assumptions, if labour and capital receive their marginal products, the total product is exhausted:

$$y = f_n n + f_k k$$

An example of a functional form for a production function which has all the above properties is the Cobb–Douglas production function. See Appendix 2.5.

2.2.3 Demand for labour and capital

The demand for labour and capital can be deduced from profit-maximizing behaviour by firms subject to the constraint of the production function, as is explained in Appendix 2.4. Since all firms are very small, they are price-takers for their products and for the services of both labour and capital. Assuming that there are no income taxes, profits are defined by

Profits $= Py - Wn - (r + q)Pk$

where P is the price at which the good is sold

W	money wage rate per hour
r	real rate of interest[8]
q	depreciation rate

The expression $(r + q)P$ is the implicit rental price of capital. In a perfectly competitive market, the rental price will equal the sum of the two costs of owning capital – the opportunity cost and depreciation. The opportunity cost of investment in real capital is the interest forgone on investment in a government bond, the only alternative form of investment in this model.

The necessary conditions for profit maximization subject to the constraint of the production function are

$$f_n = W/P = w \tag{2.2}$$
$$f_k = r + q \tag{2.3}$$

The profit-maximizing firm under conditions of perfect competition will adjust the level of employment of labour to the point where the marginal product of labour (f_n) equals the real wage rate $(W/P = w)$ and adjust the input of capital to the point where the marginal product of capital (f_k) equals the real rental price of capital. That is, in equilibrium the net marginal product of capital (the gross marginal product less the amount of capital used up in producing that output) will equal the real rate of interest (r).[9]

A word of explanation on the interpretation of 'real' may be helpful. From the viewpoint of the firm, the real wage rate is the number of units of output that it must give up as payment to a worker in order to obtain an additional hour of labour services. Hence, dividing the money wage rate by the price of a unit of output gives the 'real wage rate'. From the viewpoint of the worker, it is the number of units of output that can be bought with the money wage received for the hour's labour. In a one-good economy, the real wage is the same for both firms and workers. In a multi-good economy in which firms specialize in the production of goods, the real wage from the firm's point of view will be different from the real wage from the worker's point of view since the products produced by a firm will be different from the products consumed by a worker. Hence, bargaining in terms of real wages may not lead to a settlement if the prices of a firm's products are moving differently than the prices of the goods that workers are consuming.

In this model the real interest rate is the real rate of return on a government bond. This is also the opportunity cost of investment in real capital. In equilibrium, this will equal the net marginal product of capital. Hence, the real rate of interest is also measured in units of output. For example, $r = 0.04$ would mean that the yield would be 0.04 units of output per period of time. The units for q would be the same.

If there are constant returns to scale and if factors are paid their marginal products, the net profits (after deducting the opportunity cost of the capital used) are zero. This can be seen from the definition of profits:

$$
\begin{aligned}
\text{Profits} &= Py - Wn - (r+q)Pk \\
\text{Profits}/P &= y - (W/P)n - (r+q)k \\
&= y - f_n n - f_n k \\
&= 0
\end{aligned}
$$

An interesting implication of this is that entrepreneurs, in equilibrium, receive no reward as entrepreneurs. Their income arises entirely from any labour services they provide to the firm or the return on any capital they own which is used by the firm. It is in disequilibrium situations where there is uncertainty about the future that entrepreneurial income is generated as a residual profit.[10]

So far, the analysis has been in terms of a representative firm rather than the economy as a whole. It can be shown (see Sargent, 1987a, pp. 7–11) that the assumptions that have been made concerning the production function of firms together with the assumptions of perfect competition and profit maximization imply that the functional form of the production function and the demand-for-labour and demand-for-capital functions derived above also apply to the economy as a whole.

2.2.4 Supply of labour services

Assume that all individuals have the same utility function and that they are all utility maximizers. It can be shown (see Appendix 2.4) that utility is maximized when the hours of leisure (or hours worked) are adjusted so that the ratio of the marginal utility of leisure to the marginal utility of income equals the market real wage rate. Under the assumptions specified in Appendix 2.4, the supply of labour will be an increasing function of the real wage rate provided that the effect of an increase in the real wage rate on income is not such that the income effect outweighs the substitution effect between leisure and work. An aggregate labour supply function can be obtained by aggregating the labour supply functions of all workers.

$$n^s = h(w) \qquad h_w > 0 \tag{2.4}$$

where n^s denotes quantity supplied and h is the labour-supply function.

2.2.5 Labour market equilibrium

To complete a sub-model which will explain the determination of the level of real output (y), the level of employment (n), and the real wage rate (w), it is necessary to specify the nature of the labour market. Assume that the labour market is an auction market in which, given that all economic agents have full

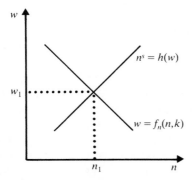

Fig. 2.2 Labour market equilibrium

information, the wage bargain is made in terms of the real wage rate and the real wage continuously adjusts to clear the market:

$$n = n^s \tag{2.5}$$

Labour market equilibrium is shown in Fig. 2.2. Since the market clears, there is, by definition, full employment.[11]

2.2.6 The effect of changes in the stock of capital

At a moment in time,[12] stocks may be regarded as constant. Thus, the solution of the model will be in accordance with 'short-period analysis' which takes the stock of capital as given. One question which can be addressed to this model is 'What effect would there be on the values of the endogenous variables if the value of the exogenous variable, k, had been slightly larger?'

This question is typical of the type of question asked in economic theory when no quantitative estimates of the parameters of the functions are available. Generally the questions are 'What will be the effect of a *change* in the value of an exogenous or predetermined variable?' or 'What will be the effect of a *change* in behaviour or technology upon the values of the endogenous variables?'. In a theoretical analysis where no empirical estimates of parameters or elasticities are available, the answers will necessarily be qualitative, rather than quantitative. The answer will be that the change leads to an increase or a decrease in the value of an endogenous variable or that the effect is indeterminate since it depends on the values of parameters.

In this particular case, treating the stock of capital as exogenous and using the equilibrium condition to replace n^s by n in the supply-of-labour equation, a three-equation model is obtained:

$$y = f(n, k)$$
$$w = f_n$$
$$n = h(w)$$

This is a set of three equations whose solutions will determine the values of the three endogenous variables: y, w, and n. The one exogenous variable whose value is determined outside the model is k.[13]

A geometrical solution of the model[14] is shown in Fig. 2.3 which depicts the production function on the left-hand side and the labour market on the right-hand side. For an initial stock of capital, k_1, the production function is shown as $f(n,k_1)$ and the demand-for-labour curve is shown as $f_n(n,k_1)$. The real wage rate w_1 produces equilibrium at a level of employment of n_1. Transferring this level of employment to the production function gives y_1 as the equilibrium level of real output. Since labour and capital are complements, an increase in the

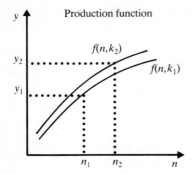 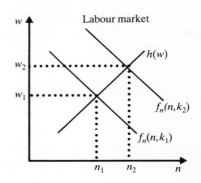

Fig. 2.3 Effect of an increase in the stock of capital

stock of capital to k_2 will shift the production function upward and the demand-for-labour curve to the right; hence, a new equilibrium level of employment n_2 will be determined. Transferring n_2 back to the production function gives a new level of output, y_2. Thus, the increase in real output is $y_2 - y_1$. Note that the effect on w and n of a change in k depends on f_{nk}. Only if capital and labour are complements is there a positive effect.

2.2.7 Investment by firms in new capital

By definition, net real investment i equals $\dot{k}$, where $\dot{k}$ is the rate of change over a short interval of time in the net stock of capital.[15] The profit-maximizing conditions can be used to derive the demand for newly produced capital goods (real investment), assuming no trading in existing capital goods. The optimal stock of capital ($k^\#$) is given by the condition $f_k - q = r$. That is, following the conditions for profit maximization, firms will add to the stock of capital until the net marginal product of capital (which, given diminishing returns, will decline as k increases) equals the opportunity cost of the investment. Hence, the desired stock of capital is a function of f_k, q, and r:

$$k^\# = k\,(f_k, q, r)$$

where (for economy of symbols) k is used as the name of the function.[16]

In equilibrium, $k = k^\#$. In disequilibrium, $k \neq k^\#$, and $i = i(k^\# - k)$. Hence, remembering that $f_k = f_k(n, k)$,

$$i = i(n, k, q, r) \tag{2.6}$$

and $i_n > 0$ if $f_{nk} > 0$, $i_k < 0$ if $f_{kk} < 0$, $i_q < 0$, and $i_r < 0$

The yield on the government bond (r) represents the opportunity cost of real investment and i will vary inversely with r. In equilibrium the net return on real investment $(f_k - q)$ will equal the yield on the government bond (r) and there will be zero net investment. The higher the depreciation rate (q), the lower will be the net return on the investment; hence, i will vary inversely with q.

2.2.8 Supply of financial assets

Equities
Under the assumptions of the model, no retained earnings are available to finance the investment of firms in new capital. Hence, all investment is financed by selling new equities (common shares) to households in an amount exactly equal in real terms to i. To keep the model simple, it will be assumed (in keeping with the assumptions of perfect information and static expectations) that these equities always have a market price of unity. Hence, the total real value of the equities held by households will exactly equal k, the real value of the capital stock of firms.[17]

Bonds
The government buys for its own consumption some of the good produced by firms, raises taxes by a lump-sum tax[18] on households, and finances any budget deficit by selling bonds to households or to the central bank. The government bond is valued in such a way that it is always worth \$1 in constant dollars to the holder. This is accomplished by stating that a bond is redeemable at P dollars at any time, where P is the price level.[19] The bond pays interest at a rate which varies continuously in accordance with market demand and supply conditions so that the bond market always clears.

The government budget equation (budget constraint) in nominal dollars is[20]

$$G + rB - T = \dot{B}^{\mathrm{T}}$$

where G is government expenditure on the good in current dollars
$\quad\quad r$ the rate of interest on the bond
$\quad\quad B$ the value of the bonds held by households ($= Pb$, where b is the number of bonds held by households)
$\quad\quad T$ the revenue from the lump-sum tax
$\quad\quad B^{\mathrm{T}}$ total value of the bonds issued by the government
and $B^{\mathrm{T}} = B + B^{\mathrm{CB}}$
where B^{CB} is the total value of the bonds held by the central bank
In real terms, the budget constraint is

$$G/P + (rB)/P - T/P = \dot{B}^{\mathrm{T}}/P$$

which may be rewritten as

$$g + rb - t = \dot{B}^{\mathrm{T}}/P \quad\quad \text{where } g = G/P \text{ and } t = T/P$$

The budget is assumed to be set by the government in real terms (constant dollars) so that g and t are exogenous variables in the model. The government is presumed to be able to forecast P accurately.

Money

The central bank can buy government bonds, either directly from the government or from households in the open market, and pay for them with fiat money which it prints. In a closed economy the central bank's balance sheet can therefore be represented by the identity:

$$B^{CB} \equiv M \tag{2.7}$$

where M is the quantity of fiat money issued by the central bank.

When the central bank buys bonds in the open market from households, the money supply increases and the holding of bonds by households decreases:

$$dM = - dB$$

Since $B^T = B + B^{CB}$ and $B^{CB} = M$, $\dot{B}^T = \dot{B} + \dot{M}$. The government budget constraint can therefore be written as

$$g + rb - t = \dot{B}/P + \dot{M}/P \tag{2.8}$$

Thus (as can be seen by transposing terms), the rate of change in the supply of money in real terms equals the real government deficit minus the net purchases (in real terms) of bonds by households.

2.2.9 Saving by households

Saving (income not spent on consumption goods) by households makes households the capitalists of the model. They are the sole source of the resources which makes additions to the net stock of capital goods possible.[21] Their saving is hypothesized to be directly related to the level of real disposable income (z) and to the real rate of interest (r) and inversely related to the level of real wealth (a). Hence, the real savings (s) of households is given by

$$s = s(z, r, a) \qquad 0 < s_z < 1, s_r > 0, s_a < 0 \tag{2.9}$$

where s_z is the marginal propensity to save out of real disposable income. It is assumed that households have a lifetime target level of wealth so that an increase in wealth, other things remaining the same, decreases the need to save in order to achieve the target. Hence, $s_a < 0$.

The real disposable income of households is

$$z = y - qk - t + rb \tag{2.10}$$

and equals the real value of wages and dividends received (total product less depreciation allowances) less taxes paid plus bond interest received.

Total wealth in nominal dollars (A) is equal to $M + B + Pk$ (since the value of equities equals the value of the net stock of capital held by firms). The real wealth of households (a) equals $M/P + B/P + k$. Total real wealth also equals the sum of all past saving.[22] By definition $\dot{a} = s$.

Household consumption (c) is defined to be

$$c = z - s \tag{2.11}$$

c_z, the marginal propensity to consume out of disposable income, equals $1 - s_z$.

The inclusion of real wealth in the saving and consumption functions is attributable to Pigou and is referred to either as the 'Pigou effect' or as the 'real balance effect'. It is common in an introductory macroeconomics course to assume that $s_a = 0$. For the remainder of Chapter 2, this assumption will be made to simplify the solution of the model. (The Pigou effect will be discussed further in Chapter 4.) Since z is a function of y, r, and t, and r appears in the saving function, the saving function will be written as $s(y,r,t)$ from now on.

2.2.10 Product market equilibrium

The market-clearing equilibrium condition for the product market is

$$y = c + i + qk + g \tag{2.12}$$

which may be rewritten as

$$i = y - qk - c - g$$

Using equations (2.9) and (2.11), this becomes

$$i = s - (g + rb - t)$$
$$i(n, k, q, r) = s(y, r, t) - (g + rb - t)$$

Since n and y have been predetermined in the labour market in conjunction with the production function, and since g, t, and q are exogenous variables and k and b are predetermined, there is only one variable in the model which independently affects the saving decisions of households and the investment decisions of firms and which can adjust to clear the product market: the rate of interest.[23] Thus, the market-clearing condition for the product market says that the rate of interest adjusts so that total saving of the private sector less the real government deficit passes into an equal amount of real investment. That is, saving never results in a reduction in the aggregate demand for goods; thus, total output is always at the full employment level. Hence, Say's Law holds: production generates an equal amount of demand. In a world in which saving and investment decisions are always made by the same economic agents, saving and investment would always be equal in amount (and by definition). In a world in which households make saving decisions and firms (entrepreneurs) make investment decisions the rate of interest adjusts to clear the product market at the level of real output that is consistent with full employment.

Pigou (1953, p. 27) cites Alfred Marshall (1920, p. 534) to show that movements in the rate of interest were considered to be the adjusting mechanism in the neoclassical model,[24] and then goes on to paraphrase Marshall:

> 'interest, being the price paid for the use of capital in any market, tends towards an equilibrium level such that the aggregate demand for capital in that market, at that rate of interest, is equal to the aggregate [flow] forthcoming at that rate'.
>
> This passage may be paraphrased: The rate of interest and the amount of real income devoted to investment tend to be so adjusted that the quantity of real income demanded for investment at that rate of interest is equal to the quantity offered at that rate; in such wise that there are no demands unsatisfied and no offers declined.

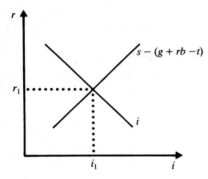

Fig. 2.4 Product market equilibrium

Figure 2.4 shows the determination of this equilibrium rate of interest. The rate of interest that produces this equilibrium at full employment may be called the 'optimum rate of interest' (Keynes, 1936, pp. 242–3). In equilibrium, the optimum rate of interest equals the net marginal product of capital ($f_k - q$). Given g, t, and b, the allocation of output between c and i is thus determined.

The Swedish economist Knut Wicksell (1936) used the term 'natural rate of interest' to refer to the rate of interest that equates saving and investment but, unless there is only one level of real income that is consistent with product market equilibrium, there will be more than one natural rate of interest. Wicksell's use of the term 'natural rate of interest' is in keeping with the classical notions of natural price and long-period equilibrium and the analysis of deviations of market price from natural price. The natural rate of interest was to Wicksell the rate that equated the supply of and demand for real capital. The market rate of interest represented the rate at which funds could be borrowed in the market place. Wicksell argued that whenever there was a divergence between natural and market rates of interest, a cumulative process of adjustment of commodity prices occurs until the two rates coincide and equilibrium is restored.[25]

Sargent (1987a, pp. 28–9) has pointed out that there is a loanable funds interpretation of the determination of the rate of interest which is consistent with the above statement of product market equilibrium. Saving provides the supply of loanable funds which, given an efficient market for financial capital which equates the demand and supply of funds, governs the amount of investment in real capital. Given that $i = s - (g + rb - t)$, it can be seen from equation (2.8) that

$$s = i + \dot{M}/P + \dot{B}/P$$

The left-hand side of this equation is the rate of private saving – the rate at which households are adding to their stock of wealth. The right-hand side is the rate of growth (in real terms) of the stock of equities, money, and bonds in the hands of households. The rate of interest adjusts to ensure that private saving exceeds the rate of net investment by precisely the amount by which the government is expanding the real value of household claims on the government in the form of money and bonds. This suggests that one rationale for levying taxes to finance government expenditure instead of printing money or bonds is to protect the rate of growth of physical capital by limiting the extent to which private saving is diverted to accumulating claims on government (money and bonds) instead of financing the net investment of firms. Taxes may, however, reduce the amount of saving because of their effect on disposable income.

2.2.11 Demand for financial assets

The saving decision determines the rate at which households desire their wealth to grow. Households must then decide in which form they wish to hold their total wealth; that is, the composition of their portfolio of assets must be determined. Two simplifying assumptions will be made. First, expectations are static so that the expected rate of inflation is zero and there is no difference between nominal and real rates of interest. Second, bonds and equities will be assumed to be perfect substitutes so that the portfolio balance decision reduces to the decision as to how much to hold as money and how much to hold as securities (bonds plus equities). Hence, there are two demand functions for the real value of financial assets which households desire to hold:

$$(M/P)^D = m(r, z, a) \qquad m_r < 0, m_z > 0, 0 < m_a < 1 \qquad (2.13)$$
$$(b + k)^D = b(r, z, a) \qquad b_r > 0, b_z < 0, 0 < b_a < 1 \qquad (2.14)$$

In the demand-for-money function, r represents the opportunity cost of holding money. An increase in the opportunity cost will reduce the demand for real money balances ($m_r < 0$). The income variable z reflects the transactions demand for money. As z increases, the demand for money will increase ($m_z > 0$). Since z is a function of y and r and r appears explicitly in the demand functions, z will be replaced in these functions by y. Since money is one of two financial assets, a portion of any increase in real wealth (a) will usually be held in the form of real money balances so that m_a will not normally equal either 0 or 1.

For securities, an increase in their yield (r) will increase the demand for them ($b_r > 0$). If an increase in income increases the demand for money, it must decrease the demand for securities ($b_z < 0$), other things remaining the same. A portion of any increase in real wealth will usually be held in the form of securities so that normally b_a will not equal either 0 or 1.

Since for the portfolio balance decision total wealth is given, the total demand for financial assets must obey the real wealth constraint:

$$(M/P)^D + (b + k)^D = a \qquad (2.15)$$

The mathematical properties of the two demand functions are related[26]:

$$m_r + b_r = 0 \qquad m_y + b_y = 0 \qquad m_a + b_a = 1$$
$$m_r = -b_r \qquad m_y = -b_y \qquad m_a = 1 - b_a$$

2.2.12 Asset market equilibrium

Portfolio equilibrium requires that the following two market-clearing conditions hold:

$$(M/P)^D = M/P \qquad (2.16)$$
$$(b + k)^D = b + k \qquad (2.17)$$

If, however, $(M/P)^D = M/P$ and $(M/P)^D + (b + k)^D = a$ then $(b + k)^D = a - M/P = b + k$. That is, the market-clearing condition for securities is implied by the equilibrium between the demand and supply of real money balances and the wealth constraint. Hence, to solve the model, only one of the market-clearing conditions need be included. The other is implied, given the constraint: Walras's Law holds. Which of the two market-clearing functions is actually omitted from the model depends on the analyst's convenience. Since the analysis here will focus attention on changes in the supply of money, it is convenient to include the money demand and supply equations and to exclude the securities market equations.

A simplifying assumption that is usually made in introductory macro-economics courses is that households desire to hold any increment in real wealth entirely in the form of securities; that is, it is assumed that $m_a = 0$ and $b_a = 1$. Hence, real wealth does not appear in the demand-for-money function. The condition for asset market equilibrium, making this simplifying assumption, is

$$M/P = m(r, y)$$

Real income (y) has already been determined by the conditions for equilibrium in the labour market in conjunction with the production function, and the rate of interest (r) has been determined by the conditions for equilibrium in the product market. The real demand for money is therefore predetermined once y and r have been determined. The nominal supply of money (M) is assumed to be determined exogenously by the policy of the central bank. Hence, there is only one variable left whose value can adjust to equate the real supply of money to the demand for real money balances: the price level (P). Figure 2.5 depicts the determination of the price level for a given nominal supply of money (M_1).

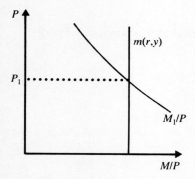

Fig. 2.5 Asset market equilibrium

2.2.13 Summary

The static neoclassical macroeconomic model is the macro counterpart of the perfect-competition microeconomic model. The principal assumptions are that all firms have the same production function; all markets are auction markets with flexible prices that will (in the absence of interference) continuously adjust to clear all markets; all economic agents are price takers; all economic agents have complete information; and expectations are static. In such an economy, the outcomes of the decisions of individual economic agents are pre-coordinated by the price system. Hence, Say's Law holds so that aggregate demand always adjusts to equal the full-employment level of output. The rate of interest is the variable that adjusts to make Say's Law hold. Under certain assumptions about the absence of nominal variables in behavioural relations (all behavioural relations are in terms of real variables), changes in the money supply affect only nominal variables and do not affect real variables. The price level is the variable that adjusts to equate the real money supply to the demand for real money balances.

The complete set of equations describing the static model is set out in Appendix 2.1. To see the essential properties of the model it is frequently simplified to a set of seven equations. Two assumptions are frequently made to do this. It is assumed that $m_a = 0$ and $s_a = 0$. Hence, household wealth does not enter into the solution of the model. To complete the exclusion of the securities market, interest on the government debt is omitted in the government budget equation. Thus, although the government may finance its expenditures by selling bonds, the quantity of bonds outstanding is ignored in solving the model.

The simplified model is a short-run model in which the stock of capital (k) is assumed to be constant. Making these assumptions and incorporating behavioural equations into equilibrium conditions, the model reduces to the following seven equations:

$$y = f(n, k) \qquad f_n > 0, f_{nn} < 0$$
$$f_n = w$$
$$n = h(w) \qquad h_w > 0$$
$$i = i(n, k, q, r) \qquad i_n > 0, i_k < 0, i_q < 0, i_r < 0$$
$$c = c(y, r, t) \qquad 0 < c_y < 1, c_t < 0, c_r < 0$$
$$y = c + i + g + qk$$
$$M/P = m(y, r) \qquad m_y > 0, m_r < 0$$

Exogenous variables: k, M, g, t, q
Endogenous variables: w, n, y, i, c, r, P

2.3 THE DICHOTOMY BETWEEN REAL AND NOMINAL VARIABLES

Under the conditions assumed in the model, an increase in M will produce a proportionate increase in P, as is demonstrated in Appendix 2.6. This result occurs because y is jointly determined by the labour market equilibrium condition and the production function, and r is determined by the product market equilibrium condition. Hence, r and y are determined independently of M.

The complete neoclassical model is required to support this proportional relation between changes in M and changes in P because the complete model is required to specify the conditions for full employment. If there is any feedback from the asset market to the values of real variables in other markets, this proportionality will not hold. Hence, it was important to define the government real budget constraint in such a way that changes in P do not affect product market equilibrium. The result is that, in this version of the neoclassical model, there is a dichotomy between the determination of real and monetary variables. An increase in the quantity of money affects only P and other nominal variables such as the money wage rate and nominal government expenditure on goods, and does not affect real variables such as real output, employment, and the real rate of interest.[27] Money is also 'neutral': relative prices are invariant to the multiplication of the initial stock of money by a scalar. (In the one-good model presented here, there are, however, no relative prices.) The implication of the dichotomy and the neutrality of money is that 'money doesn't matter' with respect to the equilibrium positions of real variables.[28] Money is really not necessary in this model since all trades could be carried out by barter, and, given the certainty about future prices, there is no need to store wealth in the form of money. Because of this, neoclassical theory tended to keep real and monetary theory separate.

This dichotomy dates back, at least, to Ricardo (1951, pp. 363–4) who stated that:

> The interest for money . . . is not regulated by the rate at which the Bank will lend, whether it be 5, 4, or 3 per cent., but by the rate of profits which can be made by the employment of capital, and which is totally independent of the quantity, or the value of money. Whether a Bank lent one million, ten millions, or a hundred millions, they would not permanently alter the market rate of interest; they would alter only the value of the money which they thus issued.

Pigou (1953, pp. 34–5) observed that Marshall's model had this property:

> In Marshall's analysis . . . there is . . . a monetary equation involving the price level, and also a further equation involving the rate of wages. For long-period problems, the rate of interest, new investment and the employment percentage being already determined . . . these additional equations together determine the price level and the money rate of wages.

Morishima (1977, p. 167) cites Walras (1954, pp. 46 and 327) to show that Walras also derived the rate of interest from the saving–investment equation and the level of prices from the quantity theory of money:

> Equality between the two sides of the equation [the saving–investment equation] is achieved through an increase or decrease in the price of new capital goods brought about by a fall or a rise in [the rate of interest].

. . . The price of the service of money [the price level] is established through its rise or fall according as the *desired cash balance* is greater or less than the quantity of money.

2.4 THE QUANTITY THEORY OF MONEY

The demand-for-money function used in the model is a descendant of the demand-for-money function developed by Marshall and Pigou at the University of Cambridge. It represents a transformation of the original Quantity Theory of Money and, in its simplest form, the 'Cambridge equation' states that the real demand for money balances is a constant proportion of an economy's real wealth. That is,

$$(M/P)^D = ka$$

where k in this equation is the 'Cambridge k' which represents the proportion of a community's total resources (other than those held by the banks) which the community chooses to keep in the form of money, and a in this equation represents the real value of the community's total resources. If k is a constant, a is given, and M is exogenously determined, then the equation can be rewritten so that

$$P = M/(ka)$$

and the direct proportionality between a change in M and a change in P results. This is the Quantity Theory of Money in its simplest and most explicit form.

Marshall (1926, p. 34, in his evidence before the Gold and Silver Commission in Great Britain in 1887) had, however, stated:

I accept the common doctrine that prices generally rise, other things being equal, in proportion to the volume of the metals which are used as currency. I think that changes in the other things that are taken as equal are very often, perhaps generally, more important than the change in the volumes of the precious metals.

Although they discussed the factors that might affect k, Marshall and Pigou never did make k an explicit function of the rate of interest – the opportunity cost of holding money. It was left to later economists, including Keynes and Friedman, to put the rate of interest explicitly into the demand-for-money function as was done in section 2.2 above. In its modern version the Quantity Theory of Money has two components: a demand-for-money function and the incorporation of that function into a model in such a way that a change in the quantity of money leads to a proportionate change in the price level.

Keynes in his *A Tract on Monetary Reform* restated the Cambridge equation and its qualifications, but then went on to criticize it as a tool for the analysis of short-run economic fluctuations[29]:

> The theory has often been expounded on the . . . assumption that a *mere* change in the quantity of currency cannot affect [k and a] – that is to say, in mathematical parlance, that [M] is an *independent variable* in relation to these quantities. It would follow from this that an arbitrary doubling of [M], since this in itself is assumed not to affect [k and a], must have the effect of raising [P] to double what it would have been otherwise. The quantity theory is often stated in this, or a similar form.
>
> Now in the 'long run' this is probably true. If, after the American Civil War, the American dollar had been stabilised and defined at law at 10 per cent below its present value, it would be safe to assume that [M and P] would be now just 10 per cent greater than they actually are and that the present values of [k and a] would be entirely unaffected. But this *long run* is a misleading guide to current affairs. *In the long run* we are all dead.

Keynes's rejection of the Quantity Theory of Money in the *Gerneral Theory* will be discussed in the next chapter.

2.5 UNEMPLOYMENT AND ECONOMIC POLICY

Unemployment (an excess supply of labour services offered for work at the going real wage rate) can exist and persist in the neoclassical model when there is an interference with the market-clearing mechanism such that the resulting real wage rate is, and stays, above the market-clearing rate as is shown in Fig. 2.6. When there is an excess supply of labour, it will be balanced by an excess demand for goods – Walras's Law holds. At the higher money wage rate firms' costs curves have moved up and firms supply less goods, as is indicated by the lower level of employment. Hence, in the product market, households find that they cannot buy as much goods as they would like. Households are thus *quantity constrained* (rationed) in both the labour market where they sell their services and in the product market where they buy goods. In a world of flexible prices, such a situation would lead to a rise in goods' prices which would decrease real wages and create a situation in which firms would find it profitable to increase employment and output. If, however, money wages are drifting up because of exogenous factors such as minimum wage laws or trade union bargaining power so that real wages are not declining significantly, a barrier to achieving full employment would exist. Another possibility that could lead to a persistence of the unemployment would be any exogenous factors in the product market which keep prices from rising sufficiently to achieve the equilibrium real wage rate.[30]

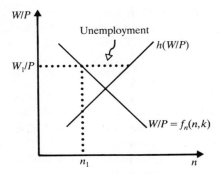

Fig. 2.6 High money wages and unemployment

The classical view of how the labour market functions had been expressed by Pigou (1949, p. 90):

> If the classical view . . . represents the facts, there must clearly exist some mechanism by which it may be supposed that, in a given environment, the trend of employment is tied, as it were by an elastic string, to the trend of the number comprised in the available labour force. . . . Advocates of the classical view would, I think, describe the mechanism which they believe to be at work more or less as follows: When the percentage of unemployment is heavy, competition among wage-earners for work, hampered and delayed as it is by frictions and elements of monopolistic policy, leads presently to the acceptance of lower money wages, whereas, on the other hand, when the percentage of unemployment is small, competition among employers for scarce labour tends to push money wages up.

Robert Solow (1980, pp. 6–7) points out that the belief that wage cuts serve to restore full employment was based on estimates, which Pigou had made, that the elasticity of demand for labour with respect to the real wage rate is greater than unity. Solow cites the results of recent research which indicate that the elasticity is 0.5 or lower and goes on to say 'smooth wage adjustment seems intrinsically unlikely in a world with such a small demand elasticity and institutions like [trade unionism and unemployment insurance]'.

Pigou, in his *Unemployment* (1913, pp. 51–2) and again, as follows, in his *The Theory of Unemployment* (1933), expressed his views on economic policy with respect to unemployment:

> With perfectly free competition among workpeople and labour perfectly mobile . . . there will always be at work a strong tendency for wage-rates

to be so related to demand that everybody is employed. Hence, in stable conditions every one will actually be employed. The implication is that such unemployment as exists at any time is due wholly to the fact that changes in demand conditions are continually taking place and that frictional resistances prevent the appropriate wage adjustments from being made instantaneously. (p. 252)

The factor that determines the long-run relation between the real wage-rate stipulated for and the real demand function for labour is best described in a general way as *wage policy.* . . . This wage policy is exercised sometimes through collective bargaining on the part of Trade Unions, sometimes through State action establishing minimum rates of pay. It is not necessary, merely because these agencies are employed, that the goal of the policy should be a system of rates higher than those which perfectly free competition among wage earners tends to bring about. If in fact the goal set were identical with the goal of free competition, the quantity of unemployment for which wage policy made would be nil. No part of the actual unemployment ruling at any time would be attributable to it. There is reason to believe, however, that the goal at which wage policy aims is sometimes . . . a wage-rate substantially higher than the rate which, if adopted, everywhere, would yield nil unemployment. (p. 253)

Students of our problems in this country before the war, while recognising maladjustments of a long-run character associated with wage policy as one of the factors responsible for unemployment, in general took the view that the part played by them was small. Unemployment, for these writers, was, in the main, a function of industrial fluctuations and labour immobility – of short-run frictions rather than of long-run tendencies. . . . Wage policy as a possible long-run determinant of unemployment calls . . . for closer study than would have been thought necessary twenty years ago. (pp. 255–6)

Keynes (1936, p. 257; italics added) summed up his view (which seems to agree with that of Pigou's) of the classical position on unemployment:

The classical theory has been accustomed to rest the supposedly self-adjusting characteristics of the economic system on an assumed fluidity of money wages; and, when there is a *rigidity*, to lay on this rigidity the blame of maladjustment.

Pigou (1913, pp. 245–6) did allow for a role by government in reducing the unemployment resulting from industrial fluctuations:

Public authorities are in a position somewhat to lessen the fluctuations that occur in the demand for labour, and hence to diminish unemployment, both by fitting that part of their own demand for goods and services, which is necessarily occasional, into the interstices of the general demand, and also by avoiding unnecessary ups and downs in that part of their demand which is, or can be made, continuous. These practices constitute remedies for unemployment in all circumstances. The policy, which recently has found advocates, of deliberately making public demands vary in such wise as to compensate variations in private demands, only constitutes such a remedy, provided that certain conditions as regards the mobility of labour are fulfilled.

Keynes (1937c, p. 259) commented later on Pigou's position on economic policy which was reiterated during the 1920s and 1930s: 'When it comes to practice, there is really extremely little between us.'

2.6 GOVERNMENT EXPENDITURE AND CROWDING OUT

That government expenditure 'crowds out' private expenditure can be seen as follows. Since in the neoclassical model real output is determined by the supply side of the market (the labour market and the production function) and is at the full-employment level, total final demand $(c + i + g + qk)$ is constrained always to equal the predetermined level of total output (y). Thus, if g increases, the sum of $c + i$ must decrease by an equivalent amount. The rate of interest is the variable which adjusts to restore equilibrium in the product market. As shown in Fig. 2.7, the increase in g shifts the s schedule to the left, r rises, and i decreases. The rise in r increases s and decreases c. The decrease in private spending $(c + i)$ exactly offsets the increase in government expenditure.

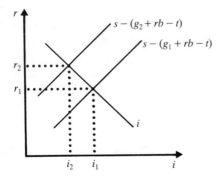

Fig. 2.7 The crowding-out effect of government expenditure

The classical (Ricardian) view against using government expenditures as a means of restoring full employment is stated by Pigou (1933), pp. 248–9:

> *Changes* in the state of demand are, of course, relevant, but, when once any given state of demand has become fully established, the real wage-rates stipulated for by workpeople adjust themselves to the new conditions. The new conditions thus operate on the wage level and perhaps also, in some degree, on the normal hours of labour, but not on the percentage of unemployment.
>
> If this broad conclusion is accepted it follows that long-run Government policies, which, whether by design or by accident, make the state of labour demand permanently better or worse than it would otherwise have been, are not, when once established, either causes of or remedies for unemployment. Thus, any lasting expansion in non-wage-earners' desire to devote their resources to the construction of capital instruments (i.e. to investment) or of other non-wage-goods will be met, not by an increase in employment, but by a shift of employment out of wage-good industries into the expanded industries, associated with an appropriate relative rise in the real wage rate there.

He went on, however, to say (p. 250):

> Our conclusion that the long-run effect of expansionist State policies . . . does not touch employment, affords, of course, no arguments against the State's *temporarily* adopting these devices as 'remedies' for unemployment in times of exceptional depression. For here it is not their long-run, but their short-run, consequences that are significant.

2.7 APPRAISAL OF THE NEOCLASSICAL MODEL

The neoclassical model is regarded by some as uninteresting in that the hard core and positive heuristic of the research programme ensure that coordinated outcomes will result (see Weintraub, 1979, pp. 75–6). Unemployment can only be generated by the *ad hoc* imposition of wage or other rigidities or by irrational behaviour by economic agents. For those that find more attractive a research programme that does not automatically produce coordinated outcomes and which explicitly looks for explanations of market failures, the Keynesian research programme is an alternative. The next chapter will examine the model of Keynes's *General Theory of Employment, Interest and Money*.

For those who do not believe that the neoclassical model provides a useful explanation of how the real world operates, the model does, however, provide a benchmark from which the functioning of the economy may be judged. As Hahn (1984, p. 308) has expressed it:

It serves a function similar to that which an ideal and perfectly healthy body might serve a clinical diagnostician when he looks at an actual body.

Hutchison (1978, p. 199) expresses the view that, in fact, this is the way that Pigou used it:

> Pigou made some use of the flexible, perfectly competitive model simply as a reference model. But he repeatedly made it clear that this model differed critically from the real-world economy of Britain in the inter-war years and he repeatedly and emphatically rejected policy conclusions drawn from such a flexible, competitive model.

2.8 FURTHER READING

An in-depth mathematical treatment of the neoclassical model is in Sargent (1987a, Ch. I). An introductory exposition is in J.A. Sawyer (1975, Chs 5–6). Hillier (1986) is a good introduction to the neoclassical and Keynesian models and to the recent controversies. Felderer and Homburg (1987, Ch. IV) is an exposition of the neoclassical model.

For an exposition of Walras's model, Morishima (1977) is recommended. Niehans (1978, Ch. 1) discusses the neoclassical tradition of the theory of money. Pigou (1917) and Keynes (1923) present expositions of the Cambridge version of the Quantity Theory of Money. Lange (1944) and Patinkin (1965) attempt to integrate the neoclassical theories of value and money.

With respect to the mathematical appendices, students who need to improve their knowledge of mathematics will find Glaister (1978), Dixit (1976), Timbrell (1985), or Weintraub (1982) useful. Kogiku (1968) is an introduction to mathematical macroeconomic models and Allen (1959) and Chiang (1984) are introductions to mathematical economics.

APPENDIX 2.1   THE EQUATIONS OF THE NEOCLASSICAL MODEL

The static neoclassical model consists of the following equations:

Production function	$y = f(n, k)$	(2.1)
Labour market		
demand (determines n)	$f_n = w$	(2.2)
supply	$n^s = h(w)$	(2.4)
market-clearing condition	$n = n^s$	(2.5)
Product market		

demand for capital goods (determines $k^\#$)	$f_k = r + q$	(2.3)
investment	$i = i(n, k, q, r)$	(2.6)
stock of capital	$\dot{k} = i$	(2.18)
household disposable income	$z = y - qk - t + rb$	(2.10)
household saving	$s = s(z, r, a)$	(2.9)
household consumption	$c = z - s$	(2.11)
market-clearing condition	$y = c + i + qk + g$	(2.12)

Asset markets

household wealth	$a = (M/P)^D + (b + k)^D$	(2.15)
money		
demand	$(M/P)^D = m(r, z, a)$	(2.13)
supply (nominal)	$M = B^{CB}$	(2.7)
market-clearing condition	$(M/P)^D = M/P$	(2.16)
securities		
demand	$(b + k)^D = b(r, z, a)$	(2.14)
supply	$\dot{B} = G + rB - T - \dot{M}$	(2.8)
market-clearing condition	$(b + k)^D = b + k$	(2.17)

Nominal dollar identities

value of output	$Y = Py$	(2.19)
government expenditure	$G = Pg$	(2.20)
tax revenue	$T = Pt$	(2.21)
money wage rate	$W = Pw$	(2.22)
household wealth	$A = Pa$	(2.23)
value of bonds	$B = Pb$	(2.24)

Exogenous variables: B^{CB}, g, t, q

Endogenous variables – real: $y, k^\#, k, i, w, n, n^s, z, s, c,$
$\qquad\qquad\qquad\qquad (b + k)^D, b, r, a$
$\qquad\qquad$ – nominal: $P, M^D, M, Y, G, T, W, A, B$

Although there are 24 equations, there are only 23 endogenous variables. The market-clearing condition for the securities market is redundant because of Walras's Law. It is implied by the wealth constraint and the equilibrium condition for real money balances as long as all securities are regarded as perfect substitutes for one another. Hence only 23 equations are required to solve the model; equation (2.17) can be omitted.

APPENDIX 2.2   THE ALGEBRA OF COMPARATIVE STATICS ANALYSIS

The effect of a change in the stock of capital on the endogenous variables of the sub-model given by equations (2.1), (2.2), (2.4), and (2.5) can be obtained using an algebraic technique that is very useful in situations where the number of variables is such that geometric analysis becomes difficult. The technique is one of linear approximations using the total differentials of equations.

Substituting equation (2.5) into equation (2.4), a three-equation sub-model is obtained:

$$y = f(n,k)$$
$$w = f_n$$
$$n = h(w)$$

The equations can be linearized around the current equilibrium values of the endogenous variables by taking total differentials of the equations and assuming, since the changes will be very small and will be in the neighbourhood of the original equilibrium, that the coefficients (the partial derivatives) are constant. The method is based on Taylor's theorem and obtains, for example, the (approximate) change in the value of f by adding the changes attributable to n and k, assuming the effects are independent. Applying this method, the following set of linear simultaneous equations is obtained, where f_n, f_k and h_w are the partial derivatives of f and h with respect to n, k and w; f_{nn} and f_{kk} are the partial derivatives of f_n and f_k with respect to n and k; f_{nk} is the partial derivative of f_n with respect to k. Note that f_n and f_k are functions and can be written as $f_n(n, k)$ and $f_k(n,k)$.

$$dy = f_n dn + f_k dk \qquad (2.25)$$
$$dw = f_{nn} dn + f_{nk} dk \qquad (2.26)$$
$$dn = h_w dw \qquad (2.27)$$

The first equation states that the change in y equals (approximately) the sum of the marginal product of labour times the change in the input of labour services plus the marginal product of capital times the change in the input of the services of capital.

Since the system is linear, methods of linear algebra can be applied to solve the system. The results are, however, only local; that is, valid only for small changes in the neighbourhood of the original equilibrium. Since the marginal product of labour is the tangent to the production function at the relevant point, as is shown in Fig. 2.1, f_n can only be regarded as a constant in the immediate neighbourhood of the original point.

A solution can be obtained by starting with the demand-for-labour equation and then substituting the labour-supply equation for dn. Thus, the following 'reduced-form equation' – the solution of the model for a particular endogenous variable which expresses that variable as a function of all the exogenous variables and the parameters of the model, all other endogenous variables having been eliminated in the solution process – is obtained for dw:

$$dw = \frac{f_{nk}}{1 - f_{nn}h_w} dk$$

Since $f_{nk} > 0$, $f_{nn} < 0$, and $h_w > 0$; $dw/dk > 0$
From the labour-supply equation, $dn = h_w dw$; hence, $dn/dk > 0$.
From the production function, $dy = f_n(h_w dw) + f_k dk$; hence, $dy/dk > 0$.

APPENDIX 2.3 MATRIX ALGEBRA SOLUTION OF A MODEL

Matrix algebra can also be used to solve equations (2.25)–(2.27). These can be written in matrix form:

$$\begin{bmatrix} 1 & 0 & -f_n \\ 0 & 1 & -f_{nn} \\ 0 & -h_w & 1 \end{bmatrix} \begin{bmatrix} dy \\ dw \\ dn \end{bmatrix} = \begin{bmatrix} f_k dk \\ f_{nk} dk \\ 0 \end{bmatrix} \qquad (2.28)$$

The left-hand-side matrix of coefficients is called a Jacobian since all the co-efficients are first partial derivatives. (A matrix whose elements are all second partial derivatives is called a Hessian.) It is post-multiplied by a vector which contains all the endogenous variables. On the right-hand side is the vector of exogenous variables, which in some cases have coefficients associated with them.

Note the zeros in the first column in the second and third rows. This indicates that dy does not appear in the second and third equations and that the last two equations may be solved by themselves to determine dn and dw. The first equation is then used to determine dy, once dn has been determined. Such a model is said to be 'block recursive'. That is, it can be separated into separate blocks of equations and solved block by block. In some cases, each block is a single equation and then the model is simply said to be 'recursive'. When the model is not recursive or block recursive, the system of equations must be solved simultaneously. When solutions for all of the endogenous variables are required, a solution would proceed as follows, ignoring the recursiveness in order to indicate the more general method of solution.
Let **A** be the Jacobian matrix

    x   vector of endogenous variables

    z   vector of exogenous variables

Equation (2.28) can now be written $\mathbf{Ax} = \mathbf{z}$.
Hence, $\mathbf{x} = \mathbf{A}^{-1}\mathbf{z}$
where $\mathbf{A}^{-1} = (1/|\mathbf{A}|)\mathbf{A}^+$
and $\mathbf{A}^{-1}$ is the inverse of $\mathbf{A}$

    $|\mathbf{A}|$ is the determinant of $\mathbf{A}$

$\mathbf{A}^+$ is the adjoint of $\mathbf{A}$ (transpose of the matrix of cofactors of $\mathbf{A}$)
In this example

$$|\mathbf{A}| = 1 - f_{nn}h_w$$

$$\mathbf{A}^+ = \begin{bmatrix} 1 - f_{nn}h_w & f_n h_w & f_n \\ 0 & 1 & f_{nn} \\ 0 & h_w & 1 \end{bmatrix}$$

Hence,

$$\begin{bmatrix} dy \\ dw \\ dn \end{bmatrix} = \{1/(1 - f_{nn}h_w)\}\mathbf{A}^+ \begin{bmatrix} f_k dk \\ f_{nk} dk \\ 0 \end{bmatrix}$$

and $dy = \{f_k + (f_n h_w f_{nk})/(1 - f_{nn}h_w)\}dk$
$\quad dw = \{f_{nk}/(1 - f_{nn}h_w)\}dk$
$\quad dn = \{h_w f_{nk}/(1 - f_{nn}h_w)\}dk$

If a solution was required only for dw, it would not be economical to calculate $\mathbf{A}^{-1}$. Instead, Cramer's rule, which involves fewer calculations, could be used. Cramer's rule involves calculating the determinant of a matrix in which the second column of $\mathbf{A}$ (since dw is the second endogenous variable) is replaced by $\mathbf{z}$. According to Cramer's rule,

$$dw = |\mathbf{B}|/|\mathbf{A}|$$

$$\text{where } \mathbf{B} = \begin{bmatrix} 1 & f_k dk & -f_n \\ 0 & f_{nk} dk & -f_{nn} \\ 0 & 0 & 1 \end{bmatrix}$$

Hence, $dw = \{f_{nk}/(1 - f_{nn}h_w)\}dk$

APPENDIX 2.4 OPTIMIZATION

The mathematics of finding the necessary conditions for the maximum or minimum of a function subject to one or more constraints using Lagrange expressions is demonstrated below for the examples in sections 2.2.3 and 2.2.4.

Profit maximization

$$\text{Profits} = Py - Wn - (r + q)Pk$$

A general way of finding the necessary conditions for profit maximization subject to the constraint of the production function is to form the Lagrangian expression L, derive the partial derivatives of L with respect to each of the variables, set them equal to zero, and solve the resulting set of equations. (In this example, the same result can be obtained by substituting $f(n,k)$ in place of y

before differentiating profits. The Lagrangian method is particularly useful when there is more than one constraint.)

$$L = Py - Wn - (r + q)Pk - \lambda[y - f(n,k)] \tag{2.29}$$

where λ is a Lagrange multiplier and the last term equals zero so that L equals total profits.

The variables from the viewpoint of the firm as a price-taker are y, n, and k. Mathematically, λ must also be treated as a variable. Hence, the necessary conditions for a maximum are

$$\partial L/\partial y = P - \lambda = 0$$
$$\partial L/\partial n = -W + \lambda f_n = 0$$
$$\partial L/\partial k = -(r + q)P + \lambda f_k = 0$$
$$\partial L/\partial \lambda = -y + f(n,k) = 0$$

Hence, $\lambda = P$
$$f_n = W/P = w$$
$$f_k = r + q$$
$$y = f(n, k)$$

Note that the Lagrange multiplier has an economic interpretation: it is the price of output, or, if the perfect competition assumption is relaxed, marginal revenue.

Utility maximization

Assume that all individuals have the same utility function and that they are all utility maximizers. Assume utility is a function of real income (y) and leisure hours (m):

$$U = h(y, m) \qquad h_y > 0, h_m > 0, h_{yy} < 0, h_{mm} < 0$$

There are two constraints that must be obeyed. Leisure hours (m) equal the total number of hours available for work and leisure combined (t) minus the number of hours worked (n). Real income equals the real wage rate times the number of hours worked:

$$m = t - n$$
$$y = wn \qquad \text{where } w = W/P$$

To obtain the necessary conditions for maximizing utility subject to the two constraints, a Lagrangian expression can be formed:

$$L = h(y, m) - \lambda_1(m + n - t) - \lambda_2(y - wn) \tag{2.30}$$

The variables that can be controlled by the household are y, m, and n. The market prices W and P must be taken as given. The necessary conditions for utility maximization are obtained by determining the partial derivatives of L with respect to y, m, n, λ_1, and λ_2, setting each of them equal to zero, and solving the resulting set of five equations.

$$\partial L/\partial y = h_y - \lambda_2 = 0$$
$$\partial L/\partial m = h_m - \lambda_1 = 0$$
$$\partial L/\partial n = -\lambda_1 + \lambda_2 w = 0$$
$$\partial L/\partial \lambda_1 = m + n - t = 0$$
$$\partial L/\partial \lambda_2 = y - wn = 0$$

From the first two equations

$$\lambda_2 = h_y \text{ and } \lambda_1 = h_m$$

Substituting these two expressions into the third equation gives

$$-h_m + h_y w = 0$$

In this case the Lagrange multipliers are the marginal utility of income and the marginal utility of leisure, respectively. The necessary condition for utility maximization is $h_m/h_y = w$.

APPENDIX 2.5 COBB–DOUGLAS PRODUCTION FUNCTION

The Cobb–Douglas production function originated in the 1920s as a result of a collaboration between Paul Douglas, a labour economist at the University of Chicago, and William Cobb, a mathematician at Amherst University. Douglas wanted a functional form which would give constant returns to scale and in which the factors of production would also obey the law of diminishing returns with respect to each factor. In addition, in order to do econometric work, it was necessary that the parameters of the function could be estimated by linear regression.

The resulting function was

$$y = e^a n^b k^{1-b} \qquad 0 < b < 1 \tag{2.31}$$

where e is the base of the natural logarithms

a and b are parameters

That the function obeys the law of diminishing returns with respect to labour can be seen. The marginal product of labour is

$$f_n = be^a n^{b-1} k^{1-b} = b(y/n) > 0$$

Note that in this function there is a proportional relation between the average product of labour (y/n) and the marginal product of labour (f_n). Similarly for the average and marginal products of capital.

The change in the marginal product of labour as the input of labour increases is

$$f_{nn} = b(b - 1)e^a n^{b-2} k^{1-b} < 0$$

Hence, there are diminishing returns with respect to the input of labour. Similarly, $f_k > 0$ and $f_{kk} < 0$.

Labour and capital are complements:

$$f_{kn} = f_{nk} = b(1-b)e^a n^{b-1} k^{-b} > 0$$

Constant returns to scale exist:

$$e^a(\mu n)^b(\mu k)^{1-b} = \mu^b \mu^{1-b} e^a n^b k^{1-b} = \mu e^a n^b k^{1-b} = \mu y$$

where μ is a scalar, $\mu > 0$.

That is, the production function is assumed to be homogeneous of degree one in both labour and capital.

Euler's theorem states that if $z = f(x,y)$ is continuous and has continuous first-order derivatives and if $f(x,y)$ is homogeneous of degree μ, then $f_x x + f_y y = \mu f(x,y)$. Thus, if labour and capital are paid their marginal products, the total product is distributed:

$$y = f_n n + f_k k = (by/n)n + (1 - b)(y/k)k = y$$

It can also be seen that if there is perfect competition the share of labour and capital in the total product is constant. In value terms, $Py = Wn + (r + q)Pk$. Labour's share is

$$(W/P)(n/y) = f_n(n/y) = b(y/n)(n/y) = b$$

Since payment according to marginal product exhausts the total product, capital's share is $1 - b$.

The function has constant elasticities of output with respect to both labour and capital. (A similar functional form will produce a demand function which has constant price- and income-elasticities of demand.) The elasticity of output with respect to the input of labour is

$$(\partial y/\partial n)(n/y) = b(y/n)(n/y) = b$$

Similarly, the elasticity of output with respect to the input of capital is $1 - b$.

The function is linear in the natural logarithms (ln) of the variables and linear regression analysis can be performed if a logarithmic transformation of the variables is done:

$$\ln(y) = a + b \ln(n) + (1 - b) \ln(k)$$

The optimal stock of capital is derived from equation (2.3), which for the Cobb–Douglas production function becomes

$$f_k = (1 - b)(y/k) = r + q$$

That is, $k^\# = \{(1 - b)/(r + q)\}y$

The profit-maximizing demand-for-labour equation (2.2) becomes

$$b(y/n) = W/P$$

This can be interpreted as a price equation

$$P = (1/b)\,(Wn/y)$$

That is, firms set prices as a markup on unit labour costs (Wn/y) where the markup is ($1/b$) which, for the Cobb–Douglas production function, is a constant.

From the profit-maximizing conditions it can be seen that

$$f_n/f_k = W/(r + q)$$

Substituting $b(y/n)$ for f_n and $(1 - b)\,(y/k)$ for f_k and rearranging the terms, this becomes

$$[1/(1 - b)]\,[(r + q)k/y] = (1/b)(Wn/y)$$

Hence, the unit capital cost is $(r + q)k/y$ and equals $[(1 - b)/b]$ times the unit labour cost (Wn/y). The price equation could also be written, therefore, in terms of unit capital cost rather than unit labour cost:

$$P = [1/(1 - b)]\,[(r + q)k/y]$$

Because of this relationship between unit labour cost and unit capital cost implied by the assumptions of the Cobb–Douglas production function and perfectly competitive markets, it is not necessary to include both labour and capital costs in the price equation.

APPENDIX 2.6   THE MONEY SUPPLY AND THE PRICE LEVEL

That an increase in the supply of money produces a proportionate increase in the price level can be seen as follows:

$$M/P = m(r, y)$$
$$d(M/P) = (P dM - M dP)/P^2$$
$$= dM/P - M dP/P^2$$
$$= dM/P - (M/P)(dP/P) = m_r dr + m_y dy$$

Hence, $dP/P = dM/M - m_r(P/M)dr - m_y(P/M)dy$
$$dP/dM = P\{1/M - m_r(P/M)dr/dM - m_y(P/M)dy/dM\}$$

Because y is jointly determined by the labour-market equilibrium condition and the production function and r is determined by the product-market equilibrium condition, r and y are determined independently of M.

Hence, $dr/dM = dy/dM = 0$ and $dP/P = dM/M$.

NOTES

1. The statement of the core and heuristics has been adapted from Weintraub (1985, p. 109, and 1979, Ch. 2) and from Blaug (1976, p. 161). The statement of their consequences for the resultant macroeconomic model have been influenced by Weitzman (1982) and Kaldor (1983). For a discussion of the hard core and heuristics of the neoclassical perfect competition model, see Latsis (1976b, pp. 22–3), Coats (1976, pp. 53–4), and Blaug (1976, pp. 167–71). Leijonhufvud (1976, p. 106) dismisses claims that there is a need to develop a separate neo-Walrasian macro-structure with the statement 'We already have a full-fledged macro-theory within this programme.' The reader might compare the hard core propositions with the assumptions set forth by Knight (1921, pp. 76–80) for his imaginary 'competitive' society and also read the discussion of perfect competition by Stigler (1957).
2. See Weintraub (1979, p. 29) and Hicks (1965, p. 20).
3. Weintraub (1979, pp. 74–5) makes this point, which is based on the earlier work of Clower and Leijonhufvud.
4. This is a common assumption. Pigou (1949, p. 4) makes it in constructing his model and uses grain as an example of a commodity which can either be eaten or used for seed.
5. A lower-case letter will be used for real variables and upper case will be used for prices and nominal dollar quantities.
6. Readers who know calculus will recognize that this is a partial derivative of the function.
7. Note that f_n, f_{nn}, and f_{nk} are all functions and could be written as $f_n(n, k), f_{nn}(n, k)$, and $f_{nk}(n,k)$ and that $f_{nk} = f_{kn}$.
8. Static expectations are assumed; hence, the expected rate of inflation is zero and real and nominal rates of interest are the same.
9. If the Cobb–Douglas production function is used, explicit demand-for-labour and demand-for-capital functions can be derived as shown in Appendix 2.5.
10. See Knight (1921) for an exposition of the role of the entrepreneur in the presence of uncertainty.
11. Weitzman (1982) has pointed out that the hard core of the model suggests a way in which the neoclassical model gives rise to full employment for all workers. Any worker who is not employed by a firm may become an entrepreneur, create a firm (which, given constant returns to scale, will be a scale replica of existing firms) and, given full information and a full set of spot a forward markets, sell, at some appropriate price, all the output he/she produces.
12. Time will be treated as a continuous variable and the model solved at a moment of time. To keep the notation simple, until Chapter 5 when dynamic analysis is introduced, the time subscript on variables will continue to be omitted.

13. Strictly speaking, this is a predetermined variable whose value is determined by the past history of the system.
14. Appendices 2.2 and 2.3 show two different algebraic methods of solving the model.
15. Generally, in this book a dot over a variable will be used to denote the rate of change of a variable over time (the derivative of the variable with respect to time).
16. It is a common practice of economists to use the same name for a function and for the endogenous variable whose value it explains. Appendix 2.5 derives the optimal stock of capital for a Cobb–Douglas production function.
17. Tobin (1982, pp. 46–73) has developed the 'Q theory of investment' which focuses attention on the ratio of the actual market value of equities to the replacement cost of the capital goods held by firms, and has termed this ratio Q. He notes that when $Q < 1$ (the market value of equities is less than the replacement cost of capital) it is cheaper for firms to acquire real capital by buying existing companies rather than buying capital goods directly. When $Q > 1$, the market is valuing the future prospects of firms highly (expected earnings exceed the cost of the new capital required to produce additional output) and firms will tend to undertake investment in new capital goods. In equilibrium $Q = 1$.
18. To keep the model simple, it is assumed that there is no income tax.
19. The price level (P) is defined to equal 1.0 in the first year that bonds were issued.
20. On a consolidated basis the government only pays interest on the bond to households since the income of the central bank is paid to the government.
21. Since firms do not retain any earnings, the saving of households is the total saving of the private sector.
22. There are no real capital gains or losses on holding financial assets since the bond is always worth 1 constant dollar, the price of an equity always equals $1, and the inflation rate is zero.
23. If real wealth (a) had been left in the saving function, this would not be true.
24. Morishima (1977, pp. 129–30) cites a passage from Walras to show that Walras also derived the rate of interest from the saving–investment equation.
25. Three English economists, Ralph Hawtrey, Frederick Lavington, and Sir Dennis Robertson, all subsequently used similar forms of analysis, as did Keynes in his *Treatise on Money* (1930). See Milgate (1982, Chs V and XI) for a discussion of these economists' arguments as well as that of Wicksell.
26. This can be seen by taking the total differentials of the two demand functions and adding them together. The real wealth constraint (2.15) must hold. Take the total differential of it and subtract it from the above equation. Then the stated properties are obtained.
27. This dichotomy follows from the original conception of the Quantity Theory of Money as formulated by Locke and Hume.
28. Money does matter for the inflation rate. This will be discussed in Chapter 6.
29. Keynes (1923, p. 65). His notation has been changed, as is indicated by the use of [#] to conform with that in this book and the context of the quotation thereby slightly altered without, however, affecting its main point.
30. See Malinvaud (1984, pp. 37–43 and 60–6) and Sinclair (1987, pp. 60–80) for a discussion of Classical and Keynesian unemployment.

3 · A MODEL FROM KEYNES'S *GENERAL THEORY*

> The economic system may find itself in stable equilibrium with [employment] at a level below full employment.
>
> John Maynard Keynes (1936, p. 30)

This chapter sets out the static model of Keynes's *General Theory of Employment, Interest and Money* modified by translating Keynes's retention of the neoclassical demand-for-labour function into an equation describing the price-setting behaviour of firms. That is why it is described as a model *from* the *General Theory* rather than as the model *of* the *General Theory*. In interpreting Keynes's *General Theory*, it is important to remember that he learned his economics from Marshall and and Pigou and he used Marshall's methodology.[1] Keynes's view of the world was that of one who had been trained in neoclassical economics but who had come to reject certain key elements while retaining the remainder. The chapter concludes with a summary of Keynes's thoughts on macroeconomic policy.

3.1 THE HARD CORE AND HEURISTICS

The hard core that may be considered to underlie Keynes's model consists principally of the hard core from which the neoclassical model of the previous chapter was derived, but with important differences which reflect in large part market failures. As Frank Hahn (1984, p. 290) remarks, the neoclassical model 'does not capture any of the market failures macroeconomists have been concerned with for forty-five years'.[2] The third and fourth components of the neoclassical hard core from Section 2.1 are therefore replaced by the following:

1. Economic agents *do not* have full information on all prices and quantities demanded or supplied; thus, there is a significant amount of uncertainty.
2. Observable economic outcomes are *not* necessarily coordinated so that the nature of an equilibrium state may be different.

In an essay entitled 'The end of *laissez-faire*', Keynes (1926, p. 291) had expressed his concern for the economic consequences of uncertainty: 'Many of the greatest economic evils of our time are the fruits of risk, uncertainty, and ignorance.' Keynes was very familiar with financial markets and well aware that there is not a complete set of spot and forward markets. Hence, long-run decisions cannot be based on prices which are assumed to be certain. Mark Blaug (1976, p. 162) points out the essential difference between the Keynesian and neo-Walrasian scientific research programmes:

> The classical and neoclassical 'hard cores' had always contained the idea of rational economic calculation involving the existence of certainty-equivalents for each uncertain future outcome of current decisions. Keynes introduced pervasive uncertainty and the possibility of destabilizing expectations, not just in the 'protective belt' but in the 'hard core' of his programme. The Keynesian 'hard core', therefore, is really a new 'hard core' in economics. . . . There is hardly any doubt, therefore, that Keynesian economics marked the appearance of a new SRP [scientific research programme] in the history of economics.

Richard Lipsey (1981, p. 546) takes the same position:

> My thesis is that Keynesian macroeconomics is a 'progressive research programme' within Lakatos's definition of the term. . . . As such it is fulfilling two criteria. First, it is continuing to prove resilient in explaining new observations which at first seemed in conflict with its basic tenets. It incorporates and explains what we see within its broad hypothesis without having to explain away inconvenient facts on a totally ad hoc basis. . . . Second, it continues to make strong predictions which conflict with those of its principal rivals. So far these predictions have a pretty good track record.

As Frank Hahn (1984, p. 13) has pointed out, Keynesian economics is about the failure of decisions made independently by economic agents to be coordinated because of the failure of the decentralized signalling system (competitive market prices) to function. This leads to economic outcomes which are not Pareto optimal. This is in contrast to the equilibrium in a Walrasian economy which can be reached by the independent decisions of economic agents and which, given the assumptions in the hard core of the model, will be Pareto optimal. In the Keynesian model there is a role for government as an economic agent which can adopt policies which will bring the economy to a more optimal position and thereby serve as a substitute for cooperation among economic agents.

The positive heuristics of the Keynesian programme are:

1. The types of economic agents are the same but the characteristics of mar-

kets and factors of production may be different. Individual industries may contain only small numbers of firms so that firms may have market power and may set prices. The mobility of factors of production may be limited. Goods and factors of production may not be infinitely divisible so that constant returns to scale may not exist everywhere. Firms have explicit forms of organization. Hence, it may not be possible for an individual to create a firm without incurring significant set-up costs.

2. Economists may construct theories in which psychological and other non-economic influences may play an important role.
3. Economic data should be developed in a form that enables them to be used to measure macroeconomic magnitudes. For example, national income and expenditure accounts should be developed.
4. The theories should make predictions of the effect of changes in economic variables.

The first two differ significantly from those of the neoclassical programme. The negative heuristics appear to be the same.

3.2 KEYNES'S METHOD

Keynes used Alfred Marshall's method of comparative statics. As Hicks (1985, pp. 44, 58–61) has pointed out, however, Marshall avoided the apparent sterility of the analysis of a stationary state by putting the difficulties of static analysis 'in the pound of *ceteris paribus*' – that is, in the other things remaining the same. There were two aspects to this. The first was his frequent attention, not to the whole economy, but to a small sector of it such as an industry or a market – the *partial equilibrium* of a single industry or market. The second was Marshall's concern with *time* and the appropriate *ceteris paribus* for different time periods. He had both a short-period and a long-period notion of equilibrium. In the short run, the stock of fixed capital was held constant within the period, whereas in the long period all variables were let out of the pound of *ceteris paribus*.

Keynes, in contrast to the emphasis of classical economics upon long-period equilibrium, concerned himself with short-period analysis, but extended it, unlike Marshall, to the economy as a whole.[3] Fixed capital was taken as a given quantity in the short period and there was no analysis of economic growth. Presumably he assumed that those interested in growth and the long period would turn to Marshall's *Principles of Economics*. A difficulty with Keynes's short-period analysis is that, if saving and investment are occurring, the capital stock cannot remain unchanged for very long, but the period must be long enough for the multiplier process to work itself out. There does not seem to be a period of time that meets both of these requirements.

Because the saving and investment which occur in each period change the stock of capital, equilibrium within a period could only be a restricted equilibrium. Keynes restricted it to the determination of real output and employment within the period under consideration. Equilibrium could then be static in the sense that employment would not be changing within the period. The change in the capital stock would not be considered and all that mattered about investment is the income and employment that it generates within the period.

3.3 THE COMPONENTS OF KEYNES'S STATIC MODEL

The simplifying assumptions to keep the solution of the model simple and to avoid aggregation problems are the same as those in Chapter 2 for the neoclassical model.

3.3.1 The marginal efficiency of capital

Keynes recognized that in the modern world investment decisions are made by the managers of business firms and that the stock market's evaluations of the worth of firms play an important role in investment decisions. He emphasized the role of expectations in determining the volume of net investment by firms. Given the incompleteness of markets in the real world, particularly those for future deliveries, it is difficult for firms to quantify their expectations of the proceeds from long-term investments. Hence, there is an important element of the states of business confidence that drive capital investment that is unexplained and unpredictable. As he phrased it (p. 161)[4]:

> Even apart from the instability due to speculation, there is the instability due to the characteristic of human nature that a large proportion of our positive activities depend on spontaneous optimism rather than on a mathematical expectation. . . . Most, probably, of our decisions to do something positive, the full consequences of which will be drawn out over many days to come, can only be taken as a result of animal spirits – of a spontaneous urge to action rather than inaction, and not as the outcome of a weighted average of quantitative benefits multiplied by quantitative probabilities.

Keynes emphasized that his emphasis on uncertainty was an important departure from the writings of Ricardo and, more recently, Pigou. He wrote (1937a, pp. 112–13):

> But these more recent writers like their predecessors were still dealing with a system in which the amount of the factors employed was given and the other relevant facts were known more or less for certain. This does

not mean that they were dealing with a system in which change was ruled out, or even one in which the disappointment of expectations was ruled out. But at any given time facts and expectations were assumed to be given in a definite and calculable form; and risks, of which, though admitted, not much notice was taken, were supposed to be capable of an exact actuarial computation. The calculus of probability, though mention of it was kept in the background, was supposed to be capable of reducing uncertainty to the same calculable status as that of certainty itself. . . .

By 'uncertain' knowledge, let me explain, I do not mean merely to distinguish what is known for certain from what is only probable. The game of roulette is not subject, in this sense, to uncertainty. . . . The sense in which I am using the term is that in which the prospect of a European war is uncertain, or the price of copper and the rate of interest twenty years hence, or the obsolescence of a new invention. . . . About these matters there is no scientific basis on which to form any calculable probability whatever.

An important distinction is made between 'risk' and 'uncertainty'. Risk refers to events for which there is an objective probability distribution which defines the probability of the occurrence of a specific event. Hence, one can compute expected values when risk exists. Uncertainty refers to the situation where no such probability distribution exists and expected values cannot be calculated. Frank Knight's book *Risk, Uncertainty and Profit* (1921) is the classic work in economics on this distinction. This distinction will be discussed again in Chapter 5 when the rational expectations hypothesis is presented.

Investment may, therefore, be thought of as having an exogenous component determined by the state of confidence, and an endogenous component. In terms of the decision with respect to endogenous investment, Keynes (p. 248) said:

There will be an inducement to push the rate of new investment to the point which forces the supply-price of each type of capital-asset to a figure which, taken in conjunction with its prospective yield, brings the marginal efficiency of capital in general to approximate equality with the rate of interest.

The 'marginal efficiency of capital' was Keynes's term for what Irving Fisher, an early twentieth-century economist at Yale University, had called the 'internal rate of return' – the discount rate that equates the present value of the *expected* future stream of income from an investment to the cost of the capital good. The only other asset in Keynes's model was a government bond. Hence, the marginal efficiency of capital was compared with the rate of return on the bond to see whether the investment in new capital goods should be undertaken.

The marginal efficiency of capital schedule thus depicts the volume of real investment that will be undertaken at each alternative rate of interest. It should be noted that the marginal efficiency of capital was used by Keynes rather than the marginal product of capital since Keynes (p. 141) wanted to emphasize the *prospective* yield on capital, not merely its current yield. The marginal efficiency of capital is the device that Keynes used to incorporate into his model the expectations of entrepreneurs about future business prospects. Changes in the state of business confidence, therefore, lead to shifts in the marginal efficiency of capital schedule. A fall in the rate of interest, given firms' expectations of profits, will, however, encourage investment. Total investment may, however, be very inelastic with respect to changes in the rate of interest if the exogenous component is large.

3.3.2 The propensity to consume

The principal endogenous component of total demand for goods is household consumption of goods and services. Keynes's explanation of the factors determining consumption expenditures was couched in terms of the 'propensity to consume' out of disposable income. In keeping with his emphasis on uncertainty and expectations, Keynes emphasized the psychological determinants of the propensity to consume.

3.3.3 The multiplier

The presence of exogenous components of net investment leads naturally to the question: What is the effect on total real output of an increase in exogenous real investment? The answer depends on the induced effects on endogenous components of aggregate demand. Simple algebra demonstrates that, in a model in which $c = c(y)$ and the economy is so far below full employment that output may increase without price increases occurring, an increase of one unit in exogenous investment increases output by $1/(1-c_y)$, where c_y is the marginal propensity to consume. This is referred to as the 'multiplier' effect of an increase in exogenous net investment.[5] The economics underlying the algebra is that original expenditure generates a dollar of income of which c_y is spent on consumption and $1-c_y$ is saved. Each subsequent amount spent on consumption similarly generates income out of which the same portion is consumed and the remainder saved. Hence, the total effect on output and income is the sum of a geometric progression in which each term is c_y times the preceding term; that is, the sum is $1/(1-c_y)$. If the economy is markedly below the full-employment point, crowding out of private expenditure may not occur.

3.3.4 Effective demand

In the static neoclassical model, in the absence of interference with the functioning of market prices, aggregate demand plays no role in determining total output. Total demand equals the total supply of goods and full employment exists. This level of demand is sometimes termed 'notional demand'. In contrast, in Keynes's model at less than full employment 'effective demand' determines output. Effective demand to Keynes was the level of aggregate demand determined by the level of exogenous demand in conjunction with the multiplier.

Two different estimates of total effective demand may exist in the market place – depending on the expectations of economic agents – and equilibrium will not exist until these two estimates are reconciled. The total demand of households and firms for consumption and capital goods is derived from their state of long-term expectations. Their demand is a *constrained* demand in that it is a function of their expected incomes based on an expected level of employment that may be less than full employment. Entrepreneurs, on the other side of the market, will base their current decisions on prices, employment and production on their expectations of total demand, which may be significantly different from those on the demand side of the market. Households as consumers and suppliers of labour are price-takers and adapt their expenditures to the prices set by firms. They will thus communicate a demand to the market. If the value of their demand equals the demand expected by entrepreneurs, firms will not have any incentive to modify their decisions on prices, output, and employment and a state of equilibrium will prevail. This equilibrium will be at less than full employment unless the exogenous component of aggregate demand happens to be at the level required for effective demand to generate full employment. If an equilibrium is not reached initially, firms will adjust their price, employment, and output decisions which will in turn affect market demand. The process will continue until expectations converge and market equilibrium is attained.[6]

3.3.5 Product market equilibrium and Say's Law

The exogenous component of investment has an important implication for the way in which product market equilibrium is achieved in Keynes's model. In the neoclassical model Say's Law held. Saving was always transformed into an equal volume of investment because the rate of interest always adjusted to equate at full employment total investment by firms to total private saving minus the amount of saving required to finance the government deficit. The equality between investment and private saving (less the government deficit) is brought about according to Keynes, not by variations in the rate of interest, but by the level of income adjusting to produce the required volume of saving. Hence, the full-employment level of output only comes about if exogenous aggregate demand is at the appropriate level. Say's Law no longer always holds and the economy no longer adjusts automatically to a full-employment position. Hence, the Keynesian model gives rise to a multiplicity of solutions, each conforming to some given level of exogenous investment and each of which may be an equilibrium position.

Because Keynes envisaged the level of output and income always adjusting so that the resulting level of saving always equalled total investment, he gave no role in the *General Theory* to the rate of interest in producing product market equilibrium. He said (1939a, pp. xxxiii–xxxiv):

> In recent times it has been held by many economists that the rate of current saving determined the supply of free capital, that the rate of current investment governed the demand for it, and that the rate of interest was, so to speak, the equilibrating price-factor determined by the point of intersection of the supply curve of savings and the demand curve of investment. But if aggregate saving is necessarily and in all circumstances exactly equal to aggregate investment, it is evident that this explanation collapses. We have to search elsewhere for the solution. I find it in the idea that it is the function of the rate of interest to preserve equilibrium, not between the demand and supply of new capital goods, but between the demand and supply of money, that is to say between the demand for *liquidity* and the means for satisfying this demand.

This represented an important change in Keynes's thinking. In his *A Treatise on Money*, he had said (Keynes, 1930, vol. I, pp. 152, 155):

> In equilibrium . . . both the value and the cost of current investment must be equal to the amount of current savings . . . the natural rate of interest is the rate at which saving and the value of investment are exactly balanced.

The change in his thinking seems to reflect the addition of a large exogenous component to investment, thus forcing saving to be the variable which adjusts and making output, rather than the rate of interest, be the variable which brings about the adjustment.

As Keynes pointed out (p. 210):

> If saving consisted not merely in abstaining from present consumption but in placing simultaneously a specific order for future consumption, the effect might indeed be different.

Morishima (1977, p. 60) remarks that Keynes's rejection of Say's law is the most important distinction between Keynes and neoclassicists; that is to say, an economist who believes in Say's law can never be a Keynesian, and no neoclassical economist can deny the law.

3.3.6 The paradox of saving

A consequence of the theory that it is the level of income that adjusts to equate saving to investment is the 'paradox of saving' whereby an increase in the marginal propensity to save, other things remaining the same, reduces the aggregate demand for goods. Output and income will fall until the level of saving again equals total investment (including the exogenous component). Thus, although the marginal propensity to save is higher, total saving will now be lower. Hence, an increase in the propensity to save could be an obstacle to full employment. As Keynes (1972, p. 123) expressed it:

> A country is enriched not by the mere negative act of an individual not spending all his income on current consumption. It is enriched by the positive act of using these savings to augment the capital equipment of the country.

Pigou (1950, p. 40) remarked on Keynes's analysis of the effect of saving:

> This conclusion is probably, as regards its effects on the attitude and policy of practical men, the most important element in Keynes's teaching.

3.3.7 Liquidity preference

Keynes included in the *General Theory* the Cambridge equation for the demand for money in his model but made the 'Cambridge k' a function of the rate of interest so that the demand for money – which he termed 'liquidity preference' – in relation to the supply of money determined the rate of interest.[7] Hence, Keynes viewed the rate of interest as being determined primarily in the asset market while the level of real output adjusted, given this rate of interest, to produce product market equilibrium.

Money is important in Keynes's model because of the need for economic agents to be able to hold a liquid asset when uncertainty about the future prices of securities exists. Changes in the degree of uncertainty produce shifts in the liquidity preference schedule. One special case to which Keynes (p. 172) attached some importance was that:

> Circumstances can develop in which even a large increase in the quantity of money may exert a comparatively small influence on the rate of interest. For a large increase in the quantity of money may cause so much

uncertainty about the future that liquidity-preferences . . . may be strengthened; whilst opinion about the future of the rate of interest may be so unanimous that a small change in present rates may cause a mass movement into cash.

The situation where the liquidity preference schedule becomes perfectly elastic with respect to the rate of interest has been termed by Keynes's followers as a 'liquidity trap'.

3.3.8 Wage rates and employment

Keynes rejected the classical supply-of-labour function which was based on the assumption that there is a single homogeneous labour market in which labour sells its services at the going real wage rate. To Keynes, the labour market was a segmented market in which the utility functions of workers in many industries included as one of the arguments their money wage relative to that of workers in other industries. The wage-bargaining process was, however, outside his formal model so that the money wage rate should be regarded as an exogenous variable in his model. As he expressed it:

> Though the struggle over money-wages between individuals and groups is often believed to determine the general level of real wages, it is, in fact, concerned with a different object. Since there is imperfect mobility of labour, and wages do not tend to be an exact equality of net advantage in different occupations, any individual or group of individuals, who consent to a reduction of money-wages relatively to others, will suffer a *relative* reduction in real wages, which is a sufficient justification for them to resist it.
> In other words, the struggle about money-wages primarily affects the *distribution* of the aggregate real wage between different labour-groups. . . .
> The effect of combination on the part of a group of workers is to protect their *relative* real wage.
> Thus it is fortunate that the workers, though unconsciously, are instinctively more reasonable economists than the classical school, inasmuch as they resist reductions of money-wages, which are seldom or never of an all-round character. (pp. 13–14)

> Ordinary experience tells us, beyond doubt, that a situation where labour stipulates (within limits) for a money-wage rather than a real wage, so far from being a mere possibility, is the normal case. (p. 9)

Thus Keynes argued that workers bargained in terms of the money-wage rate and suggested that workers might resist attempts to lower their money wage – a resistance that may be strengthened by the actions of trade unions.

The inability to forecast future prices and wages could play an important role in this reluctance to accept wage cuts. If, for example, workers in the steel industry are bargaining for a new two-year contract to replace a contract which is expiring and are being asked to accept a wage cut because aggregate demand is falling, how can they be sure that the cut is not too large? How can they be sure that workers in the chemical industry whose contracts don't expire for another six months will take a similar cut? Given the uncertainty of the future, those who adjust first may take losses relative to those of other workers. Hence, the reluctance to accept wage cuts.

3.3.9 Involuntary unemployment

Keynes's test for whether 'involuntary unemployment' existed was to ask whether unemployment would be reduced if, given the money wage rate, there was a small rise in the price of consumer goods so that the real wage rate would fall. The involuntarily unemployed would be those who were willing to work at this lower real wage rate but who were without employment at the current wage. The problem that Keynes addressed was how to increase employment in such a situation, given the way he perceived the labour market to function and given his view of the product market.

In the neoclassical model, in the absence of rigidities, full employment is expected by all – firms and workers alike. In that model, an individual worker knows that he can sell all the labour services he wishes to supply at the going wage rate. He knows, therefore, what his future labour income will be and can plan future expenditures with certainty. In the Keynesian model, this certainty about future income is missing. Moreover, in the Keynesian world constant returns to scale and infinite divisibility of factors of production do not exist. The opportunity of the unemployed worker to create a firm and sell its output, which was implicit in the assumptions of the neoclassical model, does not exist. Furthermore, the unemployed worker may have no way of signalling to firms that he is willing to work at a wage rate lower than the prevailing one. As Keynes points out (p. 13):

> There may exist no expedient by which labour as a whole can reduce its *real* wage to a given figure [the amount required for full employment] by making revised *money* bargains with the entrepreneurs.

That is, involuntary unemployment, as Keynes saw it, arises from coordination failures. Workers and firms acting independently cannot coordinate their setting of market prices so that a market-clearing wage rate is arrived at.

In Keynes's model the distinction between effective demand and notional demand is important. When the level of effective demand is less than the level of notional demand, the level of demand that firms perceive in the product market will be such that firms will suffer an excess supply of goods if they produce at full potential. Firms would employ more labour if they perceived a larger demand for their output because they would then find it profitable to produce more goods. Thus, in contrast to the situation in the neoclassical model, the excess supply of labour coexists with a potential excess supply of goods. Hence, the excess supply of labour which gives rise to involuntary unemployment must be tackled by analysing the cause of the deficiency of effective demand for goods and devising policies to increase demand. In this respect, involuntary unemployment may be regarded as unemployment resulting from a deficiency of effective demand.

Another way of viewing the existence of involuntary unemployment is to note that workers realize that there is a *quantity* constraint on the amount of labour services they can sell at the going wage rate and firms recognize that they face downward-sloping demand curves and that there is a quantity constraint on the amount of output they can sell at the going price for their product. This is in sharp contrast to the Walrasian model where all agents expect to be able to sell all they wish at the going market price and their demand functions are based on this expectation. The quantity constraints on sales in the Keynesian model mean that the demand functions of economic agents are based on expected income which reflects these quantity constraints. Workers will have adjusted their expenditure plans to the fact that they cannot sell as much labour as they would like. Appendix 3.2 spells out the nature of these constraints more explicitly.

The involuntary unemployment that exists in the Keynesian model may be regarded as being consistent with a state of equilibrium in the sense that Hahn has defined it:

> An economy is in equilibrium when it generates messages which do not cause agents to change the theories which they hold or the policies which they pursue. (1984, p. 59)

> The central element of an equilibrium is that strategies are equilibrium strategies if no rational agent will wish to deviate from his strategy given those of the other players. That involuntary unemployment leaves Pareto-improving moves unexploited is not sufficient to demonstrate its incompatibility with equilibrium . . . involuntary unemployment (in a certain range) does not lead any agent to change his actions and in particular does not lead to a change in the wage. (1987, pp. 4–5)

3.3.10 Product pricing and the price level

Keynes did not discuss explicitly the nature of firms and the structure of product markets. He was quite familiar with the business world and perhaps took it for granted that the world did not consist of very large numbers of very small firms producing a homogeneous product and acting as price-takers in all markets. Moreover, it was also apparent that constant returns to scale did not prevail everywhere. The world of Keynes's model may be regarded as one in which many firms face downward-sloping demand curves and in which some industries may be oligopolistic. For firms facing downward-sloping demand curves, the quantity demanded will depend on market incomes as well as prices. The market income varies, of course, as employment varies; hence, the firm cannot assume a stable real income at full employment levels as it would in a classical world. Hence, the firm has a vested interest in any policy which will compensate for the failure of the independently arrived at decisions of economic agents to produce a Pareto optimal solution and which will improve the economic system's outcome.

Although Pigou and Keynes in their earlier writings had related the prices firms charged for their products to their costs of production, the overall determination of the price level had been within the framework of the Quantity Theory of Money. In the *General Theory*, however, Keynes broke away from the Quantity Theory:

> In a single industry its particular price-level depends partly on the rate of remuneration of the factors of production which enter into its marginal cost, and partly on the scale of output. There is no reason to modify this conclusion when we pass to industry as a whole. The general price-level depends partly on the rate of remuneration of the factors of production which enter into marginal cost and partly on the scale of output as a whole, i.e. (taking equipment and technique as given) on the volume of employment. (p. 294)

> Money, and the quantity of money, are not direct influences at this stage of the proceedings. They have done their work at an earlier stage of the analysis. The quantity of money determines the supply of liquid resources, and hence the rate of interest, and in conjunction with other factors (particularly that of confidence) the inducement to invest, which in turn fixes the equilibrium level of incomes, output and employment and (at each stage in conjunction with other factors) the price-level as a whole through the influences of supply and demand thus established. (1939a, pp. xxxiv–xxxv)

In the *General Theory*, Keynes did keep the neoclassical demand-for-labour function. But, given the above quotation, it may be interpreted as a price-setting equation:

$$P = (1/f_n)W \tag{3.1}$$

where W is exogenously determined and $1/f_n$ may be regarded as a markup factor. In this formulation the markup is a function of n, given k. In situations of less than full employment real output is determined by aggregate demand and, given k, the production function determines the level of employment:

$$n = f^{-1}(y,k) \tag{3.2}$$

Hence, given that the marginal product of labour decreases as employment and output increase, the markup would increase as aggregate demand increases. That is, firms adjust the markup to maximize profits given the constraint of demand.

3.3.11 Summary

Keynes's model recognizes the existence of quantity constraints on the decisions of firms and households and is useful for analysing situations where effective demand is less than notional demand. Involuntary unemployment can exist and equilibrium may be at less than full employment. Neither monetary expansion nor wage cuts may be effective in restoring full employment; fiscal policy may be effective.

Two critical variables in Keynes's model are exogenous: a portion of business investment in new capital and the money wage rate. In this respect, the model is very incomplete since the determination of two key variables is not explained. Moreover, the exogeneity of the wage rate could imply, if there is markup pricing with a markup that is invariant to the state of aggregate demand, that the price level is also exogenously determined. Hence, Keynes did not have a theory of inflation for situations of less than full employment. He did agree that under conditions of full employment, the Quantity Theory of Money would function. In Chapter 5 the attempt to put a theory of inflation into the Keynesian model by means of the Phillips curve is discussed.

Keynes's model is often summarized as a set of six simultaneous equations. (The simplifying assumptions are the same as for the neoclassical model in section 2.2.13.) It is assumed that the government is able to predict, given the model and the policy of the government, the price level so that government expenditure and tax revenues are exogenous variables in real terms.

$$P = (1/f_n)W \qquad f_n > 0, f_{nn} < 0 \tag{3.1}$$
$$n = f^{-1}(y, k) \tag{3.2}$$
$$i = i(y, r) \qquad i_y > 0, i_r < 0 \tag{3.3}$$
$$c = c(y, r, t) \qquad c_y > 0, c_t < 0, c_r < 0 \tag{3.4}$$
$$y = c + i + g + qk \tag{3.5}$$
$$M/P = m(y, r) \qquad m_y > 0, m_r < 0 \tag{3.6}$$

Exogenous variables: W, g, t, q, M, k

Endogenous variables: P, n, i, c, y, r

One simple mathematical way of recognizing exogenous components of investment and consumption would be to define two additional exogenous variables: i^* and c^* for exogenous investment and exogenous consumption, respectively. The investment and consumption functions would then be written:

$$i = i(y, r) + i^* \tag{3.3a}$$
$$c = c(y, r, t) + c^* \tag{3.4a}$$

This algebraic formulation unfortunately does not incorporate expectations in an explicit way. Moreover, it makes no distinction between consumption and capital goods – it is a one-good model.[8]

Keynes summarized his *General Theory* by stating (pp. 246–7):

> Thus we can sometimes regard our ultimate independent variables as consisting of (1) the three fundamental psychological factors, namely, the psychological propensity to consume, the psychological attitude to liquidity and the psychological expectation of future yield from capital-assets, (2) the wage-unit as determined by the bargains between employers and employed, and (3) the quantity of money as determined by the action of the central bank; so that, if we take as given the factors specified above, these variables determine the national income . . . and the quantity of employment.

There is an aspect of Keynes's analysis which differentiates it from Marshall's and generally from the neoclassical model. The method of comparative statics assumes that the changes in exogenous variables or shifts in functions are small. Hence, the system is inherently stable since small changes produce small effects. But, as Hicks (1946, p. 256) has pointed out, as soon as the elasticity of expectations becomes larger than unity, large economic fluctuations may result. Keynes's psychological propensities (the marginal efficiency of capital, liquidity preference, and the propensity to consume) have the potential, given the inherent uncertainty in Keynes's world, of giving rise to large changes. When this is coupled with an exogenously determined money wage rate which determines prices, the potential for instability in the Keynesian system is much higher, although fixed wage rates would reduce instability. (See the discussion of wage policy in section 3.8.)

3.4 THE KEYNESIAN DICHOTOMY

The dichotomy between real and monetary variables in the neoclassical model made theorizing more manageable since it separated monetary theory from price theory. Similarly, there is a dichotomy in Keynes's model which simplified the analysis.[9] Total expenditure on goods determines the level of real output and employment. Independently of this (and exogenously to the model), the general level of costs (and particularly wage rates) determines the level of product prices. There is nothing within Keynes's model, however, to ensure that the amount of total expenditure will produce the desired level of real output and employment or that the level of costs corresponds to the desired level of prices.

3.5 IS–LM SOLUTION OF THE STATIC MODEL

The IS–LM solution of Keynes's model developed by Sir John Hicks (1937) has become the standard method of analysis and is depicted in Fig. 3.1. Hicks's approach was to take M and P as given, to consider separately the equilibrium

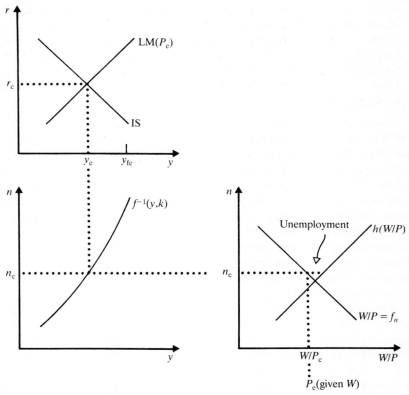

Fig. 3.1 IS–LM solution of a Keynesian model

conditions for the product and asset markets, and then the conditions for simultaneous equilibrium in both markets. It is assumed that the economy is below full employment so that the equilibrium level of output will be below the full-employment level, y_{fe}. Substituting equations (3.3) and (3.4) into equation (3.5), it can be seen that aggregate demand (y) is a function of the rate of interest (r). The alternative combinations of y and r which will produce equilibrium in the product market (equate investment (I) to saving (S), given the exogenously determined values of g, t, q, and k) can be plotted in (y,r) space as a negatively sloped curve – the IS curve.[10]

Equation (3.6) is the condition for asset market equilibrium. For a given P, a set of alternative values of y and r can be determined which will produce asset market equilibrium in that the demand for money (liquidity preference, L) equals the supply of money (M). The locus of these points in (y,r) space is the LM curve, a positively sloped curve. The slope of the LM curve depends on the elasticity of the demand for money with respect to the rate of interest. If the demand for money is perfectly inelastic with respect to the rate of interest, as has been sometimes assumed in a particular version of the Quantity Theory of Money, the LM curve will be vertical instead of being positively sloped. If there is a liquidity trap, the LM curve will be horizontal. The intersection of the IS and LM curves will determine uniquely a pair of values of y and r which, for a given M and P, simultaneously produce product and asset market equilibrium.[11]

The solution value of y – the level of effective demand – can then be fed into the production function, given k, to determine the level of employment, n. Since Keynes retained the neoclassical demand-for-labour function,[12] the real wage rate is then the rate that corresponds to the level of n implied by the level of effective demand. If a neoclassical supply of labour curve is added to the diagram, the level of unemployment can then be seen.

The solution can be generalized to allow P to be a variable. Keynes did this in two steps: In Chapter 3 (p. 29) of the *General Theory* he made a simplifying assumption that W was constant. If equation (3.1) holds (that is, if the neoclassical demand-for-labour function is retained), then for each given W, if the real wage rate varies, the price level must vary. Since different levels of effective demand determine different levels of employment, there will be, for a given W, a different level of prices associated with each level of effective demand. A higher level of employment implies, because of the decreasing marginal productivity of labour, a lower real wage rate and, therefore, a higher P if W remains unchanged. There is, however, a feedback of the price level onto the real money supply, given the exogenously determined level of M.[13] Hence, there will be a family of LM curves, one for each alternative level of P, given the level of M. Solution of the model implies that the solution price level, P_e, must be the one associated with the LM curve that intersects the IS curve at the

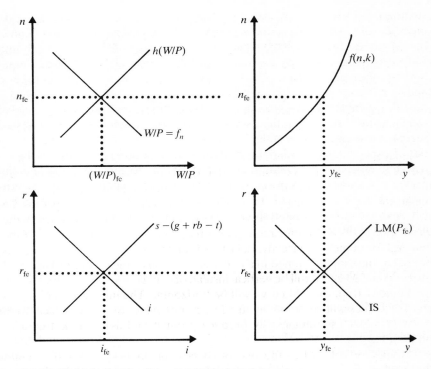

Fig. 3.2 IS–LM solution of the neoclassical model

solution level of effective demand, y_e, and must also be the one associated with the real wage rate that corresponds to the solution level of employment, n_e, given that M and W are assumed to remain constant.[14]

The holding of W constant was, however, only a simplifying assumption which was relaxed in Chapter 18 of the *General Theory*. Keynes noted (p. 249) that the wage rate will tend to rise as employment improves and an increase in output will be accompanied by an increase in prices, relative to the increase in the wage rate, because of the increased cost of production.[15] The position of equilibrium will, therefore, be influenced by these repercussions, which are not taken into account in Fig. 3.1.[16]

For comparison, the IS–LM solution of the simplified static neoclassical model specified in section 2.2.13 is shown in Fig. 3.2. The upper-left figure shows the determination of the level of employment and the real wage rate in the labour market. The production function, given the stock of capital, then determines the full-employment level of real output, y_{fe}. The real rate of interest is then determined by the condition for product market equilibrium as summarized by the IS curve. Since y has already been determined, there is only one value of r which will produce product market equilibrium. There is a family of LM curves, one for each alternative price level, given M. The equilibrium LM curve passes through this point on the IS curve. Product market equilibrium, given g, determines i and, therefore, the division of output between c and i.

Although at the time Keynes approved of Hicks's exposition of the model of the *General Theory* using the IS–LM framework, he subsequently expressed regrets, as pointed out by Kahn (1984, p. 159), that the key role of uncertainties of expectations associated with the psychological behavioural variables – marginal efficiency of capital, marginal propensity to consume, and liquidity preference – was being ignored. The uncertainty associated with expectations means that the IS–LM schedules should not be regarded as stable relations. Changes in expectations in response to random disturbances lead to unpredictable shifts in the schedules.

3.6 AGGREGATE DEMAND AND SUPPLY CURVES

The IS–LM graphical solution is designed to focus attention on changes in two variables: r and y. IS–LM can be used when the price level is varying by developing a family of LM curves, one for each alternative price level. Supply-side considerations do enter into the IS curve if the neoclassical investment function $i = i(n,k,q,r)$ is used instead of the function $i = i(y,r)$. When there is a primary interest in price level changes, however, a graphical analysis which depicts changes in P is required. To accomplish this, aggregate demand and supply schedules can be used. Figure 3.3 shows an aggregate demand (AD) curve: the locus of combinations of (y,P) which are intersection points of IS–

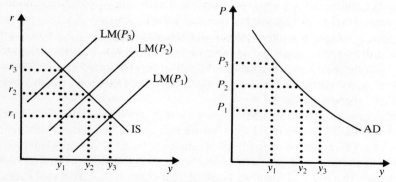

Fig. 3.3 Derivation of aggregate demand curve

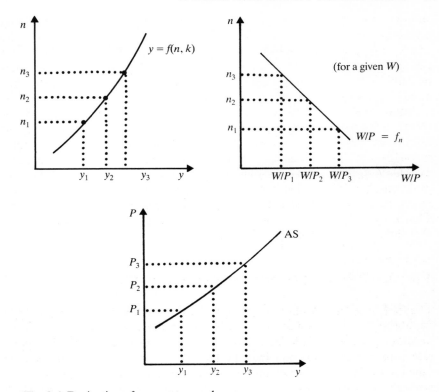

Fig. 3.4 Derivation of aggregate supply curve

LM curves for alternative levels of P. That is, the aggregate demand curve is the locus of the various alternative combinations of y and P which produce asset market equilibrium and which are consistent with total aggregate demand as determined in the product market (points on the IS schedule).

Figure 3.4 shows the derivation of an aggregate supply (AS) curve[17] as the locus of the various alternative combinations of (y,P) which, given an exogenously determined money-wage rate (W), correspond to points on the demand-for-labour curve and the corresponding point on the production function for alternative values of P. As P varies, given W, the real wage changes and, therefore, the volume of employment (n). Given the stock of capital (k), the production function then gives the level of real output (y) corresponding to each level of n. The aggregate demand curve has a negative slope and the aggregate supply schedule has a positive slope.[18] Under the usual assumptions of the model, these curves will intersect at a single point in positive (y,P) space, as shown in Fig. 3.5. This point will give the values of y and P which result from the solution

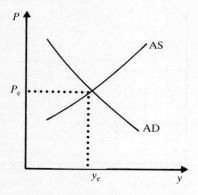

Fig. 3.5 Aggregate demand and supply solution

of the complete model. In the neoclassical model, the solution is always at the full-employment level of real output and the price level is determined by the nominal quantity of money and is independent of the level of real output. The aggregate supply curve for the neoclassical model is, therefore, depicted in (y,P) space as a vertical line at the full-employment level of real output as is shown in Fig. 3.6.

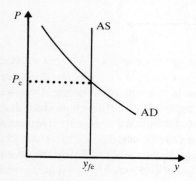

Fig. 3.6 Neoclassical aggregate supply curve

3.7 POLICIES TO INCREASE EMPLOYMENT

The effectiveness of three policies which might increase employment are examined below in the light of the *General Theory*.[19]

Policies to increase investment

Any policies which would reduce uncertainty and increase anticipated future profits from investment by business firms would increase the marginal efficiency of capital. Such an increase shifts the IS curve to the right and induces a movement along the LM curve so that both y and r rise. The adjustment proceeds as follows. The increased orders by firms for capital goods and the induced increase in consumption expenditures (the multiplier effect) leads business firms to perceive that the demand for their products has increased. Since the wage rate is fixed by the wage bargain, they choose to expand output and increase employment at unchanged prices. At the original r, the increase in y creates an excess demand for real money balances. Households try to sell bonds but the central bank does not accommodate them so the supply remains unchanged. Bond prices fall and interest rates rise until the quantity demanded of real money balances falls to equal the available supply. The rise in r induces a decrease in real investment, thus reducing somewhat the initial increases in aggregate demand, real output, and employment. As output increases, the marginal productivity of labour decreases and some increase in prices may occur. If the new level of aggregate demand is sustained, in the long run there may be an increase in the wage rate and a further increase in the price level.

Given the uncertainty concerning the future, it is difficult to see how, in practice, such a policy might be formulated although tax changes may be beneficial. Hence, policies to increase exogenous private investment may not be a practicable way of increasing employment.

Monetary policy

An increase in M brought about by open-market purchases of bonds by the central bank will shift the LM curve to the right and induce a movement along the IS curve so that r declines and y increases. At the initial r and y, the increase in money balances held by households disturbs their portfolio balance since there is now an excess supply of money. Households attempt to buy more bonds, but since the supply is not increasing, bond prices rise and interest rates fall[20] – the magnitude of the decline in interest rates depending on m_r. The deline in interest rates will lead to increases in i and c – the magnitude of the increases depending on i_r and c_r. Again the perceived increase in aggregate demand will lead producers to increase output and employment. As a consequence there will be some increase in the price level and ultimately in the money wage rate, thereby inducing further price increases.

Keynes (p. 173) was sceptical, however, that an increase in M would have a significant effect on employment:

> If, however, we are tempted to assert that money is the drink which
> stimulates the system to activity, we must remind ourselves that there

may be several slips between the cup and the lip. For whilst an increase in the quantity of money may be expected, *cet. par.*, to reduce the rate of interest, this will not happen if the liquidity-preferences of the public are increasing more than the quantity of money; and whilst a decline in the rate of interest may be expected, *cet. par.*, to increase the volume of investment, this will not happen if the schedule of the marginal efficiency of capital is falling more rapidly than the rate of interest; and whilst an increase in the volume of investment may be expected, *cet. par.*, to increase employment, this may not happen if the propensity to consume is falling off. Finally, if employment increases, prices will rise in a degree partly governed by the shapes of the physical supply functions, and partly by the liability of the wage-unit to rise in terms of money.

Hicks (1946, p. 259) has expressed the opinion that Keynes's conclusion regarding monetary policy is:

> From some points of view . . . the most important thing in his *General Theory*, since it finally explodes the comfortable belief . . . that in the last resort monetary control (that is to say, interest control) can do everything.

Wage policy
If producers set prices as a markup on costs, a decrease in the money wage rate resulting from the wage-bargaining process will lead to a decline in prices which will ultimately have the effect of increasing employment. This effect, which has come to be termed the 'Keynes effect', was described by Keynes as follows:

> The reduction in the wage-bill, accompanied by some reduction in prices and in money-incomes generally, will diminish the need for cash for income and business purposes; and it will therefore reduce *pro tanto* the schedule of liquidity-preference for the community as a whole. *Cet. par.* this will reduce the rate of interest and thus prove favourable to investment. (p. 263)[21]

> We can, therefore, theoretically at least, produce precisely the same effects on the rate of interest by reducing wages, whilst leaving the quantity of money unchanged, that we can by increasing the quantity of money whilst leaving the level of wages unchanged. It follows that wage reductions, as a method of securing full employment, are also subject to the same limitations as the method of increasing the quantity of money. . . . Just as a moderate increase in the quantity of money may exert an inadequate influence over the long-term rate of interest, whilst an immoderate increase may offset its other advantages by its disturbing effect on confidence; so a moderate reduction in money-wages may prove

inadequate, whilst an immoderate reduction might shatter confidence even if it were practicable.

There is, therefore, no ground for the belief that a flexible wage policy is capable of maintaining a state of continuous full employment; – any more than for the belief that an open-market monetary policy is capable, unaided, of achieving this result. The economic system cannot be made self-adjusting along these lines. (pp. 266–7).

3.8 POLICY CONCLUSIONS

The major message of Keynes's analysis is that, in a market economy in which uncertainty prevents the calculation of long-term expectations, there is a problem of coordination between economic agents, particularly savers and investors, which prevents the buyers and sellers of labour from arriving at a mutually satisfactory level of output and employment. Because wage cuts and money supply increases would not, in his opinion, work, Keynes argued that there was a role for government in fiscal and wage policy to serve as a substitute for the coordinating role of prices in a perfectly competitive Walrasian economy.

In 'The end of *laissez-faire*' written in 1926, Keynes (1972, p. 292) had commented:

> I believe that some coordinated act of intelligent judgement is required as to the scale on which it is desirable that the community as a whole should save, the scale on which these savings should go abroad in the form of foreign investments, and whether the present organization of the investment market distributes savings along the most nationally productive channels. I do not think that these matters should be left entirely to the chances of private judgement and private profits, as they are at present. . . .
>
> These reflections have been directed towards possible improvements in the technique of modern capitalism by the agency of collective action. There is nothing in them which is seriously incompatible with what seems to me to be the essential characteristics of capitalism, namely the dependence upon an intense appeal to the money-making and money-loving instincts as the main motive force of the economic machine.

Fiscal policy
In the *General Theory* Keynes stated (p. 378):

> I conceive, therefore, that a somewhat comprehensive socialization of investment will prove the only means of securing an approximation to full employment; though this need not exclude all manner of compromises

and of devices by which public authority will co-operate with private initiative.

Referring back to Figs 3.1 and 3.2, it can be seen that the Keynesian model can lead to the same solution – full employment – as the neoclassical model if, given the money wage rate, the level of government expenditure on goods is such that the level of effective demand leads to a full-employment solution. In this respect, the given (exogenously determined) money wage then becomes the neoclassical equilibrium money wage. A decrease in income tax rates which increased the disposable income of households would similarly have a stimulative effect. The very utilitarian view of public finance taken by Keynes and his followers became the source of debates between the neo-Walrasians and Keynesians. Some of these debates will be summarized in Chapter 8.

Wage policy

With respect to wage policy, Keynes (pp. 269–70) concluded that:

> if labour were to respond to conditions of gradually diminishing employment by offering its services at a gradually diminishing money-wage, this would not, as a rule, have the effect of reducing real wages and might even have the effect of increasing them, through its adverse effect on the volume of output. The chief result of this policy would be to cause a great instability of prices, so violent perhaps to make the business calculations futile in an economic society functioning after the manner of that in which we live. To suppose that a flexible wage policy is a right and proper adjunct of a system which on the whole is one of *laissez-faire*, is the opposite of the truth.
>
> In the light of these considerations I am now of the opinion that the maintenance of a stable general level of money-wages is, on a balance of considerations, the most advisable policy for a closed system; whilst the same conclusion will hold good for an open system, provided that the equilibrium with the rest of the world can be secured by means of fluctuating exchanges.

Keynes advanced another argument for wage stability. He argued (p. 304) that there should be some factor, 'the value of which is, if not fixed, at least sticky, to give us any stability of values in a monetary system'. His recommendation was that money-wage rates should be the sticky factor to provide this stability.

It should, however, be borne in mind that the existence of involuntary unemployment in Keynes's system is not solely a result of wage rates being set at non-market-clearing levels. The problem is one of coordination (signalling). How do workers signify their willingness to work at a lower real wage? Rather than try to solve this signalling problem, Keynes gave government the role of providing the necessary increment in effective demand. Having then relieved wages of the necessity of adjusting, as they would have to in the neoclassical model, he presented the argument for stable wages on other grounds. In the neoclassical system, the quantity of money is controlled by the central bank and is the anchor for nominal values in the economy. In Keynes's system, the money-wage rate is seen as the anchor. He did not say that money-wage rates were fixed; he said it was desirable that they be stable.

3.9   A DISTINCTIVE RESEARCH PROGRAMME

The view taken here is that Keynes's *General Theory* marked the beginning of a research programme which had a hard core and positive heuristic that were distinct from that of the neo-Walrasian programme. Both programmes are concerned with specifying rigorously how a market economy works and how that economy comes to an equilibrium position. Keynes's model differed in its view of the information available to economic agents, how the economy worked, and the notion of equilibrium. Keynes's model was, however, incomplete in that important variables (money wages and long-term expectations) were exogenously determined and the failure to reach a full-employment equilibrium position seemed to rest on the fact that exogenously determined wage rates and prices are set at non-market-clearing levels. Failure to reach equilibrium because of interference with the market mechanism was, of course, recognized by the neoclassical economists and if that was the only explanation of unemployment to come out of the *General Theory*, then it was nothing new. The key distinction is that coordination failures exist in Keynes's system whereas they do not in the Walrasian system and prices and wage rates are set by economic agents at non-market-clearing levels. In the Walrasian system prices perform the signalling and coordinating function. Why don't they in Keynes's system, and what prevents prices from ultimately adjusting to achieve full employment? Variables can only be exogenous and unchanging in the short run. Clearly the incompleteness of the *General Theory* means that there is an agenda for further work on putting theoretical foundations under Keynes's economics and explaining why there can be equilibrium at non-market-clearing prices and wages. Some of the subsequent work of the New Keynesian Economists is discussed in Chapter 7.

3.10   FURTHER READING

Harrod (1951) and Moggridge (1976) are biographies of Keynes, and Moggridge gives an annotated guide to the literature on Keynes. Harris (1947) presents a collection of early papers on Keynes's *General Theory* and Wood (1983) a complete collection of assessments of the *General Theory*. Hansen (1953) is an early interpretation of the *General Theory* with many quotations and Klein (1966) is an early exposition of Keynes. Some early textbook presentations of the *General Theory* are Timlin (1942) and Dillard (1948). A recent thorough analysis is Chick (1983). Mathematical treatments of the Keynesian model are in Sargent (1987a, Ch. II) and Turnovsky (1977). Fender (1981), Kahn (1984), and Kaldor (1983) give recent sympathetic interpretations of Keynes's *General Theory*. Tobin (1983a, pp. 28–37) provides a list of market failures that he perceives in Keynes's *General Theory*. Coddington (1983, especially Ch. 6) should be read for a somewhat different view. Some recent textbook treatments are Cuthbertson and Taylor (1987), Felderer and Homburg (1987), and Hillier (1986).

Frank (1986) and Sinclair (1987) discuss the theory of unemployment in relation to both neoclassical and Keynesian models. Dow and Dow (1985) and Hodgson (1985) discuss the role of expectations in Keynes's *General Theory*. Coddington (1983), Dow (1985), and Weintraub (1979, 1985) discuss the foundations of Keynesian economics. Clower (in Walker, 1984), Hahn (1984), and Leijonhufvud (1981) are collections of papers which comment critically on neo-Walrasian and Keynesian economics.

APPENDIX 3.1   COMPARATIVE STATICS OF THE KEYNESIAN MODEL

The model is equations (3.1)–(3.6). The comparative static effects of changes in variables are obtained, as in Appendix 2.2, by taking the total differentials of the equations and solving the resulting set of simultaneous equations. The solution is a short-run one in which it is assumed that the stock of capital (k) is constant. Hence, $dk = 0$.

From the production function $y = f(n, k)$,

$$dy = f_n dn \tag{3.7}$$

From the demand for labour $W/P = f_n(n)$,

$$(PdW - WdP)/P^2 = f_{nn}dn$$

Replacing W/P by f_n,

$$dP/P = dW/W - (f_{nn}/f_n)dn \tag{3.8}$$

From equations (3.3)–(3.6):

$$\mathrm{d}i = i_y\mathrm{d}y + i_r\mathrm{d}r \tag{3.9}$$
$$\mathrm{d}c = c_y\mathrm{d}y + c_r\mathrm{d}r + c_t\mathrm{d}t \tag{3.10}$$
$$\mathrm{d}y = \mathrm{d}c + \mathrm{d}i + \mathrm{d}g \tag{3.11}$$
$$\mathrm{d}M/P - (M/P)(\mathrm{d}P/P) = m_y\mathrm{d}y + m_r\mathrm{d}r \tag{3.12}$$

To obtain the total differential of the IS curve, substitute equations (3.9) and (3.10) into (3.11) and collect terms in dy and dr:

$$\mathrm{d}y = (c_y + i_y)\mathrm{d}y + (c_r + i_r)\mathrm{d}r + c_t\mathrm{d}t + \mathrm{d}g \tag{3.13}$$

The slope of the IS curve is the partial derivative of r with respect to y. (The partial derivative is the ratio of the differentials of the two variables obtained by holding the other variables constant – by setting their differentials equal to zero – and dividing through by the second differential. In this case, set dt = dg = 0, divide through by dy, and rearrange terms. The result is written as a partial derivative to signal that other variables are being held constant.)

$$\partial r/\partial y = (1 - c_y - i_y)/(c_r + i_r)$$

The slope is negative if $(1-c_y) > i_y$; that is, if the marginal propensity to save is greater than the marginal propensity to invest.

To see how the IS curve shifts in response to changes in the exogenous variables, obtain the appropriate partial derivatives from equation (3.13):

$$\partial r/\partial t = -c_t/(c_r + i_r) < 0$$
$$\partial r/\partial g = -1/(c_r + i_r) > 0$$

The IS curve shifts downward when t increases and upward when g increases.

The total differential of the LM curve is equation (3.12). The slope is

$$\partial r/\partial y = -m_y/m_r > 0$$

The LM curve shifts as follows:

$$\partial r/\partial P = -(1/m_r)/(M/P^2) > 0$$
$$\partial r/\partial M = 1/(m_r P) < 0$$

An increase in P shifts the LM curve upward and an increase in M shifts it downward.

The total differential of the AD curve can be obtained by equating the IS and LM equations (3.13) and (3.12) and eliminating dr:

$$\mathrm{d}y = 1/H\{\mathrm{d}g - c_y\mathrm{d}t + ((c_r + i_r)/m_r)(\mathrm{d}M/P - M\mathrm{d}P/P^2)\} \tag{3.14}$$

where $H = (1-c_y - i_y) + (m_y/m_r)(c_r + i_r)$ and H is positive if $(1-c_y) > i_y$.

The slope of the AD curve is

$$\partial P/\partial y = -H/\{[(c_r + i_r)/m_r](M/P^2)\}$$

The slope is negative if H is positive.

To see the shifts in the AD curve obtain the appropriate partial derivatives from equation (3.14):

$$\partial y/\partial g = 1/H > 0$$
$$\partial y/\partial t = -c_y/H < 0$$
$$\partial y/\partial M = (c_r + i_r)/(m_r P) > 0$$

The AD curve shifts to the right when g or M increases and to the left when t increases.

The total differential of the AS curve is obtained from equations (3.7) and (3.8):

$$dy = (f_n^2/f_{nn})[dW/W - dP/P] \tag{3.15}$$

The slope of the AS curve is

$$\partial P/\partial y = -P(f_{nn}/f_n^2) > 0$$

The slope of the AS curve is positive.

A change in the wage rate shifts the AS curve as follows:

$$\partial P/\partial W = P/W > 0$$

An increase in W shifts the AS curve upward.

The reduced-form equation for dy can be obtained from equations (3.14) and (3.15) by eliminating dP.

$$d = 1/X\{dg + c_y dt + ((c_r + i_r)/m_r)[dM/P - MdW/PW]\} \tag{3.16}$$
where $X = (1 - c_y - i_y) + ((c_r + i_r)/m_r)[m_y - (M/P)(f_{nn}/f_n^2)]$
and $X > 0$ if $(1 - c_y) > i_y$.

The multipliers

The multiplier effect of a change in an exogenous variable on real output (y), holding the values of all other exogenous variables constant, can be obtained from the reduced-form equation for dy (equation (3.16)). The multipliers are:

$$\partial y/\partial g = 1/X > 0 \text{ if } (1 - c_y) > i_y$$
$$\partial y/\partial t = -c_y/X < 0 \text{ if } (1 - c_y) > i_y$$
$$\partial y/\partial M = (1/P)((c_r + i_r)/m_r X) > 0$$
$$\partial y/\partial W = -((c_r + i_r)/m_r X)(M/PW) < 0$$

The effect on the price level can be obtained by using the above multipliers and the information contained in the AS curve. From the AS equation (equation (3.15)),

$$dP = (P/W)dW - (Pf_{nn}/f_n^2)dy$$

Hence,

$$\partial P/\partial g = - (Pf_{nn}/f_n^2)\partial y/\partial g > 0$$

Similarly,

$$\partial P/\partial t < 0, \partial P/\partial M > 0, \partial P/\partial W > 0$$

Increases in g or M or decreases in t increase the price level (P). Since increases in g or M shift the AD curve upward, the change in the price level resulting from such increases is often referred to as 'demand-pull' inflation. Increases in W (or in other costs, such as the price of imported oil) shift the AS curve upward generating 'cost-push' inflation.

If i^* and c^* had been added to the model (as indicated at the end of section 3.3.11), the multipliers for these exogenous variables would be identical to those with respect to changes in g.

Special cases

A number of special cases are featured in the Keynesian literature. These special cases occur when specific partial derivatives of behaviourial equations are either equal to zero or approach infinity. The former corresponds to perfectly inelastic response of one variable to a change in another; the latter to perfectly elastic response.

Liquidity trap: The liquidity trap case occurs when at very low interest rates economic agents expect bond prices to fall so that the demand for money becomes perfectly elastic at the going interest rate: $m_r \longrightarrow \infty$. Hence, $\partial y/\partial M$ and $\partial y/\partial W \longrightarrow 0$ and monetary policy and wage cuts are ineffective as policies to increase aggregate demand and employment.

Perfectly inelastic demand for money: When $m_r = 0$, $X \longrightarrow \infty$ and fiscal policy completely crowds out private spending:

$$\partial y/\partial g \text{ and } \partial y/\partial t = 0$$

Interest-insensitive investment: When c_r and $i_r = 0$, monetary policy and wage cuts are ineffective in increasing aggregate demand and employment:

$$\partial y/\partial M \text{ and } \partial y/\partial W = 0$$

Simple multipliers: When c_r and $i_r = 0$ and $m_r \longrightarrow \infty$, the fiscal policy multipliers are independent of asset-market behavioural parameters:

$$\partial y/\partial g = 1/(1-c_y-i_y)$$
$$\partial y/\partial t = -c_y/(1-c_y-i_y)$$

The textbook multiplier: If in addition to the assumptions made for the simple multipliers shown above, $i_y = 0$, then the introductory textbook multipliers are obtained:

$$\partial y/\partial g = 1/(1-c_y)$$
$$\partial y/\partial t = -c_y/(1-c_y)$$

Balanced-budget multiplier: The assumptions of the previous case enable the 'balanced-budget multiplier' to be obtained. When $dt = dg$,

$$\partial y/\partial g + \partial y/\partial t = 1/(1-c_y) - c_y/(1-c_y) = 1$$

APPENDIX 3.2 QUANTITY CONSTRAINTS

The model from Keynes's *General Theory* presented in this chapter is a model in which households and firms are subject to quantity constraints in their expenditure and production decisions when *effective* demand is less than *notional* demand (the full-employment demand of the neoclassical model). The mathematical notation of this chapter and Appendix 3.1 did not, however, explicitly reflect this. This appendix draws on Muellbauer and Portes (1978) and the summary of their work by Cuthbertson and Taylor (1987, Ch. 2) to make the constraints explicit. Muellbauer and Portes derive the behaviour of households from utility functions which incorporate the constraints and derive the behaviour of firms from profit functions which recognize the constraints.

Consider a model in which product prices and wage rates remain constant during a period of time (a fixed-price model), there are no taxes or transfers, and in which, for simplicity, total demand, y, equals $c + g$. If $n^S > n^D$ so that there is unemployment, the real income of households will be less than if full employment existed. Denote this constrained level of income by $\bar{y}$ and the constrained level of employment by $\bar{n}$, where

$$\bar{y} = w\bar{n} + rk \tag{3.17}$$

and $\bar{n} = n^D < n^S$

Consumer demand will now be a function of the quality constraint from the labour market.

$$c^D = c^D(\bar{n}) \tag{3.18}$$

The constrained level of consumer demand (c^D) will be less than c^S, the quantity of consumption goods that would be supplied if firms were producing at the full-employment level. Hence, there is a potential excess supply in the product market.

Actual consumption will be

$$c = \text{Min}(c^D, c^S) \tag{3.19}$$

When effective demand equals notional demand, $c = c^S$. Otherwise, $\bar{c} = c^D < c^S$. In the latter case where consumption is constrained, actual consumption will be denoted by $\bar{c}$.

Similarly, the labour market may be quantity constrained. The demand for labour by firms will depend on their expectations as to the level of effective demand. If $c = c^S$, then the level of effective demand equals the level of notional demand and $y = y^S = c^S + g$, where y^S is the notional level of output. If however, $c = \bar{c} = c^D$, then $y = \bar{y} = \bar{c} + g$ and $\bar{y} < y^S$, where $\bar{y}$ is the constrained level of effective demand. In the latter case, the constrained demand for labour will be:

$$\bar{n} = n^D = n^D(\bar{y}) < n^S \tag{3.20}$$

Equilibrium within a period, for a given g, will be achieved when the expectations of firms as to the level of effective demand and the expectations of households as to the level of employment are such that the quantity of goods supplied by firms equals the amount that household and government will buy. This equilibrium is determined by the interaction between the labour and product markets and is affected by the multiplier process. The existence of the constraints leads economic agents to form their decisions by a 'dual decision process'. For example, households may first form their plans in accordance with the price signals from the product market and then revise them to take into account the quantity constraint imposed from the labour market.

In a quantity-constrained equilibrium $c^D < c^S$ and $n^D < n^S$. That is, there is excess supply in both the product and labour markets. This is 'Keynesian unemployment' in contrast to the 'classical unemployment' which is characterized by excess supply in the labour market and excess demand in the product market.

In this simplified exposition, the quantity-constrained model can be summarized by three equations:

$$\bar{n} = n^D(\bar{y}) \tag{3.21}$$
$$\bar{c} = c^D(\bar{n}) \tag{3.22}$$
$$\bar{y} = \bar{c} + g \tag{3.23}$$

These equations can be combined into a reduced-form equation for $\bar{y}$:

$$\bar{y} = c^D\{n^D(\bar{y})\} + g \tag{3.24}$$

Totally differentiating (ignoring the bars over the variable names for simplicity of notation):

$dy = (\partial c^D/\partial n)(\partial n^D/\partial y)dy + dg$

Hence, $dy/dg = 1/\{1 - (\partial c^D/\partial n)(\partial n^D/\partial y)\}$

The right-hand side is the reciprocal of one minus the marginal propensity to consume. If $n^D < n^S$, increases in g will increase both y and n until the level of effective demand equals the level of notional demand. Hence, increased government expenditure is a remedy for Keynesian unemployment.

When there is classical unemployment, $c = y^S - g$ and $dc/dg = -1$ and government expenditure simply crowds out an equivalent amount of private expenditure.

NOTES

1. See Hicks (1965, pp. 49–57), for comments on Marshall's method.
2. Kaldor (1983, p. 13) makes a similar point.
3. Kaldor (1983, pp. 47–9) comments that the real author of the 'neoclassical synthesis' was Keynes himself. It was Keynes who synthesized Marshall's short-period analysis with his own theory. Kaldor remarks that it was in long-period analysis, which Keynes never fully developed, that he parts company with the neoclassical economists.
4. Unless stated otherwise, page references refer to the *General Theory*. All English-language printings of the *General Theory* have the same pagination.
5. The first calculation of the multiplier was by Kahn (1931) to demonstrate Keynes's assertion (Keynes, 1929, p. 106), in a political tract written jointly with Hubert Henderson to aid in the election of David Lloyd George, that increases in exogenous aggregate demand would have multiplier effects on employment.
6. See Fitoussi (1983, p. 18) for this description of how the equilibrium level of effective demand is attained. Kregel (1976, pp. 210–17) discusses the role of expectations in Keynes's model in some depth. With respect to short-run expectations, Keynes (1937b, p. 181) remarked that 'if I were writing the book again I should begin by setting forth my theory on the assumption that short-run expectations were always fulfilled; and then have a subsequent chapter showing what differences it makes when short-period expectations are disappointed.'
7. Strictly speaking, this is the short-run rate of interest. In Keynes's model there is only one rate of interest: the yield on a government bond. In retrospect Pigou and others have noted that Keynes's model would have been better if he had included both a long-term and a short-term rate of interest and had made it explicit that it was the short-term rate that affected liquidity preference. Long rates are, of course, equivalent to a succession of short rates and if there is no uncertainty about the future, a single interest rate will suffice for purposes of the model. In the presence of uncertainty about long-term inflation rates, however, the distinction between the long- and the short-term rate becomes important.
8. James Meade (1937) had written an exposition of Keynes's model which was a two-sector model and which gave a more explicit role to expectations. It was, however, Hicks's (1937) exposition using IS–LM curves which caught the profession's attention and which became the basis for textbook Keynesian economics. See Darity and Cottrell (1987) for a geometric presentation of Meade's model.

9. This has been pointed out by Coddington (1983, pp. 5–6).
10. An algebraic solution which derives the slopes of the curves is presented in Appendix 3.1.
11. The same solution is obtained if equation (3.1) is replaced by an equation which makes P a constant markup on W. Then, for a given W, there will be only one P and only one LM curve.
12. Early expositions of Keynes's model in the *General Theory* all recognized this critical assumption. See Hicks (1937), Meade (1937), Modigliani (1944), and Smithies (1947). The retention by Keynes of the neoclassical demand-for-labour function created an anomaly in terms of the observed behaviour of employment and wages and prices during the business cycle. This is discussed in section 4.3.
13. There may also be a feedback onto the IS curve if a change in P affects the expected profits of firms and, therefore, their investment plans.
14. This statement concerning the solution of the model does not imply that price is the adjusting variable that restores equilibrium after a disturbance. All it means is that, if the model consists of six linear equations in six unknowns, the simultaneous solution of the equations will generally give rise to a set of unique values for the six variables.
15. At this point Keynes treats the wage rate as an endogenous variable. He does not, however, provide a behaviourial equation for the wage rate. He never sets out mathematically a complete model and solves it. Because of this, economists have been forced to interpret Keynes's system and set out a set of equations to represent it. Hence, there have been debates over what Keynes really meant. Keynes's notion of how a model should be used is set out in section 4.2.
16. One reader has suggested that it is possible that the interaction between wages and prices could produce an 'explosive' solution. An increase in prices shifts the LM curve upward to the left. This could cause output to fall to a level which depresses real wages to a point where, if the money wage is sticky, firms raise prices even higher.
17. This is a different derivation and concept of aggregate supply from that used by Keynes.
18. The slopes of the IS, LM, AD and AS curves are derived algebraically in Appendix 3.1.
19. The discussion is adapted from Sargent (1987a, pp. 60–1).
20. The original open-market operations produced a temporary increase in bond prices.
21. It is the lower need for money balances for transactions purposes, given the lower level of prices, that reduces the demand for money and shifts the LM curve outward to the right.

4 · AFTER THE *GENERAL THEORY*

> The fundamental assertion of the *General Theory* was that [the] destabilizing effects of demand shocks could be readily offset by appropriate stabilization policies.
>
> Franco Modigliani (1986, p. 11)

The model in Chapter 3 is a static model from the *General Theory*. This chapter begins with some brief comments on Keynes's business cycle theory. This is followed by two subsequent discussions by Keynes relevant to the static model. The first relates to Keynes's view of economic science and the second to the cyclical movement of real wages and employment. Then follow some comments on markup pricing and the role of prices as a signalling device. Pigou's criticism of Keynes's argument that neither wage nor monetary policy may significantly reduce unemployment is then presented. The chapter concludes with two alternative views of the *General Theory*. The immediate response was that of trying to develop a synthesis of Keynes's theory and neoclassical theory. More recently, there has been the development of Post Keynesian economics. The recent development of the 'New Keynesian Economics' is summarized in Chapter 7.

4.1 THE BUSINESS CYCLE

Neoclassical economists had a theory of the business cycle which was quite separate from their theory of long-run tendencies. Frederick Lavington, a University of Cambridge economist, had written a monograph on *The Trade Cycle* (1922) in which, after outlining his theory, he said:

> it leads to the conclusion which is apparently accepted by such economists as Dr. Marshall and Professor Pigou: the conclusion, namely, that the active principle animating business cycles is to be found in the level of business confidence. (p. 60)

What does seem certain, however, is that such rhythmical fluctuations as do occur are strongly reinforced when there is added to these conditions the influence exerted by changes in the level of business confidence: changes which lead to the cumulative growth of an error of optimism or pessimism in business judgments, which in periods of rising general activity unduly stimulates enterprise and in times of declining activity unduly depresses it. (p. 90)

Keynes followed the neoclassical tradition in that he had a separate chapter in the *General Theory* on the trade cycle. Keynes's model could, however, be used to explain economic fluctuations. His explanation was similar to Lavington's but he gave the marginal efficiency of capital an explicit role (p. 313):

> The essential character of the trade cycle and, especially, the regularity of time-sequence and of duration which justifies us in calling it a *cycle*, is mainly due to the way in which the marginal efficiency of capital fluctuates. The trade cycle is best regarded, I think, as being occasioned by a cyclical change in the marginal efficiency of capital, though complicated and often aggravated by associated changes in the other significant short-period variables of the economic system.

It was, of course, within the marginal efficiency of capital that Keynes included the forecasts of business about future economic prospects.

Other economists were writing on the business cycle in the early 1930s. Many of the ingredients of Keynes's model were independently developed by Michal Kalecki who published a paper on his macroeconomic model in Polish in 1933 and a subsequent paper in English in *Econometrica* in 1935 entitled 'A macrodynamic theory of business cycles'. There are marked similarities in the treatment of saving and investment by Kalecki and by Keynes although they had not seen each other's work. Kalecki paid more attention to market imperfections in the price-setting process. Kalecki was, however, primarily concerned with developing a *dynamic* theory of the business cycle while Keynes was primarily concerned with developing his theory of effective demand and showing that the assumption of the classical economists that the economic system, if left alone, always tended in the long run to full employment was not necessarily valid.[1]

The Swedish economists Erik Lindahl and Bertil Ohlin were also making major contributions to business cycle theory and the development of dynamic time-period analysis, as was Sir Dennis Robertson at Cambridge. Keynes regarded, however, the main objective of the *General Theory* to be the analysis of equilibrium positions, not trade-cycle theory. As he expressed it (Keynes, 1937b, p. 183): 'I'm more classical than the Swedes, for I am still discussing the conditions of short-period equilibrium.'

4.2 KEYNES'S VIEW OF ECONOMIC SCIENCE

Keynes, trained in mathematics, was well aware of the distinction between variables and parameters. Although he was a founding member of the Econometric Society, he was distressed by the pioneering work of econometricians in the 1930s (Henry Schultz, Jan Tinbergen, and Jacob Marschak) to estimate the parameters of economic models. In letters to Roy Harrod of Oxford University in 1938 Keynes wrote (1938):

> Economics is a science of thinking in terms of models joined to the art of choosing models which are relevant to the contemporary world. It is compelled to do this, because, unlike the typical natural science, the material to which it is applied is, in too many respects, not homogeneous through time. The object of a model is to segregate semi-permanent or relatively constant factors from those which are transitory or fluctuating so as to develop a logical way of thinking about the latter, and of understanding the time sequences to which they give rise in particular cases . . . economics is essentially a moral science and not a natural science. That is to say, it employs introspection and judgments of value. (pp. 296–7)

> In chemistry and physics and other natural sciences the object of experiment is to fill in the actual values of the various quantities and factors appearing in an equation or formula; and the work when done is once and for all. In economics, this is not the case, and to convert a model into a quantitative formula is to destroy its usefulness as an instrument of thought. (p. 299)

4.3 THE MOVEMENT OF REAL WAGES AND EMPLOYMENT

In the *General Theory*, Keynes's retention of the neoclassical demand-for-labour function implied that there is an inverse correlation between the movement of real wages and the volume of output and employment. This view was challenged by John Dunlop (1938) and Lorie Tarshis (1939). Observation of real-world business cycles suggested, as Pigou had pointed out (1929, p. 217, and 1933, p. 296; cited by Keynes, 1939b, p. 399) that in recessions both employment and real wages fall, while in prosperous periods, they both rose. Keynes accepted this criticism and in a 1939 article (1939b, pp. 406–7) said:

> It may be the case that the practical workings of the laws of imperfect competition in the modern quasi-competitive system are such that, when output increases and money wages rise, prices rise less than in proportion

to the increase in marginal money cost. . . . It might be, in a sense, merely an extension in the stickiness of prices. . . . Apart from those prices which are virtually constant in the short period, there are obviously many others which are, for various reasons, more or less sticky.

In commenting on Pigou's view, Keynes said (1939b, p. 399; italics added) that 'like Marshall, Pigou based his conclusion primarily on the *stickiness* of money wages relative to prices'. The quotation is noteworthy in emphasizing that the view that wages and prices are sticky is not a distinctive Keynesian view. It was a neoclassical view of the behaviour of prices and wages in the business cycle.

It is also noteworthy that in the 1939 article Keynes explicitly recognizes (pp. 406–7) the existence of imperfect competition and that the 'individual producer is normally operating subject to decreasing average costs'.[2]

4.4 MARKUP PRICING

Later formulations of the price-setting equation by Keynes's followers remove the direct link between the markup and productivity and, in many cases, treat the markup as a constant not related to the level of aggregate demand. A more general price-setting equation may be used in this case:

$$P = h(W) \qquad h_w > 0 \tag{4.1}$$

Support for this form of markup pricing came from a survey of British firms done in the 1930s by two Oxford University economists, R.L. Hall and C.J. Hitch (1939). They found that firms set prices as a markup on 'full costs' (average variable plus 'normal' fixed costs) instead of setting prices at the point where marginal revenue equals marginal cost. That is, firms are regarded as trying to achieve a target rate of return by setting prices at a markup over full costs at normal levels of output. Under certain assumptions this price may be the same as the price that maximizes profits.[3] Coutts, Godley, and Nordhaus (1978) presented further evidence that firms calculate the level of costs at a normal level of output and set prices as a markup on normal costs without references to temporary variations in demand.

For a firm which sets prices as a constant markup on costs, if costs are constant, prices will also remain constant.[4] If this pricing behaviour is inserted into Keynes's model it can be regarded, using Hicks's terminology, as a 'fixprice model', in contrast to the Walrasian 'flexprice model'. If prices tend to remain stable, the reaction to cyclical fluctuations to demand will be one of quantity adjustment rather than price adjustment. The response to transitory events which affect the demand for a firm's products when demand is less than capacity will be to reduce output. When demand is greater than normal capacity, inventories are drawn down so that quantity supplied in the market may still equal the quantity demanded by a firm's customers.

When prices tend to be constant, price changes are no longer able to serve as a signalling device to tell economic agents how to adjust their plans. In Keynesian models, in the short run, it is inventory changes, not prices, that signal changes in market conditions to firms. When there is excess demand in a market, inventories will be run down and there will be unanticipated decreases in inventories. Retailers and wholesalers will respond by increasing their orders to manufacturers and ultimately increased output will result. When there is excess supply, there will be unanticipated increases in inventories and retailers and wholesalers will respond by reducing their orders to manufacturers so that ultimately decreased output will result. Hence, even in the absence of price changes, there may be a tendency to equilibrium.[5]

4.5 PIGOU'S RESPONSE

Keynes's criticism of classical economics (which to him included what is termed neoclassical economics in this book) was directed mainly at Pigou's exposition of classical theory (p. 279):

> not because he seems to me to be more open to criticism than other economists of the classical school; but because his is the only attempt with which I am acquainted to write down the classical theory of unemployment precisely.

As explained in section 2.2.10, the classicists assumed that the rate of interest would always adjust to produce a level of investment which was consistent with full employment. Keynes's introduction of a large exogenous component of investment meant that in his model saving depends on income and it is saving that adjusts, by means of income adjustment, to make saving equal investment. Hence, Keynes argued that the economy could settle into a state of unemployment for a considerable period of time and that wage and monetary policy may not restore full employment.

Pigou (1943, 1947) countered by pointing out that Keynes had not taken into account the effect of changes in wealth on the level of consumption. If real wealth is added as a variable in the consumption function, then a wage cut which leads to a reduction in the price level will lead to an increase in real wealth. This will induce a decrease in saving and an increase in consumption and shift the IS curve to the right – the so-called 'Pigou (or real-balance) effect'.[6] Thus, y will increase even if the LM curve is horizontal, as is shown in Fig. 4.1. The only circumstance in which the Pigou effect will not operate is if

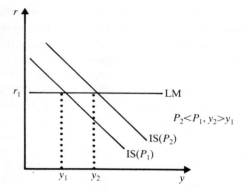

Fig. 4.1 The Pigou effect on the IS curve

the LM curve is vertical. It is surprising that Keynes ignored the real-balance effect since the effect of an increase in the value of real money balances on spending on consumption goods was implicit in the Cambridge version of the Quantity Theory of Money.

Pigou (1945, p. 24) was not of the opinion that the real-balance effect would necessarily be strong enough to bring the economy back to full employment equilibrium, but said that it would bring the economy much nearer to full employment equilibrium than Keynes's low-level equilibrium. Patinkin (1951, p. 273) concluded that it is impractical to depend on the Pigou effect as a means of policy. His reasons were:

1. The possibility that the effect of an increase in real money balances on consumption would be so small that very large price declines would be necessary in order that there be any significant effect.
2. The effect of a price decrease on expectations may offset the potential stimulative effect on consumption.

If one regards Keynes's objective as that of providing an analytical framework for studying the workings of an economy when the labour market does not necessarily clear, then the failure of Keynes to take into account the real-balance effect does not seriously damage his framework of analysis. As John Fender (1981, p. 109) points out, the fact that the neoclassical result depends on the real-balance effect enables economists 'to delimit the (extremely restrictive) conditions under which the [economic] system will continuously generate full employment'.

4.6 THE NEOCLASSICAL SYNTHESIS

The mathematical expositions of the *General Theory* by Hicks (1937) and

Modigliani (1944) focused attention on two special cases: the case where the liquidity trap exists and the case where investment is inelastic with respect to the rate of interest (see Appendix 3.1). If either of these cases holds and if the Pigou effect is insufficient, neither monetary nor wage policy would be effective in restoring full employment. Fiscal policy would, however, be effective. This led to the view that the central difference between Keynes and the classic economists was not one of theoretical foundations, but one of parameter values. Hence at the theoretical level there was a view that a synthesis of Keynesian and neoclassical theory was possible. This contrasts with the later concern of Hahn and Weintraub on developing the theoretical underpinnings of the models.

This view gave rise to a debate between Milton Friedman (and other Monetarists) and Keynesians such as Franco Modigliani. The Keynesians took the position that there are stable relations at the aggregate level such as the marginal propensity to consume, which enables government to perform a stabilizing function using fiscal policy. Hence, the battleground has been at the level of applied econometrics rather than at the level of basic theory and the content of the hard core. Two examples are the econometric work of Jerome Stein in his book *Monetarist, Keynesian and New Classical Economics* (1982) and the work using the MPS (MIT–Penn–Social Science Research Council) econometric model summarized by Modigliani in his *The Debate over Stabilization Policy* (1986).

Modigliani sums up the argument with respect to real (as opposed to monetary) shocks to the economy as follows:

> It must be recognized that the extent of contraction in output . . . resulting from a given demand shock depends on the value of certain crucial parameters of the system, a conclusion that can be readily established from the classic IS–LM paradigm of John R. Hicks. Indeed because of the presence of amplifying and offsetting mechanisms, it could range from a fraction of the shock to a substantial multiple of it. There are three essential parameters:
>
> i) The marginal propensity to save or its reciprocal, 'the multiplier'. The larger the multiplier, the larger will be the response of output to a given demand disturbance, and hence the more unstable the system.
>
> ii) The elasticity of aggregate demand with respect to the interest rate or required rate of return on capital. The greater the elasticity of demand the larger the offset to the initial shock that will be produced by the fall in interest rates resulting from a given fall in income. . . . Thus, a higher elasticity implies a smaller response of income to demand shocks.
>
> iii) The elasticity of demand for money with respect to interest rates. If the elasticity is small, [a contraction in output] will tend to be accom-

panied by a large change in interest rates which will increase demand and tend to offset the initial disturbance. An inelastic demand for money is thus also stabilizing.

The fundamental assertion of the *General Theory* was that these destabilizing effects of demand shocks could be readily offset by appropriate stabilization policies. (pp. 10–11)

Monetarists certainly rejected the idea that there was a clear need for stabilizing the system but this rejection can be seen as resting on a radically different assessment of the very parameters on which the Keynesians base their case. (p. 14)

. . . this evidence [from the MPS model] unmistakably supports the monetarist position – only up to a point. The estimated values of the parameters imply a far less unstable economy than assumed by the early Keynesians, but still not a very stable one. (p. 17)

From this Modigliani draws the policy conclusion which marks the essential difference from a policy point of view between the Keynesians and the neo-Walrasians:

the role of stabilization policies can be summarized in three points. Firstly, there is a *need* for stabilization policies, though the relevant parameters suggest that the instability with respect to demand shocks is substantially less than might have appeared forty, thirty, or even twenty years ago. Secondly, fairly successful stabilization policies are *possible*, although again the danger of poor timing and parameter uncertainty is sufficiently serious to counsel against attempts at 'fine tuning'. Thirdly, under these circumstances whether or not one should trust the government with the required discretionary power is a question that I personally would, unhesitatingly, answer in the affirmative, at least with reference to existing United States institutions. However, I will not try to defend this conclusion because it is a value judgement, not a matter of economic analysis. (p. 39)

4.7 POST KEYNESIAN ECONOMICS

The Post Keynesians reject the notion that Keynes's theory can be viewed as being in the neo-Walrasian spirit of a research programme in which economic agents make rational choices among alternatives and the economic system then moves to an equilibrium position. They see Keynes's work as an attack on this position, whereas the view in this book is that it is in the neo-Walrasian spirit but the presence of serious market failures requires a different explanation of the functioning of a market economy. This view is developed in Chapter 7.

In a sense, Post Keynesian economics is a fundamentalist view of economic theory which goes back to the Ricardian theory of production and distribution and interprets Keynes's economics in this light. Post Keynesian economics also draws on the work of Michal Kalecki. Kalecki was explicit about the price-setting behaviour of firms and about the fact that many manufacturing industries are characterized by monopoly or oligopoly. Investment played an important role in Kalecki's model and he linked it to technological developments and the growth of output. Kalecki also argued that the propensity to save out of investment income was substantially higher than that out of labour income.

The Post Keynesians argue that individual choice is restricted by income and social class and by technical conditions of production. These are more important than relative prices. Monopoly power by manufacturing firms means that they control their markups and set prices. Moreover, firms also have power over wages. Hence firms, to a certain extent, control their profits and use these profits for new investment in plant and equipment. Financial institutions also have market power and have an impact on the terms at which firms can raise additional capital.

Post Keynesians place great emphasis on the changing role of institutions. The ability to forecast using econometric models is therefore regarded as limited and the primary task of model builders is to capture structural change. The models must be continually revised as new facts become evident. Indeed, it may be impossible to specify completely a model of the economy in which there is great uncertainty and in which long-term expectations are largely exogenous.

The Post Keynesians distinguish sharply between short- and long-period analysis. Long-period analysis is concerned with establishing the equality of planned saving and investment and these conditions define a centre of gravitation towards which the economy is tending. Short-period analysis emphasizes the state of expectations in asset markets and determines the nature of business cycles.

Since the type of investment by firms determines the nature of economic growth, Post Keynesians are concerned with the conditions for balanced growth. Moreover, they recognize and advocate that governments should play a role in influencing the nature of investment and thereby the components of economic growth. Moreover, given the market power of corporations, regulation of product, labour, and financial markets may be required.

Another aspect of Post Keynesian economic thought is the concern with *historical* time. That is, there is a recognition that decisions are made in periods of real time and not arbitrarily divided into periods of time convenient to economic analysis. The uncertainty with respect to expectations of economic agents reflects current history.

4.8 FURTHER READING

Haberler (1937) is a survey of business cycle theory up to the mid-1930s. Modigliani (1986) and Stein (1982) present econometric evidence relevant to the neoclassical synthesis. Dow (1985) has a detailed account of Post Keynesian economics and Gram and Walsh (1983) summarize Joan Robinson's economics. Davidson (1981) presents a broad survey of macroeconomics since Keynes and uses the term Post Keynesian much more broadly than here. Milgate (1982) presents a summary of the classical writings on natural price and equilibrium and their relevance to a Post Keynesian interpretation of the *General Theory*. Lawson and Pesaran (1985) contains a number of papers sympathetic to the Post Keynesian interpretation of Keynes. Coddington (1983) comments on Post Keynesian economics. M.C. Sawyer (1982) presents a Kaleckian view of macroeconomics as an alternative to the Keynesian model. Fine and Murfin (1984) and Morishima (1984) analyse the workings of an industrial economy in a way that has Kaleckian elements. Feiwel (1975) summarizes the economic theories of Kalecki. A general theory of non-Walrasian equilibrium economics is explained by Benassy (1986), who treats Keynes's model as a special case.

APPENDIX 4.1 THE ALGEBRA OF THE KEYNES AND PIGOU EFFECTS

The mathematics of the 'Keynes effect' of a cut in the money wage rate modified to allow for the 'Pigou (or real-balance) effect' can be demonstrated as follows.[7] Respecify the consumption function (equation (3.4)) as

$$c = c(y, r, t, k + (M + B)/P) \qquad c_a > 0 \qquad (4.2)$$

where c_a is the partial derivative of c with respect to $\{k + (M + B)/P\}$.

Keeping the stock of capital constant so that $dk = 0$, the total differential of the IS curve is now

$$dy = c_y dy + c_r dr + c_t dt + c_a d[(M + B)/P] + i_y di + i_r dr + dg \qquad (4.3)$$

To obtain the effect on the IS curve of a change in W, use $P = h(W)$ as the price equation so that $dP/P = h_w dW/P$, set $dy = dg = dt = 0$, and then obtain $\partial r/\partial W$:

$$0 = (c_r + i_r)dr - c_a[(M + B)/P]h_w dW/P$$
$$\partial r/\partial W = \{c_a[(M + B)/P]h_w/P\}/(c_r + i_r) < 0$$

A decrease in W shifts the IS curve upwards so that y will increase as long as the LM curve is not vertical.

The rate of interest is now determined simultaneously by the equilibrium conditions for the asset and goods markets. To obtain the effect of an open-market operation by the central bank on the real rate of interest, set $dM = -dB$, and obtain $\partial r/\partial M$. The asset market equilibrium condition (equation (3.6)) can be used to obtain an expression for dP/P:

$$dP/P = -m_r(P/M)dr + dM/M$$

Making this substitution for dP in equation (4.3) and setting $dy = dg = dt = 0$, the following is obtained:

$$0 = \{c_r + i_r + c_a[(M - B)/M]m_r\}dr - c_a[(M + B)/P]dM/M$$
$$\partial r/\partial M = \{c_a[(M + B)/P]/M\}/\{c_r + i_r + c_a[(M + B)/M]m_r\} < 0$$

An increase in the money supply decreases the real rate of interest; hence, the dichotomy between the determination of real and nominal variables is destroyed.

NOTES

1. Kaldor (1983, p. 15), however, was of the opinion that Kalecki's model was superior to Keynes's in explaining unemployment equilibrium.
2. Keynes also refers the reader to Kalecki (1938) for a discussion of distributional problems between factors of production in conditions of imperfect competition, and to Pigou (1929).
3. If the Cobb–Douglas production function is used (see Appendix 2.5), the neoclassical model's profit-maximizing labour-demand equation can give rise to a constant markup interpretation of the relation between product price and unit labour costs: $P = (1/b)Wn/y$, where the markup is a constant and equal to the reciprocal of the elasticity of output with respect to the input of labour services.
4. See Lipsey (1981, pp. 551–2), for an elaboration of this argument.
5. Blinder (1980) incorporates inventories into the Keynesian model.
6. The Polish economist Oscar Lange (then at the University of Chicago) independently developed the real-balance effect in a book which was ultimately published in 1944 after Pigou's first paper appeared. Sargent (1987a, pp. 67–8) presents an analysis of the real-balance effect which is summarized in Appendix 4.1.
7. See Sargent (1987a, pp. 67–70).

5·EXTENSIONS TO THE MODELS

The basic asymmetry which . . . distinguishes Keynesian models from major competing paradigms: in the Keynesian model, fluctuations in demand bring predominantly quantity responses below full-capacity output and predominantly price responses at or above full-capacity output.
Richard G. Lipsey (1981, p. 548)

The models considered in Chapters 2 and 3 were static models which defined equilibrium positions but which gave no information about rates of change in variables over time. Hence, the models say nothing about the rate of inflation, the rate of change in money-wage rates, or their relation to the unemployment rate. Moreover, expectations were assumed to be static or to be exogenously determined. This chapter begins by defining the difference between nominal and real interest rates and explaining the effect of inflation on the real burden of the government debt. Then the neoclassical and Keynesian models are expanded to include a Phillips curve to explain the short-run rate of change of the money-wage rate. Two hypotheses about how economic agents form expectations are then presented. This is followed by the derivation of an aggregate supply function based on the rational expectations hypothesis.

5.1 NOMINAL INTEREST RATES AND INFLATION

The after-tax real rate of return on an investment of $1 for one period of time (r^a) is

$$r^a = \{[1 + R(1-\tau)]/(1 + \pi)\} - 1 \tag{5.1}$$

where R is the nominal rate of interest
τ is the income tax rate
π is the rate of inflation expected today to hold in the next period of time
Hence,

$$R = (1 + \pi)r + \pi/(1 - \tau) \tag{5.2}$$

where $r = r^a/(1 - \tau)$: the before-tax real rate of interest.

If $\tau = 0$ and π is small, this relation is approximated by

$$R = r + \pi \tag{5.3}$$

This is the 'Fisher equation' named after Irving Fisher. It says that the nominal rate of interest will (approximately) equal the real rate of interest plus the *expected* rate of inflation.

5.2 INFLATION AND THE GOVERNMENT DEFICIT

Consider the government budget constraint (equation (2.8)), but note that the nominal and real rates of interest will be different in the presence of inflation. Hence, the real interest payments will be the nominal interest paid out deflated by the price level. The government budget constraint in real terms is then

$$g + (r + \pi)(B/P) - (T/P) = \dot{B}/P + \dot{M}/P \tag{5.4}$$

where the terms on the right-hand side are the nominal increases in bonds and money held by households deflated by the price level.

In equilibrium, the actual and expected rates of inflation will be equal so that $\pi = \dot{P}/P$. It can be shown[1] that when this takes place the budget constraint can be re-written as

$$g + r(B/P) - (T/P) - (M/P)(\dot{P}/P) = (\dot{B}/P) + (\dot{M}/P) \tag{5.5}$$

where the last term on the left-hand side is an 'inflation tax' which reduces the *real* deficit of the government. The terms on the right-hand side are the increases in the real quantity of bonds and money held by households and firms. Inflation reduces the real value of money balances held by private economic agents. Hence, inflation transfers control over resources to the government by means of the inflation tax.

5.3 THE NEO-WALRASIAN PHILLIPS CURVE

A. William Phillips, a New Zealander who became an electrical engineer and then studied economics at the London School of Economics and subsequently was Professor of Economic Science and Statistics there, published in 1958 a paper on 'The relation between unemployment and the rate of change of money wage rates in the United Kingdom, 1861–1957', which was an empirical study of the relationship and presented evidence of a negative correlation between the two variables – the Phillips curve. Richard Lipsey, a Canadian then at the London School of Economics and now in Canada at Queen's University and the C.D. Howe Research Institute, published a paper in 1960 which gave a theoretical framework to the Phillips curve. The underlying theory was subsequently expanded by Milton Friedman (1968, 1977), Edmund Phelps (1967) of Columbia University, and Edwin Kuh (1967) of the Massachusetts Institute of Technology to make it fit into a neoclassical mode of analysis by shifting the emphasis from the money wage rate to the real wage rate, introducing expectations into the analysis, and allowing for productivity change.[2]

Rather than following the historical evolution of the Phillips curve, its ultimate form can be quickly seen if one starts with the static labour-demand equation of the neoclassical model (equation (2.2)) and then transforms it into a dynamic equation.[3]

$$W = f_n P \tag{5.6}$$
$$\dot{W}/W = (f_n \dot{P} + P\dot{f_n})/f_n P = \dot{P}/P + \dot{f_n}/f_n \tag{5.7}$$

In wage bargaining a contract is made for a period of time into the future. It is therefore the expected rate of inflation and the expected rate of change in labour productivity that determine the rate of change in the money wage rate. Defining these as π and ϕ, respectively, the equation becomes

$$\dot{W}/W = \pi + \phi \tag{5.8}$$

In equilibrium, actual and expected rates of change become identical and equation (5.8) gives the market-clearing nominal wage rate. Situations may arise, however, in which the money wage rate is disturbed from its market-clearing level. How can equation (5.8) be modified so as to describe the short-term money wage rate as it adjusts to its equilibrium level? Lipsey suggested that the 'law of supply and demand' could supply an answer. According to this law, in an auction market,

$$\dot{P} = h(x^D - x^S)$$

where h is the adjustment function
$\quad\quad x^D$ is quantity demanded in the market at the current price
$\quad\quad x^S$ is quantity supplied in the market at the current price
and $\quad \dot{P} > 0$ if $x^D - x^S > 0$
$\quad\quad\quad \dot{P} < 0$ if $x^D - x^S < 0$
$\quad\quad\quad \dot{P} = 0$ if $x^D - x^S = 0$

The problem in applying the law of supply and demand is that excess demand or excess supply are not observable. Hence, a proxy (substitute variable) must be found. It was Lipsey's suggestion that the unemployment rate be used as the proxy for excess supply or excess demand in the labour market and that the rate of change in the money wage rate in a disequilibrium situation be written as

$$\dot{W}/W = \pi + \phi + h(u) \tag{5.9}$$

where u is the unemployment rate.

At this point, however, imperfections in the labour market must be recognized. The macroeconomic conditions for full employment may exist but imperfections in individual labour markets unrelated to macroeconomic conditions may result in frictional unemployment. While the number of job vacancies and the number of persons looking for jobs may be identical at the going wage rate, the vacant jobs may require job skills which the lookers do not have, or the geographical location of jobs and lookers may be different, or lookers may not have information on the job vacancies. These frictional problems in the labour market must be taken into account. Friedman took Wicksell's term 'the natural rate of interest' and used the phrase 'the natural rate of unemployment' to describe the rate of unemployment that exists because of frictional problems in the labour market at macroeconomic full employment. The Phillips curve equation thus becomes

$$\dot{W}/W = \pi + \phi + h(u - u^N) \tag{5.10}$$

where u^N is the natural rate of unemployment. If $u = u^N$, there is macroeconomic equilibrium in the labour market and when actual and expected rates of change are equal, the Phillips curve is vertical at u^N since (see section 2.3) a change in the price level results only from a change in the money supply and, therefore, the rate of change in money wages is independent of the unemployment rate.

When $u \neq u^N$, a short-run negatively sloped Phillips curve exists. The short-run curve will shift as expectations about the rate of inflation change or as expectations about the rate of change in labour productivity change. (In most of the Phillips curve literature, it is implicitly assumed that labour productivity is constant.) Figure 5.1 shows short- and long-run Phillips curves.

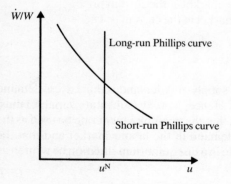

Fig. 5.1 Short- and long-run Phillips curves

A form of the Phillips curve which allows for empirical testing of the neo-Walrasian hypothesis is

$$\dot{P}/P = \alpha\pi + \beta\phi + \gamma[1/(u - u^N)] \tag{5.11}$$

where α, β, and γ are parameters. Under the neo-Walrasian hypothesis the two parameters α and β should both equal unity. The reciprocal of $(u - u^N)$ in the expression is one way of allowing for nonlinearity in the relation and γ will provide a measure of the strength of the relationship.

If prices are set by a constant markup on unit labour costs, then the rate of change in prices (the rate of inflation) can be substituted for the money wage rate and a 'trade-off equation' derived[4]:

$$\dot{P}/P = \pi + \phi + h(u - u^N) \tag{5.12}$$

This equation gave rise to a notion that, if one could determine the parameters of this equation, governments could select a rate of inflation by adjusting monetary policy to achieve the corresponding rate of unemployment. Friedman and others pointed out, however, that in the neo-Walrasian model this would not be true at macroeconomic full employment because at that point the Phillips curve, and hence the trade-off curve, would be vertical. Moreover, if the parameters of the curve changed under different policy regimes or in response to other changes in circumstances, a predictable relation between the unemployment rate and the inflation rate would not exist and monetary policy would not achieve its target inflation rate. Monetary policy is discussed further in Chapter 6.

5.4   THE KEYNESIAN PHILLIPS CURVE

Because in the *General Theory* the money wage rate was usually exogenously determined, the *General Theory* lacked a theory of inflation. When a Phillips curve is added to Keynes's model, however, it provides a theory of wage rate determination. The resulting model differs from the similarly augmented neo-Walrasian model in an important way. A strict application of the law of supply and demand implies a response of wage rates to a given amount of excess supply that is equal in magnitude but opposite in direction to an equivalent amount of excess demand. The Keynesian model however, is not symmetrical with respect to a comparable amount of excess supply of labour and a comparable amount of excess demand for labour. This asymmetry stems from Keynes's hypothesis that workers resist wage cuts because they are concerned with the money wage rate relative to that of workers in other industries. Hence, it may take a large amount of unemployment to initiate a wage cut whereas a small amount of excess demand may quickly trigger a rise in the wage rate.[5]

In comparing Keynes's model with the neo-Walrasian model, it is important to remember that in Keynes's model (see the *General Theory*, p. 295) the effect of a change in the quantity of money on the price level is composed of the total of the effects on employment (through the effect on the rate of interest and thereby on effective demand) and on the wage rate. This is not the same direct influence on the price level as postulated by the Quantity Theory of Money unless there is full employment. When there is unemployment, Keynes argued (p. 296) that employment will change in the same proportion as the quantity of money changes. Keynes pointed out (p. 303) that there is an asymmetry on the two sides of the point at which 'true inflation' sets in – true inflation occurring when an increase in effective demand results solely in an increase in unit costs proportional to the increase in effective demand.

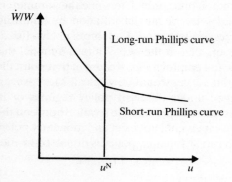

Fig. 5.2 Keynesian kinked Phillips curve

Figure 5.2 shows the resulting kinked Phillips curve in which the slope of the curve changes sharply at the point at which the unemployment rate equals the natural rate. Increasing aggregate demand above the full-employment output can increase output in the short run, but money wage rates and the inflation rate rise sharply. When the unemployment rate rises above the natural rate, the stickiness of the money wage rate implies that the unemployment rate may have to rise markedly to produce a significant reduction in wage-rate growth and thereby in the rate of inflation.

Many Keynesians, recognizing the asymmetrical nature of the Phillips curve, argue that monetary policy is not an appropriate means for lowering the rate of inflation. Since, as they argue, prices are set by firms on the basis of a markup on costs and particularly on unit labour costs, control over labour costs should imply control over the rate of inflation. They advocate,[6] therefore, that an 'incomes policy' which controls the rate of increase in money wage rates is more appropriate. Although an incomes policy may produce a misallocation of resources, the social cost of the misallocation effects, they argue, is lower than that of the unemployment and loss of real output produced by monetary policy.

The Keynesian model provides for the effect of external shocks as a source of inflation or disinflation through the effect of the shock on costs. Examples of such shocks are the increases in petroleum prices brought about by the Organization of Petroleum Exporting Countries (OPEC) in the 1970s and the decreases arising from the collapse of OPEC's market power in the mid-1980s.

5.5 UNCERTAIN EVENTS AND STOCHASTIC MODELS

The statement of the hard core of the neo-Walrasian research programme in Chapter 2 included the sentence: 'Economic agents have full information on current and future market prices and on other relevant economic matters.' Thus, expectations are as if perfect foresight existed. The model of Chapter 2 is deterministic in that it gives a complete explanation of the behaviour of endogenous economic variables, given the values of the exogenous variables and the behavioural equations. In this model there is always, in the absence of interference with the market mechanisms, a coordination of economic decisions and a tendency to full employment and, hence, no need for an outside agency such as the government to intervene to maintain full employment. Keynes, in sharp contrast to this position, gave a major role to uncertainty and its effect on long-term expectations and distinguished between uncertainty and risk. Long-term expectations were exogenous to his model. In the Keynesian system the coordination of the decisions of economic agents could break down and the system could be in a position with unemployment for long periods of time unless an outside agency performed a function which offset the effects on effective demand of this lack of coordination. Keynes gave a role to government in performing this function primarily through fiscal policy.

In the *General Theory* (p. 161), Keynes had attributed some investment decisions to 'animal spirits'[7] and in his model a large portion of net investment was exogenously determined. To neo-Walrasians, however, classifying variables as exogenous 'constitutes a throwing in of the explanatory towel' (Dow and Dow, 1985, p. 57). Keynes's references to uncertainty and animal spirits raise two fundamental questions:

1. Given that decisions must be made in the business world and in everyday life, how does one deal with uncertainty?
2. Does the presence of uncertainty preclude rational behaviour?

In current writings, the widespread use of decision theory and of subjective probabilities or 'degrees of belief' to form expected values has led to the proposition that decision makers should assign expected values to all 'uncertain' events. The statistician Dennis Lindley (1987, p. 17) in commenting on the design of expert systems has stated that 'the only satisfactory description of uncertainty is probability' and takes issues with those that argue that 'a serious short-coming of probability-based methods is that they are not capable of coming to grips with the persuasive fuzziness of information in the knowledge base' (p. 20). How Keynes would have responded to this argument must unfortunately remain a matter of pure speculation. The concept of rationality that follows from a probabilistic interpretation of uncertainty is that the decision maker should always choose so as to maximize his *expected* utility. Hence, 'the theory of rationality is intrinsically probabilistic'.[8]

It is now, and has been since the late 1940s, the standard practice of econometricians to add to each of the behavioural equations in their models a disturbance or error term which has the properties that it is a random variable, its expected value is zero, its variance is finite and constant over time, its correlations with its own previous values for lags of various lengths are all zero, and its correlation with the values of exogenous variables zero. To facilitate hypothesis testing, the probability distribution of the error term is frequently assumed to be normal. Such an error term is sometimes called 'white noise'. The solution values of all endogenous variables from models with error terms will be functions of both the values of the exogenous variables and of the error terms. The endogenous variables therefore become random variables. Such models are called *stochastic* models in contrast to the *deterministic* models of pure economic theory which have no error terms attached to behavioural equations. The observed values (or realizations) of the endogenous variables are then analyzed by econometricians as if they were generated by a stochastic process.

5.6 EXPECTATIONS HYPOTHESES

Expectations had been brought explicitly into macromodels through the expectations-augmented Phillips curve. The hypothesis about the way in which expectations were formed by economic agents was initially a very simple one. Expectations were based on the past behaviour of the relevant economic variables. One explicit form of this hypothesis was the 'adaptive expectations hypothesis' developed by Phillip Cagan (1956) and Milton Friedman (1957).

In 1961 John Muth published a landmark paper, 'Rational expectations and the theory of price movements'. The rational expectations hypothesis is an extension of optimizing behaviour to the making of forecasts (the forming of expectations about future events). Economists then began to consider the complete information set available to economic agents in formulating hypotheses about how economic agents form their expectations.

The adaptive expectations and rational expectations hypotheses may be explained by considering a simple model of an auction market for an agricultural commodity. Suppliers make a decision at point of time $t-1$ of how much to plant based on their expectation of the market price at point of time t when their product comes to market. The quantity supplied at time t (q_t^S) therefore depends on this expected or forecast price ($_tF_{t-1}$) and on the weather at harvest time (w_t):

$$q_t^S = \alpha_0 + \alpha_1(_tF_{t-1}) + \alpha_2 w_t + \varepsilon_t, \quad \alpha_1 > 0, \alpha_2 > 0 \tag{5.13}$$

where ε_t is a white-noise error and the α_i are parameters. Price is the *real* price (nominal price deflated by an index of commodity prices).

Quantity demanded (q_t^D) is a function of the prevailing market price (P_t) and real income (y_t):

$$q_t^D = \beta_0 + \beta_1 P_t + \beta_2 y_t + \eta_t, \quad \beta_1 < 0, \beta_2 > 0 \tag{5.14}$$

where η_t is a white-noise error term and the β_i are parameters.

The market clears:

$$q_t^D = q_t^S \tag{5.15}$$

The endogenous variables are q_t^S, q_t^D, and P_t; the exogenous variables are y_t and w_t.

Assume that forecasts of y_t and w_t are available and economic agents treat these forecasts as if they were certain. Agents forecast the market price in order to decide at planting time the quantity that they would like to bring onto the market. Consider now the solution of the model under the two alternative hypotheses concerning how economic agents form their price expectations.

5.6.1 Adaptive expectations

According to the adaptive expectations hypothesis, economic agents keep revising their forecasts on the basis of the observed forecast error in the last period:

$$\begin{aligned}
_tF_{t-1} &= {}_{t-1}F_{t-2} + (1-\lambda)(P_{t-1} - {}_{t-1}F_{t-2}) \\
&= \lambda(_{t-1}F_{t-2}) + (1-\lambda)P_{t-1}
\end{aligned} \tag{5.16}$$

where $0 \leq \lambda \leq 1$, and P_{t-1} is the realized (observed) price at point of time $t-1$.

If the forecast error for the previous period, $P_{t-1} - {}_{t-1}F_{t-2}$, equals zero, then the same forecast continues to be used. Otherwise, the forecast is either raised or lowered by a fraction $(1-\lambda)$ of the forecast error. In the two limiting cases, the previous forecast is used without adjustment ($\lambda = 1$) or the previous period's actual price is used as the forecast ($\lambda = 0$).

Since each forecast is a function of the previous realization, it can be shown for the cases where $0 < \lambda < 1$ that by repeated substitution the one-period forecast is a geometrically weighted average of all past realizations where the weights are λ, λ^2, λ^3. . . . Since $0 < \lambda < 1$, the weights on distant realizations decline in numerical value.[9]

Substituting the adaptive forecast of P_t from equation (5.16) into equation (5.13),

$$q_t^S = \alpha_0 + \alpha_1\{\lambda(_{t-1}F_{t-2}) + (1-\lambda)P_{t-1}\} + \alpha_2 w_t + \varepsilon_t \tag{5.17}$$

From (5.13) it can be seen that

$$\alpha_1(_{t-1}F_{t-2}) = q_{t-1}^S - \alpha_0 - \alpha_2 w_{t-1} - \varepsilon_{t-1}$$

Multiplying this expression through by λ and substituting into the previous equation,

$$q_t^S = (1-\lambda)\alpha_0 + \alpha_1(1-\lambda)P_{t-1} + \alpha_2(w_t - \lambda w_{t-1}) + \lambda q_{t-1}^S + \varepsilon_t - \lambda\varepsilon_{t-1} \tag{5.18}$$

Hence, q_t^S will be a function of the current and previous period's weather and of all previous values of P_t.

The solution of the model for P_t may then be obtained by using equation (5.15) to replace q^D in equation (5.18) by q^S and then substituting equation (5.17) for q^S and transposing so that P_t is on the left-hand side. It can be seen then that P_t will be a function of the current values of real income and weather and of all previous values of P_t (with geometrically declining weights).

5.6.2 Rational expectations

The rational expectations hypothesis (REH) is that the predictions of economic agents about the future values of economic variables are essentially the same as the predictions from the relevant economic model. Hence, the REH requires for its testing knowledge of the model which explains the behaviour of the variables, and the hypothesis can only be stated with reference to a specific model. The hypothesis does not require that economic agents know the model. It does require that the forecasts be the same as would be generated by the model. How can this occur if agents do not know the model? If the hard core and heuristics underlying the model are such that market prices contain the information required to pre-coordinate the decisions of economic agents and there are no significant market failures, then the resulting outcome will be Pareto optimal. For this to be the result, the expectations of economic agents must have been such that arbitrage has eliminated all profitable opportunities. That is, there must be a sufficient number of agents who use the available information in such a way that all opportunities to make profits from commodity speculation, running a firm, or selling information (market forecasts) have been eliminated. Such a use of the available information to form expectations is what is meant by the rational formation of expectations. That is, the essence of the Muth rational expectations hypothesis is that the expectation of economic agents of a variable x based on all the information which is available at the time that the expectation is formed will be the same as the expected value of x as determined by the relevant economic model in which x is explained. This will be achieved by the operation of market forces and the use of the available information by arbitrageurs.

The solution for P_t of the model described by equations (5.13–5.15) is

$$P_t = (1/\beta_1)\{(\alpha_0 - \beta_0) - \beta_2 y_t + \alpha_1(_tF_{t-1}) + \alpha_2 w_t + (\varepsilon_t - \eta_t)\} \tag{5.19}$$

The expected market price is the mathematical expectation of equation (5.19) (noting that $E(\varepsilon_t) = E(\eta_t) = 0$). Hence,

$$\begin{aligned} _tF_{t-1} &= (1/\beta_1)\{(\alpha_0 - \beta_0) - \beta_2 y_t + \alpha_1(_tF_{t-1}) + \alpha_2 w_t\} \\ &= [1/(\beta_1 - \alpha_1)]\{(\alpha_0 - \beta_0) - \beta_2 y_t + \alpha_2 w_t\} \end{aligned} \tag{5.20}$$

In equilibrium, the market price will equal this expected value plus the value of the error term:

$$P_t = [1/(\beta_1 - \alpha_1)]\{(\alpha_0 - \beta_0) - \beta_2 y_t + \alpha_2 w_t + (\varepsilon_t - \eta_t)\} \tag{5.21}$$

The contrast with the forecast from the adaptive expectations hypothesis is striking. The forecast which uses the information contained in the model makes the forecast (in this particular case) entirely a function of current values of the variables. That is, it is wholly dependent on the forecasts of the two exogenous variables, y_t and w_t. The past history of P_t has no influence on the forecast, whereas the adaptive expectations forecast allows the past history of P_t to affect the forecast.

Note that this is the same solution for P_t as one would obtain if $_tF_{t-1}$ had been replaced in the supply equation by P_t. That is, if suppliers had perfect foresight, the supply equation could be written:

$$q_t^S = \alpha_0 + \alpha_1 P_t + \alpha_2 w_t + \varepsilon_t \tag{5.22}$$

Thus, if the expected values of all the error terms are zero and if they are independently distributed, the expected value of a variable derived from the model will be the same as the solution value of the variable from the deterministic portion of the model.[10] The REH asserts that the subjective probability distributions of agents about future outcomes will be the same as the objective probability distribution of outcomes generated by the model, assuming that the same information set is available to all agents. Thus, the REH replaces the perfect foresight hypothesis of the neoclassical model and allows for uncertainty that can be described by probability distributions; that is, it allows for risk. Economists (see Lucas, 1981, pp. 223–4) do not, however, apply the REH in cases of true uncertainty where no probability distributions can be applied to future outcomes. Keynes's exogenous treatment of long-run expectations has not, therefore, been made endogenous by the adoption of the REH.

To sum up, the REH asserts (Muth, 1961, p. 5) that:

1. Information is scarce and economic agents do not waste it.
2. The way expectations are formed depends on the structure of the model describing the economy.
3. A publicly made forecast will have no substantial effect on the outcome from the economic system since it will have been based on information available to all economic agents. The exception will be an 'insider forecast' based on information not yet publicly available.

A corollary of the last statement is that sellers of economic forecasts must claim to have inside information, usually in the form of a model which is purported to be more accurate in its forecasts than those that are publicly available. Hence, commercial economic forecasters rarely make their complete models publicly available. The desire of firms to reduce their uncertainty about the future ensures that there is a large market for such forecasts.

An important implication of Muth's rational expectations is that economic agents should not make systematic errors in their forecasts; the forecast error should be white noise. Thus, the forecast error will be uncorrelated with the complete set of information that is available to the economic agent at the time that the forecast is made. Any future event whose occurrence can be predicted from the current information set will be included in the current information set. Hence, future events which cannot be predicted are not in the information set and their future occurrence is a random (unpredictable) event. Forecast errors will result only from the occurrence of these unpredictable events (surprises) and the errors will be uncorrelated with the current information set.

A forecast formed according to the REH makes no claim to being an accurate forecast. Unforeseen (random) events occurring between the time at which the forecast was made and the observation of the realization of the economic system will undoubtedly make the actual outcome different from the expected outcome. What the REH does claim is that the forecast will have made the best use of the information available at the time that the forecast was made. Forecast errors will be essentially unpredictable because the events which make the outcome diverge from the forecast were random events whose occurrence could not have been predicted from the information available at the time that the forecast was made. If the behaviour of the economic system was not subject to stochastic shocks, the expected values would correspond with the actual outcomes and there would be perfect foresight.

5.7 EFFICIENT MARKETS HYPOTHESIS

Related to the rational expectations hypothesis, although developed independently, is the 'efficient markets hypothesis' which states that in an auction market the current price of the good will be an equilibrium price that reflects all the available information about that good. Its price will change only in response to new information and since that new information is, by definition, unpredictable, changes in price will follow a 'random walk'.[11] Its future price changes will have two components:

1. An anticipated change based on known or anticipated future events such as a dividend payment. The price change will be such as to keep the return on holding the asset in equilibrium with respect to the rate of return on other assets.
2. A change in response to new information.

Hence, unless one has private (inside) information that is not available to the market, one cannot expect on average to beat the market since, if arbitrageurs are active and the market is an auction market, there will be no unexploited profit opportunities. The expected price is, in this sense, an unbiased predictor of the future price given the current information set. The only thing that one can say for certain is that the forecast of specific realizations will be expected to be incorrect but that the direction of the error cannot be forecast. Profits and losses will be made but the expected profit (in the probability sense) will be zero.

5.8 EXPECTATIONS AND AGGREGATE SUPPLY

If the economy is at the natural rate of unemployment and the actual and expected rates of inflation are equal, then the economy is on the long-term (vertical) Phillips curve. If, however, because of lack of information or failure to perceive the full implications of events, the expected rate of inflation is different from the actual rate, some economic agents may take actions which take the economy away from the level of output associated with the natural rate of unemployment. If the actual price level exceeds the expected level, firms may regard this as an unexpected profitable opportunity and increase output above normal levels. Similarly, if the actual price level is below the expected level, firms may be disappointed and decrease output below normal levels. Hence, the rate of change in real output may be described by the following equation (which is sometimes referred to as the 'Lucas aggregate supply equation', named after Robert Lucas, Jr. of the University of Chicago):

$$(\dot{y}/y)_t = h\{(\dot{P}/P)_t - {}_t\pi_{t-1}\} \tag{5.23}$$

where h is the function

${}_t\pi_{t-1}$ is the expectation formed at time $t-1$ by economic agents concerning the rate of inflation at time t

and $(\dot{y}/y)_t > 0$ when $h\{\ \} > 0$. Thus, the Lucas aggregate supply function implies that the level of real output can only be changed if a disturbance or economic policy lead to a change in the actual inflation rate that is different from the change in the expected inflation rate.

Since the unemployment rate is negatively correlated with the level of real output, the Lucas aggregate supply curve also implies that the unemployment rate is explained by the difference between the actual and expected rate of inflation:

$$u_t = u_t^N - \alpha\{(\dot{P}/P)_t - {}_t\pi_{t-1}\} \tag{5.24}$$

where α is a positive real number. Thus, the current unemployment rate deviates from the natural rate only if the actual and expected inflation rates are different (that is, if the position of the economy on the short-run Phillips curve is off the long-run Phillips curve). In the long run the information gap will disappear, the expected and actual rates of inflation will become equal, and the rate of change in real output will become zero and unemployment will return to its natural rate.

5.9 FURTHER READING

Friedman (1977) presents a history of the Phillips curve that is valuable reading for its emphasis on economic methodology. Lipsey (1981) presents the asymmetrical view of the Phillips curve. Benassy (1986, Part II) is good reading for the mathematically inclined. Sheffrin (1983) is an excellent exposition of the rational expectations hypothesis. Lovell (1986) reviews some of the literature on expectations hypotheses and evaluates the hypotheses. Malkiel (1981) is an entertaining application of the efficient markets hypothesis to forecasting stock market prices. McCallum (1980a) is a non-technical presentation of the rational expectations hypothesis and the Lucas aggregate supply curve.

NOTES

1. By differentiating the right-hand side of equation (5.4) with respect to time and rearranging the terms.
2. Friedman (1977) gives a history of the development of the Phillips curve from the viewpoint of the methodology of economics.

3. Equation (5.7) is obtained by differentiating equation (5.6) with respect to time, dividing through by W, and then, on the right-hand side, replacing W by $f_n P$.
4. Some writers refer to this trade-off equation as the Phillips curve.
5. Lipsey (1981) develops this asymmetry and reviews the inflationary experience of the 1970s in its light. Some alternative hypotheses that have been advanced to explain why money wages may remain at non-market-clearing levels are discussed in Chapter 7.
6. See, for example, Hahn (1983a, p. 106).
7. Dow and Dow (1985) present an interesting discussion of animal spirits and rationality.
8. Patrick Suppes, Professor of Philosophy at Stanford University (1984, p. 184). Suppes goes on, however, to point out two serious limitations to the workings of the expected-utility model:

> One is that even in the most deliberate circumstances we do not really understand how to make the calculations required by the model. A head of state, assisted by all the technical expertise of the modern bureaucracy, is still faced with a very poor estimate of the consequences of any particular set of economic decisions that he may make. . . . The second and deeper difficulty . . . is that [the model] can be satisfied by cognitive and moral idiots. Put another way, the consistency of computations required by the expected-utility model does not guarantee the exercise of judgment and wisdom in the traditional sense. (pp. 207–8)

Keynes would have agreed with Suppes!

Suppes makes another relevant point. He argues (p. 3) that 'randomness and probability are real phenomena, and are therefore not to be accounted for by our ignorance of true causes'. Hence (p. 10), 'the fundamental laws of natural phenomena are essentially probabilistic rather than deterministic in character' and that 'certainty of knowledge is unachievable'.

9. Mathematically, the adaptive expectations method is identical to exponential smoothing of current and past realizations. If the realizations are regarded as being generated by a stochastic process, it is also equivalent to an ARIMA(0,1,1) model.
10. In this sense, the expected value of a variable may be treated as a certainty equivalence by economic agents. This assumes that the loss function is quadratic (the common assumption of statisticians who minimize variances). In this case, the variance and other moments of the probability distribution of outcomes may be ignored. See Simon (1956) for a proof of this proposition about certainty equivalence and Sheffrin (1983, p. 2).
11. An ARIMA(0,1,0) process.

6·NEO-WALRASIAN MONETARY AND BUSINESS CYCLE THEORY

> Prices and quantities at each point of time are determined in competitive equilibrium.
>
> Robert E. Lucas, Jr. (1981, p. 179)

The primary objectives of central bank policy in most countries are to follow a disinflationary policy when the rate of inflation is deemed to be too high and then to keep the inflation rate at the new lower level. This chapter begins with a discussion of the effects of a disinflationary monetary policy under various assumptions concerning expectations and the existence of market-clearing wage rates. A distinction is made between the conditions under which monetary policy may be ineffective and when it may have effects on the level of employment. In the latter case, it can be argued that the policy maker should pursue a discretionary or activist monetary policy. This is followed by the presentation of a theory of optimal monetary policy for an activist policy maker. The chapter concludes with a review of recent developments in 'equilibrium business cycle theory'.

6.1 DISINFLATION AND MONETARY POLICY

An important problem of a disinflationary policy is the calculation of the correct speed of deceleration of the growth of the money supply. To understand the adjustment that is required in response to a reduction in the rate of growth of the money supply, consider the adjustment mechanism in the context of the static neoclassical model when there is a decrease in the money supply. The impact effect, when the period of time considered is so short that interest rates and the price level are still at their original level, is that households desire to re-establish portfolio balance by increasing their holdings of money balances. They try to sell bonds; this drives bond prices down and interest rates up. The higher interest rates decrease the demand for goods and the price level falls. When interest rates have risen to the point where demand has fallen enough so that the price level has decreased in the same proportion as the money supply decreased, the real money supply will have returned to its original level and portfolio balance will have been restored. Interest rates will return to their original level.

Consider now the adjustment to a permanent decrease in the rate of growth of the money supply in the neoclassical model augmented by the rational expectations hypothesis and the expectations-augmented Phillips curve. Assume that:

1. The economy is at full employment.
2. The labour, goods, and securities markets are all auction markets.
3. A policy statement is made that the central bank is lowering the rate of growth of the money supply to a specific lower rate.
4. All economic agents know that the Quantity Theory of Money holds and they form their expectations about future price levels accordingly.
5. All economic agents act as if there is no uncertainty.

Economic agents will then immediately adjust their expectations about the expected rate of inflation downward in response to the lower rate of growth of the money supply and will anticipate no change in the rate of growth of the *real* money supply. That is,

$$\pi = E(\dot{M}/M)$$

The actual rate of inflation will equal the expected rate and the conditions for no change in the rate of growth of real output as specified by the Lucas aggregate supply curve will be satisfied. There will be no effects on real variables if changes in the expected real value of securities resulting from the lowered expected rate of inflation do not affect the IS curve. When there are no effects on real variables from a change in the rate of growth of the money supply, money is said to be 'superneutral'. Under these circumstances, the Quantity Theory of Money stills holds when stated in a dynamic form: a change in the rate of growth of the money supply, other things remaining the same, produces an equal change in the rate of inflation. The nominal rate of interest falls because of the lowered expected rate of inflation.

Under these conditions, the 'policy ineffectiveness proposition' of the New Classical Economics holds: a fully anticipated change in monetary policy in a situation where markets continuously clear will have no effect on real variables; only nominal variables will be affected. The full anticipation of the policy change can result either from a policy statement from the central bank which has 100 per cent credibility or from a situation in which private economic agents know the central bank's reaction to economic conditions and can predict without error the policy that it will follow. More generally, the position of the New Classical Economics is that deviations of the unemployment rate from its equilibrium value (the natural rate) are totally insensitive to demand management policies.

Now consider what happens if the assumptions are changed:

1. No policy announcement is made.
2. Economic agents are risk averse.

Economic agents do not know whether the current change in the rate is transitory or permanent. They will wait for an accumulation of evidence and adjust their expected rate of inflation slowly towards the apparent rate of growth of the money supply, after allowing for the effect on the rate of growth of real output. In such a case the long-run expected rate of inflation may be approached asymptotically rather than being attained instantaneously. With uncertainty and risk aversion there may be unexploited profit opportunities until long-run equilibrium is established. Forecast errors will now be serially correlated because the anticipated price converges slowly to the mathematical expectation of the equilibrium price. The portfolio adjustment will go on for a long period of time as the realization that there has been a permanent decrease in the rate of growth of the money supply slowly becomes recognized. The fall in nominal interest rates resulting from the lowered expected rate of inflation will take place slowly over a long period of time. There would be a significant cost in terms of unemployment and lost real output by a disinflationary monetary policy under these assumptions.

The lack of information may be asymmetrical. It may be that only business firms know the Quantity Theory of Money and form their price forecasts in accordance with it. Labour, to illustrate with an extreme example, may know no economic theory and base its forecasts on the past behaviour of prices. Now when there is a decrease in the money supply, firms forecast that the prices of their products will decrease while workers do not expect the prices of the products they buy to change. Workers will be reluctant therefore to accept any reduction in their money wage rates since they would view such a cut as a decrease in their real wage. Firms faced with an unchanged money wage but falling prices of the goods that they are producing are therefore experiencing rising real wage rates. They will respond to the decrease in aggregate demand and the higher real wage rates by reducing output and employment. As unemployment rises, the short-run Phillips curve comes into play. If the labour market approximates an auction market, the excess supply of labour (as evidenced by the rising unemployment rate) will lead to a willingness of labour to accept lower money wages. The recognition that product prices are falling will make labour recognize that a reduction in their money wage may not mean a reduction in their real wage. Hence, over time money wages and product prices will fall and the real money supply will start rising. The process of adjustment will continue until the real money supply has risen to the point where it is equal to its original level before the aggregate demand shock occurred. Equilibrium will again be restored with aggregate demand back to its original level and unemployment back to the natural rate.

With respect to disinflation, the neo-Walrasians agree that there may be a temporary trade-off between deceleration of inflation and the unemployment rate – derived from the short-run Phillips Curve – when the change in monetary policy is not fully anticipated. Hence, there would be a cost in terms of unemployment and lost real output by reducing the rate of inflation through reducing the rate of growth of the money supply. Keynesians would not disagree that the full-employment rate of inflation is closely related to the rate of growth of the money supply and that the rate of growth of the money supply cannot affect the natural rate of unemployment or the full-employment rate of growth of real output. The disagreements concern the dynamics of the adjustment to a monetary shock – the slope of the Phillips curve, the path of the unemployment rate, the inflation rate, the growth rate of real output in the transition between full-employment steady states – and the magnitude of the resultant social costs.

6.2   A CASE FOR ACTIVIST MONETARY POLICY

Models which explain the role of monetary policy usually assume that wages, prices, and monetary policy are set at the beginning of a time period on the basis of the available information. Nominal wages are set to achieve an expected constant real wage rate and employment. Demand shocks may occur, however, which increase prices and decrease real wages and employment. The policy ineffectiveness proposition is based on the assumption that there are no long-term contracts for wages or prices which last beyond the period for which the current monetary policy applies; hence, there is no room for policy to offset the effects of the demand shocks. Models which involve wage contracts which extend over two or more periods of time imply, however, that the effects of money on output will extend for more than one period of time. At the beginning of each period the policy maker will now have information available which can be used to adjust monetary policy so as to reduce the fluctuations in output. Hence, there is now a role for an activist monetary policy. Fischer (1977) and Taylor (1980) have articulated such models and made the case for an activist monetary policy even when expectations are rational. Too quick a deceleration of the rate of growth of the money supply will, in the presence of long-term contracts, result in reductions in real money balances, higher interest rates, and unemployment.

It should be noted that the existence of wage policies, such as those implied by the existence of trade unions, were recognized by neoclassical economists such as Pigou (see the quotation in section 2.5, page 48). They were regarded by the neoclassicists as interferences with the working of perfectly competitive markets and the unemployment resulting from them was accounted for in the neoclassical theories of industrial fluctuations. There is nothing in them to imply that the long-run tendency is not towards equilibrium at full employment. If Keynesian economics is interpreted as the economics of economies with 'sticky' wages and prices, then such a policy may also be regarded as Keynesian. But if Keynesian economics is interpreted as being concerned with explaining behaviour which results in non-market clearing *equilibrium* prices and/or wage rates being set, then monetary policies designed to reduce the unemployment resulting from sticky wages may be regarded as more neo-Walrasian than Keynesian. Moreover, in seizing on nominal price and wage stickiness or rigidity as a key feature of Keynesian economics, the neo-Walrasians seem frequently to ignore Keynes's analysis (see section 3.7) of why a wage cut may not restore full employment (the Keynes effect).

With respect to situations where unemployment is above the natural rate, Keynesians attempt to push the economy down to the natural rate, not beyond it. They give an important role to monetary policy, particularly interest-rate policy which can affect investment through its relation to the marginal efficiency of capital, in moving the economy from a position of less than full employment to one that is closer to full employment. As Keynes (1936, pp. 295–6) stated:

> If there is a perfectly elastic supply as long as there is unemployment, and perfectly inelastic supply as soon as full employment is reached, and if effective demand changes in the same proportion as the quantity of money, the quantity theory of money can be enunciated as follows: 'So long as there is unemployment, *employment* will change in the same proportion as the quantity of money; and when there is full employment, *prices* will change in the same proportion as the quantity of money.'

The basic disagreement comes over the answers to two questions:

1. Would the economy have moved to the natural rate without central bank intervention?
2. If the central bank intervenes, what is the magnitude of the increase in the price level resulting from the money supply increases? (The quotation from Keynes assumed a perfectly elastic supply curve. This, of course, is not the normal situation at less-than-full-employment positions.)

It has also been a general feature of the Keynesian approach that when exogenous shocks to prices occur, such as the increase in oil prices attributable to the actions of OPEC, the shocks should be validated by an increase in the money supply. Otherwise as the increase in costs will generally lead to higher prices, real money balances will decline, and a recession will develop.

6.3 A THEORY OF OPTIMAL MONETARY POLICY

Given that there may be a short-run trade-off between the rate of inflation and the unemployment rate, Barro and Gordon (1983) have developed a theory of the optimal monetary policy for a policy maker. The basic equation is equation (5.24) which is repeated below:

$$u_t = u_t^N - \alpha\{(\dot{P}/P)_t - {}_t\pi_{t-1}\} \tag{6.1}$$

where α is a positive real number.

The natural rate of unemployment can be affected by random shocks but it is assumed to converge to its long-run average rate $(\bar{u}^N)$. The rate of convergence will depend on the value of λ, where $0 \leq \lambda \leq 1$):

$$u_t^N = \lambda u_{t-1}^N + (1 - \lambda)\bar{u}^N + \varepsilon_t \tag{6.2}$$

where ε_t is a white-noise error term.

The policy maker's objective is to choose a policy to minimize the discounted value of a socially accepted cost function where the total cost of inflation and unemployment in each period is measured by the following quadratic loss function:

$$Z_t = a(u_t - cu_t^N)^2 + b(\dot{P}/P)_t^2$$

where a and b are positive real numbers which measure the cost of departures of the unemployment rate from its natural rate, and the cost of inflation. The presence of unemployment compensation and the implications of income tax may mean that the natural rate of unemployment is higher than it would be in the absence of these distorting factors. The factor c ($c < 1$) reduces the natural rate in the cost function to allow for this.

The determination of the rate of inflation and the unemployment rate may be regarded as a game between the policy maker, who uses the central bank as its agent, and the economic agents in the private sector. The central bank influences the inflation rate through the rate of growth of the money supply and the following relation is assumed to exist:

$$(\dot{P}/P)_t = (\dot{M}/M)_t + \eta_t \tag{6.3}$$

where η_t is a white-noise error term.

Both the policy maker and the private economic agents form their expectations about outcomes in period t on the basis of an information set (I) available at time $t - 1$ which provides current information about inflation and unemployment rates and their costs. The policy maker has a reaction function based on this information set and chooses an inflation rate which it would like to exist at period t ($_t\pi_{t-1}$) as a function of the information set:

$$_t\pi_{t-1} = h(I_{t-1}) \tag{6.4}$$

The private-sector economic agents form their expectation about the inflation rate on the basis of how they expect the policy maker to react to the information set:

$$_t\pi_{t-1} = h^e(I_{t-1}) \tag{6.5}$$

It can be shown[1] that

$$_t\pi_{t-1} = (a\alpha/b)(1-k)E_{t-1}(u_t^N)$$

where E_{t-1} refers to the value expected at time $t-1$. Equilibrium will exist when the rate of inflation expected by the private-sector economic agents equals the inflation rate chosen by the policy maker and the actual unemployment rate equals the natural unemployment rate.

The amount of inflation that the policy maker can choose depends on the relative costs (the magnitude of b relative to a) and the slope of the Phillips curve (α). It may be in the interest of the policy maker to fool the public by choosing a higher inflation rate than the public expects. The short-run benefits of such a policy could include:

1. A temporary lowering of the unemployment rate and an increase in real output.
2. Increased revenue from the creation of money.
3. A reduction in the burden of the public debt.
4. An offset to an increase in the natural rate of inflation.
5. An offset to distortions which reduce the value of c.

The long-run cost of such benefits may, however, be a loss of reputation and the credibility of the central bank which may have adverse effects on the ability of the central bank to implement policy.

It might seem that the optimal policy is to choose an inflation rate of zero. This, however, is not true when the policy maker optimizes subject to a loss function that penalizes both inflation and departures of the unemployment rate from the natural rate. Zero inflation would not, therefore, be a reasonable expectation for private economic agents to hold and equilibrium would not be achieved at that rate. Equilibrium will only hold when the inflation rate chosen by the policy maker is sufficiently high that raising the chosen inflation rate does not lower the unemployment rate to such an extent that Z_t is lowered. That is, equilibrium will exist when the marginal cost of inflation equals the marginal gains from reducing unemployment. Following such a policy, however, does impart an upward bias to the long-term inflation rate.

In conclusion, there could be a role for an active policy on the part of the policy maker. Although the unemployment rate is invariant to the systematic part of monetary policy, as is implied by the long-run vertical Phillips curve, shocks to the system which introduce surprises bring costs which can, in part, be offset by the choice of an appropriate rate of inflation. The policy maker could optimize in each period subject to the parameters of the cost function and the information set upon which expectations are based.

6.4   EQUILIBRIUM BUSINESS CYCLE THEORY

Business cycles occur when real output and employment fluctuate about their long-term trend. Associated with these fluctuations in real output are movements of prices, nominal interest rates, and the share of output devoted to investment. Although the neo-Walrasian economists have used several different approaches to finding the causes of business cycles, all their models have a common characteristic in that they view the path of the economy as the outcome of a stochastic process. The basic assumption is that the economic system is being continually shocked by random events but that it is in stable equilibrium so that it always tends to return to equilibrium after the adjustment to a shock has been made.[2]

There have been two approaches:

1. One approach has been an almost pure statistical attempt to determine 'causality' by using Box–Jenkins methods on economic time series. The first step is to find variables that do not follow a random walk and which cannot be explained by their own past history (autocorrelation). The next step is to try to explain the unexplained variation in these variables by the past history of other variables. Where this is successful, the other variables are said to 'cause' the explained variable in the sense that the past history of the other variables explained a significant portion of their variability. The only input from economic theory that is required is a listing of the relevant variables to put into the model. This approach to causality is known as 'Granger causality' after Clive Granger who first advocated it, and the statistical model is referred to as a 'vector autoregressive' (VAR) model.

2. The second approach draws on neo-Walrasian economic theory in which economic agents optimize, and regards economic time series as the response to external shocks of a competitive system which tends to a moving equilibrium.[3] A satisfactory business cycle model captures both the dynamics and randomness of economic fluctuations. An essential and distinguishing characteristic of neo-Walrasian models is that fluctuations can occur but, at the same time, persistent, recurrent, unexploited profit

opportunities do not exist. Their models are constructed 'so as to predict how agents with stable tastes and technology will *choose* to respond to a new situation' (Lucas, 1981, pp. 220–1). The models aim to account for 'the observed movements in *quantities* (employment, consumption, investment) as an optimizing response to observed movements in *prices*' (Lucas, 1981, p. 222). That is, the neo-Walrasian business cycle models have three distinguishing characteristics (Lucas, 1981, pp. 179–80):

Prices and quantities at each point of time are determined in *competitive equilibrium*.

Economic agents form their expectations *rationally*, given the information available to them.

The information available to agents is *imperfect*. Not only is the future unknown, but no agent is perfectly informed on the current state of the economy.

The first characteristic implies that all prices and wages are flexible in that they adjust quickly to all shocks to the economy. Thus, the concepts of excess demand and excess supply play no role in the models.

Such models are referred to as equilibrium business cycle (EBC) models. Such models have often been criticized for their reliance on continuous market clearing, but, as Robert Barro (1981, p. 60) points out, the equating of supply to demand implies that market transactions have been undertaken up to the point where all trades that have been perceived as being mutually advantageous have been completed. Imperfect information about trading opportunities, production conditions, and so forth, or transactions and mobility costs could be taken into account, but they would be specific influences on the supply and demand functions. If continuous market clearing is rejected, Barro places the onus on those who reject it to substitute a satisfactory alternative mechanism.

A central question of business cycle theory is 'Why, in the face of moderately fluctuating nominal wages and prices, should households *choose* to supply labor at sharply irregular rates through time?' (Lucas, 1981, p. 220). In EBC models there is no such thing as 'involuntary unemployment' since all economic agents are deemed to make decisions about the supply of labour at market-clearing wages and prices. Workers who are not currently working are viewed as voluntarily substituting leisure for work because they think that the current real wage is low relative to what the labour market will offer in the future (appropriately discounted at the real rate of interest), and plan to substitute future work for current work.

There is an important point about unemployment. In Chapters 2–5, n and n^S referred to the number of hours of labour services employed or supplied at a given wage rate. The number of hours that workers are willing to supply could exceed the number of hours employers were purchasing without any person being without work. Hence, the social implications (and costs) of unemployment cannot be directly inferred from the fact that $n < n^S$ at a given wage rate. EBC models. however, do not concern themselves with explaining unemployment. The objective of business cycle models is seen as one of 'accounting for volatility in *employment* and real output' (Lucas, 1987, p. 48; italics added).

EBC models can be broadly grouped into two classes:

1. Real business cycle (RBC) models in which the initiating disturbance that leads to the departure from the long-run growth path is an exogenous technological shock (such as the introduction of new products or changes in the factors that affect the industrial composition of output) or a shift in preferences of individuals, combined with various sources of endogenous dynamics including adjustment costs and the time lags involved in putting new capital goods in place.
2. Monetary models in which the initial shock is an unexpected change in the rate of growth of the money supply or other disturbance relating to monetary institutions.

6.4.1 Real business cycle models

Bennett McCallum (1986, p. 398) states that:

> The distinguishing characteristic of RBC models is a denial that monetary policy actions have any *significant* impact on aggregate output and employment magnitudes. . . . The RBC point of view does not deny . . . that there is any association between output and monetary magnitudes. But it attributes the observed money–output correlation to so-called 'reverse causation', i.e., responses of the money stock, via the monetary authority and/or the banking sector, to variations in aggregate output. Thus, the RBC theories in effect claim that observed Phillips-type correlations stem from the monetary system's reaction to output fluctuations that are induced by real shocks to tastes or technology – not from the non-bank private sector's reaction to monetary shocks. (Italics added.)

The denial of the RBC modellers that monetary shocks have been an important source of business cycle fluctuations is based, in part, on statistical studies that money does not 'Granger cause' real output. This conclusion is similar to Keynes's argument in the *General Theory*. In the RBC models, however, the sources of the cyclical disturbances differ from those of Keynes. An example of an RBC model is the study of Kydland and Prescott (1982) which attempts to replicate the actual post-war quarterly economic fluctuations in the United States. Their model is a one-good model in which competitive equilibrium is achieved in each period. The only source of cyclical fluctuations is changes in technology which occur in the model through random shocks to the aggregate production function. The shock is a composite of white noise and autocorrelated components in a mix that cannot be observed by economic agents. The characteristic of the model that is important to the behaviour of output and employment is the lags in investment between the creation of the profitable opportunity for investment in new capital and when the capital is put in place.

The RBC models differ from Keynes's model in another important way. In Keynes's model there are significant uncertainties and market failures that lead to a lack of coordination among the decisions of economic agents. This created, in Keynes's opinion, a need for government to play a role – the 'socialization of investment'. In EBC models, it is usually assumed that there is a complete set of spot and future markets and that prices are perfectly flexible. Hence, the allocation of resources is Pareto optimal and it is then argued that there is no role for government to play in economic stabilization.

Barro (1986, p. 137) comments that real disturbances may not be large enough to account for the magnitude of observed economic fluctuations and notes that RBC models, unlike Keynesian models, lack important multipliers. RBC models need large disturbances to generate large movements in real output. Examples of large disturbances cited by Barro are the increases in oil prices brought about by the OPEC cartel in 1973 and 1979 and the decline in oil prices associated with the collapse of the market power of the cartel in 1985–87. These, and other commodity shocks, may be an important source of business cycles.

6.4.2 Monetary models

The Kydland–Prescott model contains no nominal variables (such as the quantity of money, the general price level, and nominal interest rates) and therefore it can shed no light on the problems arising from inflation or the observed movements in money and prices and real economic activity. Lucas and Stokey (1987) outline a model that does this. The procedure is 'to introduce money into a neoclassical dynamic framework in such a way as to restate in modern terms the quantity theory of money, inflation and interest'. This will also lead to a theoretical statement of 'what the problem of accounting for money-induced depressions seems to involve' (Lucas, 1987, p. 72). Information about a change in the money supply may contain information about future changes in the money supply and this can have real effects. In the absence of any anticipations about future changes, an increase in the money supply simply induces a proportional change in all prices which has no effect on relative prices or on real magnitudes – the static Quantity Theory of Money result. There will, however, be an anticipation effect which may work as follows. Suppose that the central bank undertakes open-market operations in the bond market randomly and that the timing of a change in the money supply is not known until the operation has taken place. At that time it becomes publicly known. Suppose it has been observed that increases in the money supply tend to be positively autocorrelated. The observed increase in the money supply will then lead to an anticipation of further increases and a rise in nominal interest rates. The 'inflation tax' effect encourages people to economize on money holdings by substituting against activities that require its use. Economic agents consume more leisure (employment falls) and more goods are bought on credit. Thus, there are non-neutralities resulting from monetary changes. Lucas (1987, p. 88), however, finds 'it difficult to believe that these effects can contribute very much to the explanation of major depressions or even of relatively minor post-war recessions'.

Lucas (1987) expresses a preference to pursue the more conventional view that a monetary contraction (or expansion) has real effects:

> not only through its *information effects*, but also through a *direct* effect, the latter arising because nominal prices do not respond in proportion to movements in money as they occur. That is to say, I would like to consider the prospects for monetary business cycle models based on some sort of nominal price *rigidity*. Exactly because this point of departure is so widely shared, I had better be clear on what I mean by a *rigidity*, and about what would be required to incorporate such an effect in a useful economic model.

> I use the term price rigidity to refer to a particular prediction error in classical models . . . in which the model predicts that a change in money will have a pure units effect, moving prices in proportion and quantities and relative prices not at all, but in which prices are observed to respond *less* than proportionately, and quantities similarly react 'inappropriately'. (pp. 88–9)

> The integration of monetary elements of the sort I have been discussing with the kind of real dynamics in the Kydland and Prescott model is, at present, slightly beyond the frontier of what is technically possible. (p. 85)

Lucas's preferred approach might seem to be a Keynesian modelling strategy except that Lucas is working within the confines of a model of a competitive economy without significant market failures whereas modern Keynesians, as explained in the next chapter, introduce theories of non-market-clearing equilibrium wage rates and restrictions on the availability of credit.

6.4.3 Progress within a scientific research programme

The work of the neo-Walrasians on equilibrium business cycle models is a clear illustration of the way in which a scientific research programme proceeds. Starting from the hard core of the neo-Walrasian programme, new theories are developed to explain facts not satisfactorily explained by the existing model. The static model of Chapter 2 could not explain the dynamic behaviour of the economy as exhibited by recurring business cycles observed in the real world. Hence, there was a need to develop a dynamic theory which retained the original hard core (somewhat modified) as an alternative to the Keynesian programme which had rejected some components of the neo-Walrasian hard core. The neo-Walrasian hard core's perfect foresight assumption was translated by the New Classical Economists into modern statistical terms by introducing the notion of a stochastic process and the expected value of a probability distribution as a certainty equivalent. Hence, both dynamics and randomness were added to the neoclassical model: equilibrium is a moving Walrasian equilibrium which is disturbed by stochastic shocks. Information was assumed to be used efficiently and this was translated into the rational expectations hypothesis. In this way the part of the hard core dealing with the maximizing behaviour of economic agents was given more content. The heuristic of markets in which market-clearing prices are quickly achieved so that the economy reaches an equilibrium in each time period was retained as a key feature of their business-cycle models. The major limitation to developing models which explain the full range of observed phenomena has been the technology available to model builders. As economists have added to their mathematical kit bag, it has become possible to construct and solve more complex models. As econometric theory has progressed, the testing of these theories has been able to proceed.

6.5 FURTHER READING

Friedman (1968, 1977), Mayer *et al.* (1978) and Laidler (1981) present the Monetarist view of monetary policy. Desai (1981) and Hahn (1983a) give critical assessments. Lipsey (1981) presents the Keynesian view. Phelps *et al.* (1970) has a number of theoretical papers on the dynamics of the inflation process. Blinder (1979) and Cagan (1979) have some analyses of the inflation of the 1970s. Taylor (1982) is an interesting analysis of disinflationary monetary policy with particular attention to the speed of deceleration. Darby (1976) is a good textbook presentation of the dynamics of the effects of a change in monetary policy. Barro and Fischer (1976) is a survey of developments in monetary theory up to the mid-1970s. Blanchard (1988), Fischer (1988) and McCallum (1988) are excellent surveys of recent neo-Walrasian research which include references to econometric findings. McCallum (1979) discusses the policy ineffectiveness proposition.

Lucas (1981, pp. 179–239 and 271–96) and (1987) presents his views on business cycles and Barro (1981, Ch. 2) provides a survey of equilibrium business cycle theory. Eichenbaum and Singleton (1986) survey the recent literature on real business cycle models and present some econometric findings, and Barro (1986) comments on their paper. Sargent and Sims (1977) is a time-series approach to business cycle modelling. Zellner (1984) contains an interesting discussion of causality and its role in econometrics which is relevant to the time-series approach.

Sargent (1987b) uses dynamic programming to discuss a number of topics related to monetary economics and government finance.

NOTES

1. See Barro and Gordon (1983, p. 597)
2. This framework for the study of business cycles originates with the work of Frisch (1933) and Slutzky (1937). Thus, the business cycle is regarded as serially correlated divergences of output from a smooth growth path. There have been attempts (for example, Nelson and Plosser, 1982) to show that real output follows a random walk, but this has not been convincing. See West (1988).
3. See the statement by Lucas in Klamer (1984, pp. 40–1).

7·THE NEW KEYNESIAN ECONOMICS

> When quality depends on price, market equilibrium may be characterized by demand not equaling supply.
>
> Joseph E. Stiglitz (1987, p. 4)

The equilibrium business cycle approach of the neo-Walrasian economists drew on standard neoclassical microeconomic theory which models the economy as having flexible prices in all markets so that markets clear in each period of time and there are no significant market failures. Economic agents make decisions about the supply of labour over time at market-clearing wages and prices. There is no involuntary unemployment and there is no need for government fiscal or monetary policies to reduce unemployment. The problems that Keynes addressed are not problems to the equilibrium business cycle theorists. They ask why, if fluctuations are costly, do not economic agents make arrangements that avoid such costs? Why don't the unemployed bid wages down to market-clearing levels?

The New Keynesian Economics, as stated by Greenwald and Stiglitz (1987a, p. 120), asserts that involuntary unemployment, credit rationing, and observed business cycles are inconsistent with standard microeconomic theory, and therefore seeks the development of a micro-theory which explains these phenomena. The elements of their theories include the understanding of the consequences of imperfect information and incomplete markets and the implications of the dependence of quality on price. The components of their perspective are

1. Efficiency wage theories which lead to the setting of non-market-clearing equilibrium wage rates.
2. Capital market imperfections which lead to capital rationing and the setting of interest rates at non-market-clearing equilibrium levels.
3. A view of monetary policy that is consistent with this view of capital markets.

The theories are relatively new, and to some extent incomplete (as are the equilibrium business cycle theories), and this is reflected in the following description of the theories. Since there is, as yet, no consensus among Keynesian economists as to which are the successful components of this approach, a number of different theories are surveyed briefly so that the reader can obtain a notion of the various directions in which the research programme is moving.

7.1 INSIGHTS FROM AND PROBLEMS WITH THE *GENERAL THEORY*

Greenwald and Stiglitz (1987a, pp. 120–3) point out four insights of Keynes which are useful to them in constructing a model of business cycles which, among other things, explains involuntary unemployment:

1. A general theory must explain the *persistence* of unemployment. Keynes included relative money wage rates in the utility functions of workers so that workers resisted downward movements of their money wage rate. The critical insight was that real wages may not fall to market-clearing levels. The recently developed 'efficiency wage theories' (explained below) provide an explanation which is more satisfactory to many modern Keynesians of why wages do not reach market-clearing levels.
2. A general theory must explain the *fluctuations* in unemployment. Keynes explained economic fluctuations in terms of variations in the level of investment which result from unforeseen changes in long-term expectations (changes in 'animal spirits'). Keynes did not successfully explain, however (in the view of modern Keynesians), why interest rate changes did not occur to offset the effects of these changes in long-run expectations. The New Keynesians Economics provides a theory of capital markets which explains this. Taken along with the efficiency wage theory, this provides an explanation of why interest rates, wage rates, and prices may not adjust to market-clearing levels and shows why certain exogenous disturbances are multiplied by the economic system instead of being dampened.
3. Keynes recognized that saving and investment must be distinguished and pointed out the difficulty of transforming saving into investment. He did not, however, discuss credit rationing and, more generally, the importance of capital market imperfections. The New Keynesian Economics has focused attention on this aspect of financial markets.
4. Keynes focused on demand disturbances, rather than supply disturbances, as the major cause of economic fluctuations. He worked, however, within Marshallian theory which saw equilibrium as being at the intersection of demand and supply so that firms were on their supply curves. Hence, given the neoclassical demand-for-labour function, real wages would rise as employment falls. But empirical observation suggests

that during the business cycle, employment and real wages move together, not in opposite directions. Keynes recognized this subsequent to the publication of the *General Theory* (see section 4.3). The New Keynesian Economics tries to provide a more satisfactory explanation of the pricing policies of firms.

Greenwald and Stiglitz (1987a, pp. 127–31) point out what, in their opinion, are the shortcomings of Keynes's *General Theory*. To them, the most important weaknesses were in Keynes's theory of the firm and in his explanation of the role of money in determining the level of economic activity. They suggest that both of these relate to Keynes's failure to understand fully the nature of capital markets. The shortcomings are:

1. Keynes did not distinguish between long-term bonds and equities and lumped the two together as if they were perfect substitutes. They are very different to the firm, however, since it is committed to paying back the principal amount and the interest on bonds at fixed dates whereas no such commitment is made when equities are issued. Moreover, in recessions firms seldom issue equities since they may be regarded as a sign that their financial position is such that they cannot raise capital from banks or other sources. From the viewpoint of the purchaser, bonds and equities have different risk properties.

2. Keynes's reliance on demand considerations to explain economic fluctuations, posed two quandaries:
   (a) Why don't firms use price policy to increase sales?
   (b) How could a small open economy (a price-taker in international markets) ever face unemployment problems since, by changing its exchange rate, it could face unlimited demand for its products?

3. Keynes argued that, given an exogenously determined set of long-term expectations, the only endogenous influence on investment was the rate of interest. But, real interest rates, until the 1980s, fluctuated very little. Hence, they could not serve to explain fluctuations in the endogenous component of investment. Moreover, Keynes (and neoclassical theory) did not explain inventory fluctuations.

4. Keynes's theory of how the monetary authority could affect the level of effective demand was implausible. In his model, a change in the supply of money brought about by open-market operations undertaken by the central bank leads, given the demand-for-money function of individuals, to a change in the rate of interest which, in turn, affects the investment decisions of firms. This points up the importance of distinguishing between the short-term interest rate, which is the one that enters the demand-for-money function, and the long-term rate, which is the one that influences investment decisions.

7.2 EQUILIBRIUM WITH NON-MARKET-CLEARING WAGE RATES

Neo-Walrasian models predict that individual firms will react to a reduction in the demand for their products by decreasing employment and the real wage paid to workers, but that full employment will be maintained because the laid-off workers will find employment with other firms at lower wage rates. In the real world, one observes that firms lay off redundant workers but the wage paid to the remaining workers tends to remain unchanged. Moreover, many laid-off workers remain unemployed. What alternative theory will explain this tendency to wage rigidity and involuntary unemployment? Moreover, a satisfactory theory of unemployment should explain both the level of unemployment and its form and composition. Recent attempts are of two types: implicit contract theories and efficiency wage theories.

7.2.1 Implicit contract theory

In implicit contract theory, firms, who are regarded as risk neutral, provide some degree of insurance for a reasonable period of time to workers who are risk averse against fluctuations in their incomes attributable to the business cycle. Workers usually cannot buy such insurance from insurance companies and therefore look to their employers for protection. Firms put together an employment package which offers wage and employment insurance in return for a wage that is somewhat lower (less than the value of the marginal product of the worker) than the wage that would prevail in an auction market. The risk is thereby transferred from wages to profits and, via capital markets, to the income streams of the holders of equity in the firm (and possibly its creditors). If, then, there is a shock which reduces the demand for the firm's products so that the value of the marginal product of labour falls slightly, the lack of wage flexibility imposes no cost on the firm if the wage rate is still less than the value of the marginal product. Only if the value of the marginal product falls enough will the rigid wage lead to some unemployment. The question is, under what conditions will this happen and why do other firms not hire the laid-off workers? A theory of unemployment must explain the behaviour of the market as a whole, not simply the behaviour of individual firms. Moreover, it should distinguish between reductions in the hours worked per week and lay-offs.

As an aside, it should be pointed out that in a situation where the government provides unemployment compensation to unemployed workers, it may pay firms to take advantage of this and to lay off workers when their productivity has fallen to low levels. If the firm supplements the compensation of individuals, then the laid-off workers may be regarded as voluntarily unemployed if the level of utility they get from leisure plus the unemployment compensation is at least equal to the level of utility they would have obtained from employment income. If this were the case, however, one would expect to see job rotation as individuals exhaust their unemployment benefits.

It can be argued (see Stiglitz, 1986, pp. 164–74) that, as long as firms are risk neutral, implicit contracts will lead to full employment (or overemployment in the sense that employment exceeds the level that would prevail in a Walrasian equilibrium), but not to underemployment. If, however, firms are very risk averse, underemployment may result. Such risk-averse behaviour of firms is inconsistent with a well-functioning capital market, but firms may behave in a risk-averse manner when shareholders are imperfectly informed concerning the actions of managers. This can provide an explanation of underemployment under special assumptions concerning the utility functions of workers and the degree of risk aversion of firms.

Another approach to explaining unemployment (see Newbury and Stiglitz, 1987) is to examine the sources of restrictions on the set of feasible contracts. There are three:

1. *Information*: Contracts can only be made on the basis of information available to the firm and the workers.
2. *Enforcement*: Implicit contracts differ from explicit contracts in that there is no legal mechanism for enforcement. The available mechanisms are (a) reputation mechanisms whereby bad behaviour by the firm leads to difficulties in hiring new workers, and (b) self-enforcement mechanisms whereby current workers punish the bad behaviour of firms by withdrawing their services.
3. *Complexity*: Observed contracts usually only have a limited degree of complexity.

Plausible versions of the restrictions implied by limitations on information, enforcement, and complexity, taken one at a time, do not lead to unemployment. But combinations of these restrictions do enable implicit contracts to explain unemployment.

Even if implicit contract theory provides an explanation of why lay-offs occur, it must explain why those laid off are not hired by other firms. One approach to this (see Stiglitz, 1986, pp. 179–82) is to assume that it is costly for those laid off to search for new jobs and that the process of gathering information is stochastic, so that some individuals are successful in locating suitable job vacancies and others are not. Thus, for the worker the risk that must be insured against is not just that the firm is not prosperous for a period of time but also that the laid-off worker is not successful in the search for employment. If the firm provides complete wage and employment insurance, the worker whose productivity is low will have no incentive to search for another job. Moreover, the firm cannot observe the search activities of an employee. If it could, it could make the contract provide for employment insurance conditional upon the search process. Thus, there is a moral hazard problem: the insured worker can, by not searching fully, increase the actual benefits he receives from the contract. The firm can, however, use two instruments for inducing search: (1) lower the wage of workers who are retained, and (2) lay off workers. Thus, the model can explain the simultaneous occurrence of wage reductions and unemployment and provide a model of the labour market in which there is an equilibrium level of unemployment.

To sum up, simple implicit contract models do provide an explanation of the lack of variability in real wages, but do not explain unemployment. More complicated models can explain unemployment and why unemployment takes the form of lay-offs rather than work sharing, but the combination of assumptions required for this makes the models less than fully satisfactory. Hence, other theories are being sought.

7.2.2 Efficiency wage theory

The basic hypothesis of the efficiency wage theories of unemployment is that the net productivity of workers is a function of the wage that they receive. If this is so, the wage rate may be an indicator of the quality of the worker. Hence, firms may be reluctant to lower wages when there is an excess supply of labour since lowering the wage may lower productivity more than proportionately. Equilibrium may be consistent with a situation in which there is an excess supply of labour; that is, with involuntary unemployment. In other words, the law of supply and demand may be repealed in the labour market (Stiglitz, 1987, p. 4).

A simple model explains the theory (see Yellen, 1984; Stiglitz, 1986). Consider an economy in which firms operate in competitive markets and each firm has the same production function:

$$y = f\{h(w)n\} \tag{7.1}$$

where n is the number of workers
  w is the real wage rate
  $h(w)$ is the efficiency per worker where efficiency is a function of the real wage, w

A profit-maximizing firm will choose a wage w^* that minimizes the wage cost per efficiency unit. Each firm will then hire labour up to the point where its marginal product equals the real wage rate. If w^* exceeds the minimum wage at which this supply of labour services will be forthcoming, there will be an excess supply of workers willing to work at w^* and the firm will not be constrained by labour supply conditions in choosing the level of employment which maximizes profit. Firms will not hire them at a lower wage if that would lower the productivity of those workers already on the job. Hence, the efficiency wage theory explains why the wage may not fall to the market-clearing level. Unemployment occurs if there are workers who would work at $w*$ but who cannot find work elsewhere at that rate or at a somewhat lower rate.

The theory must, however, explain why labour productivity is a function of the real wage paid by firms. A number of different explanations have been suggested:

1. *Nutrition*: At low levels of nutrition, which may be common in less developed countries as well as in the poorer classes in developed countries, productivity may improve as nutrition improves as a result of workers receiving a higher real wage.

2. *Shirking*: The payment of a wage in excess of the market-clearing wage may be an effective way for firms to give workers an incentive to work and to reduce shirking. It is difficult to monitor on-the-job performance because of incomplete information; hence, shirking cannot be eliminated simply by firing shirking workers. As long as unemployment compensation is at levels that are close to the market wage rate, the threat of laying off a worker for shirking may not be an effective disciplinary device. Indeed, it has been suggested that the increased levels of unemployment compensation in the last twenty years has contributed significantly to a slowdown in productivity growth.

3. *Labour turnover*: Offering a wage above the market-clearing wage may reduce labour turnover and thereby reduce costs to the firm.

4. *Adverse selection*: If workers are heterogeneous in their quality and if a worker's performance on the job is an increasing function of the wage rate, firms with higher wages will attract more competent workers. Firms will optimally not hire workers who are willing to work for less than the efficiency wage.

5. *Sociological*: A worker's performance may depend on whether he/she thinks he/she is being treated 'fairly'. A higher wage may be regarded as a symbol of fair treatment.

6. *Union threat*: The threat of collective action by workers in situations where there are significant costs to replacing workers may induce firms to pay higher wages so that workers will not have an incentive to forming a coalition. (Strictly speaking this is not related to the productivity of workers, but it is sometimes included as a factor leading to the setting of a non-market-clearing wage.)

In addition to giving an explanation for unemployment, wage efficiency theories provide insights into the pattern of observed unemployment. If the function $h(w)$ differs for different groups of workers, the highest productivity group will be fully employed, the middle group will be partially employed, and the lowest group may not find employment.

In a simple fixed-wage, fixed-price model an increase in unemployment compensation always has desirable effects on effective demand since (by assumption) wages and prices remain unchanged while total income increases. In contrast, in the 'shirking' version of the efficiency wage model an increase in unemployment compensation leads firms to raise the wage rate in order to induce workers not to shirk. This causes a higher equilibrium level of unemployment. In the 'adverse selection' version, an increase in unemployment compensation may affect differentially the amount of searching activity of workers with different abilities. Low-productivity workers may reduce their search activity.

The efficiency wage theory can provide an explanation of fluctuations in the unemployment rate. Other things remaining the same, the economy will settle, as explained above, into an equilibrium level of involuntary unemployment. Changes in the productivity of workers, in technology, in the capital stock, or in unemployment compensation will all lead to changes in the equilibrium level of unemployment. If these changes occur randomly, then a pattern of random fluctuations in the unemployment rate will occur. If there are frictions in the adjustment process, then the adjustment will be spread out over time and a cyclical response to changes may be observed.

To many economists the efficiency wage theory seems to have replaced the implicit contract theory as an explanation of the setting of non-market-clearing wage rates and of unemployment. Thus, the Keynesian research programme apparently has tried to replace an unsatisfactory theory with one which may be more fruitful. As Stiglitz (1986, p. 193) has expressed it:

> We have just begun the exploration of the full implications of these efficiency wage models. In the end, they may prove as unsatisfactory as the earlier versions of the implicit contract theory; empirical predictions of the theory may be shown to be inconsistent with the observed facts. But for now, they seem to provide the most fruitful direction of research, in extending our understanding of wage rigidities.

7.3 PRICE-SETTING POLICIES

Price setting is an important aspect of Keynesian economics and imperfect competition is regarded by Keynesians as the typical description of market structure in many industries. The model in Keynes's *General Theory* was not consistent, however, in that Keynes retained the assumptions of a competitive neoclassical economy in much of the micro-theory that would be implied by the *General Theory* while presenting results that can only be explained under the assumption that imperfect competition prevails.[1] In some respects it is surprising that he made no comment on imperfect competition until his 1939 *Economic Journal* article since at the time he was working on the *General Theory*. Joan Robinson, also at Cambridge, was writing her *Economics of Imperfect Competition*.

Some of the recent contributions to an explanation of why firms may not set prices at non-market-clearing levels are presented below. In part, they represent an attempt to shift the explanation of unemployment away from the wage-setting behaviour of firms to their price-setting behaviour in the hope that this will result in a more satisfactory explanation (see Mankiw, 1987, especially pp. 105–6; and Rotemberg, 1987). When the emphasis is shifted to price setting, the hypothesis is then that firms lay off workers in recessions not because of wage rates that are too high, but because prices have not been adjusted downward in response to market conditions and sales are too low.

7.3.1 Implicit contract theory

The late Arthur Okun (1981) tried to explain why prices are much more responsive to changes in costs than to shifts in demand. He suggested (pp. 169–70) that this pricing behaviour is a result of implicit contracts or conventions that introduce a concept of 'fairness' in the relation between sellers and buyers whereby price increases based on cost increases are generally accepted as fair, but those that are perceived of as taking advantage of short-run market conditions on the demand side are deemed to be unfair. Okun used the term 'customer markets' to distinguish markets in which this type of pricing may be prevalent. Customer markets are in contrast with auction markets where prices are continuously adjusting in response to the law of supply and demand.

When there is a tendency towards constancy of price, short-run fluctuations in consumer demand will lead to quantity adjustments or rationing. When demand falls, firms will initially experience an unanticipated increase in inventories which, if sustained, will lead to a reduction in output and possibly in employment. When demand rises above normal levels, firms may not be able to increase output in the short run. Hence, firms may ration output by setting quotas for customers or selling on a first-come first-served basis.

7.3.2 Non-market-clearing pricing

If current prices affect both the current and future demand for a firm's products, the current price which will maximize profits will be set below the firm's short-run marginal costs. The current 'loss' will be offset by the contribution of today's lower prices to future profits. An increase in the cost of capital to the firm will, however, increase the discount rate used to arrive at the current value of future profits and lower their current value. This would lead to a tendency for firms to increase current prices. Thus, if the cost of capital rises when a recession begins, then the reductions in prices that might accompany the fall in demand for the firm's products may be offset by the tendency to raise current prices to offset the rise in the cost of capital. Hence, prices may not adjust downwards to reflect fully changes in market conditions.

Another argument that leads to a downward rigidity of prices relates to the fact that firms could increase sales by cutting prices but the increase in profits to the firm may be so small[2] that, to the firm as an individual economic unit, it may be rational not to lower its price (see Parkin, 1986; Akerlof and Yellen, 1985; Mankiw, 1987). Firms in imperfect markets may, therefore, choose to change quantity, rather than price, to satisfy demand changes. In some models of the economy, however, relatively small deviations from optimal price have been shown to lead to large fluctuations in output. The cost to society, as measured by the induced unemployment, may be high. Hence, there is a disparity between private and social objectives and the outcome is non-Pareto optimal.

7.4 CAPITAL MARKET IMPERFECTIONS AND CREDIT RATIONING

The absence of forward markets combined with limitations on the ability to raise funds in the equity market in Keynes's model meant that production decisions may involve uncertainty. Because of this, there was a large exogenous component of investment. However, endogenous investment played an important role in the *General Theory* and movements in the rate of interest played a key role in determining the level of the endogenous component of investment. Total investment was not highly sensitive to interest rate fluctuations, however, because of the large component of exogenous investment or the possibility of a low elasticity of investment to interest rate movements. Moreover, a liquidity trap might prevent money supply or money wage rate changes from influencing the rate of interest.

The hypothesis has been advanced (see Greenwald, Stiglitz and Weiss, 1984, pp. 194–5) that Keynes incorrectly analysed the determinants of investment behaviour:

1. It is constraints on the availability of credit, not the cost of borrowing money, that restrict the amount of investment or curtail the amount of working capital so that production is limited.
2. The *effective* marginal cost of debt capital to firms is the monetary cost of interest plus the marginal increase in expected bankruptcy cost associated with the additional debt and possible bankruptcy. In situations where the credit constraint is not binding, firms may experience an increase in the effective cost of capital which results in a reduction in investment.

When firms raise capital by borrowing from banks or by issuing new equity, the problem facing banks is that they are never certain how the money that they lend will be used. When banks raise the interest rate charged to borrowers, this may generally increase the average riskiness of the projects that the banks are financing. They may be financing riskier projects or borrowers with safer projects may reduce their loan applications. Thus, raising the interest rate may reduce the banks' profits because the defaults on the riskier loans may offset the increased revenue from the higher interest rate. Again price, in this case the price of credit, is an indicator of quality. If so, the banks' profits may be maximized at a lower interest rate at which there is an excess demand for loanable funds. This results in a rationing of funds which may contribute in three ways to an explanation of fluctuations in investment by firms in real capital and thereby induce fluctuations in business generally.

1. It provides an explanation for the persistence of a situation in which a market does not clear.
2. The amount of credit rationing a firm will face will, at the given interest rate, vary at different phases of the cycle so that it may be severely rationed in a recession because of the greater uncertainty concerning the prospects of firms and the losses associated with bankruptcies. A firm may be forced to seek other sources of financing; thus, there may be variations in a firm's cost of capital which are unrelated to interest rate variations.
3. Credit rationing may explain how monetary policy is likely to work. It explains why policies which seek to increase investment by lowering interest rates are not likely to have the desired effect. If banks have set the interest rate lower than the market-clearing rate, then there already is an excess demand for funds and the banks are rationing credit. If, however, the monetary policy increases the availability of funds, this may lead to increased investment even if there is no effect on the level of interest rates.

This explanation may not, however, be a sufficient explanation of cyclical fluctuations in investment. Firms who are constrained in their borrowing from banks may raise capital by issuing equities. Moreover, it has been observed that some firms who are not credit constrained do vary their investment markedly during the course of the cycle.

A firm's ability to raise equity may be limited by informational imperfections for two reasons:

1. An important characteristic of the modern corporation is that the firm's managers are distinct from the firm's shareholders. Managers may receive only a small share of any increase in profits so that there may be

incentive problems when a firm is equity financed. Managers may divert some of the 'profits' to uses which increase the utility of managers rather than to uses which increase the value of the firm. Debt financing, on the other hand, gives managers less discretion in the use of funds and the threat of a bankruptcy, which may cost the managers their jobs, may serve as a spur to increasing their efforts to improve the position of the firm. Moreover, banks usually monitor the actions of managers of firms who are large creditors of the banks and may withdraw their funding if the managers do not appear to be efficient. This may be more effective than shareholder control which, in the absence of a strong board of directors, may be exercised only at annual meetings by majority vote.

2. There may be a signalling effect which restricts a firm's access to equity markets. The managers of a 'good' firm may be more willing to assume the responsibility of a debt burden and the additional debt may have a small incremental effect on the probability of the firm going bankrupt. 'Good' firms may therefore find it easier to borrow from banks. Hence, a firm attempting to raise capital in equity markets may convey a negative signal about the firm's quality and thereby reduce the market value of the firm. This may make the cost of capital prohibitive for many firms.

The effective marginal cost of capital for firms who are not credit constrained does not bear a simple relation to the long-term interest rate (as implied by Keynes's *General Theory*) or to the market price of equities. The effective marginal cost of capital may therefore have a much wider amplitude of fluctuations than either of these variables and these fluctuations may play an important role in explaining the behaviour of both investment and prices.

7.5 MONETARY POLICY AND BUSINESS CYCLES

A basic question is: how does monetary policy affect real economic activity? Traditional answers have focused attention on the central bank's ability to change the money supply. In the neoclassical model, there is a direct link between changes in the money supply and nominal magnitudes such as total spending. In Keynes's analysis, the change in the money supply might operate, if offsetting conditions did not exist, through affecting the rate of interest and thereby the level of investment. The quantity of money has, however, become a very difficult concept to define. Moreover, effectiveness in controlling the economy through an attempt to control the magnitude of any defined concept of the money supply is weakened markedly because of the existence of ready substitutes for money. Again, it is credit rationing that appears to be the operative mechanism (see Blinder, 1987b).

It is through the operation of the commercial banking system that the central bank's creation of fiat money enters the analysis. Commercial banks operate on a fractional reserve system and create a 'credit multiplier'. A scenario of economic expansion can be described in which the demand for the products of firms rises. Firms then borrow more and increase production. Their demand for money balances increases and their bank deposits rise. As money flows into the banking system, the supply of bank credit increases and fuels the increase in demand and the increase in supply by easing credit constraints. The credit multiplier – whereby more credit leads to firms hiring more workers and investing in more capital, producing more, increasing bank deposits, and increasing credit – operates alongside the Keynesian income-expenditure multiplier to further the expansion of economic activity. Depending on the relative magnitudes of the central bank's creation of fiat money and aggregate demand, the economy may become credit constrained. If there is a binding credit constraint, the expansionary effect of an increase in exogenous aggregate demand may be reduced from that which would otherwise exist in the simple Keynesian model.

What will be the effect of a binding credit constraint? The desired supply of goods by firms is based on current and expected relative prices, incomes of customers, and so forth. The absence of forward markets for most goods means that most firms cannot sell the goods that they plan to produce until after they have produced them. Thus, firms will likely need working capital obtained through credit in order to produce the goods, and every decision to produce goods involves a risk (including that of bankruptcy). If the supply of credit becomes rationed during the expansion, firms find their working capital reduced and they will therefore be unable to produce all the goods that they desire. Hence, there may be what Alan Blinder (1987b) describes as a 'failure of effective supply'. If a recession is initiated by declines in supply rather than declines in demand, there may be a tendency for prices to rise rather than to fall and this makes the *real* supply of credit decline. This may have a different impact than the cost–push mechanism of higher real interest rates that is usually mentioned as a factor in the cyclical downturn.

It is possible that the instability of the economy resulting from credit rationing may be offset by other stabilizing influences such as the real balance effect and the Phillips curve so that credit rationing may be a self-correcting malady. A theory of effective supply based on credit rationing (and perhaps on other phenomena) may be an area for further development. Perhaps, as Blinder (1987b, p. 351) says 'the principle of effective supply may take its place alongside the Keynesian principle of effective demand as the twin pillars' of the New Keynesian Economics.

7.6 SUMMARY

The New Keynesian Economics, as sketched above, provides a new general theory of economic behaviour derived from microeconomic principles – thereby contributing to an integration of the two branches of economics, as does neo-Walrasian economics. According to its proponents, it provides a more satisfactory explanation of wage and price setting and the resulting involuntary unemployment than did Keynes and a more satisfactory explanation of the cyclical fluctuations in investment in physical capital and in inventories.

In contrast to the conclusions of neo-Walrasian economics, Greenwald and Stiglitz (1987a, p. 132) conclude that:

> Unemployment is but the worst manifestation of pervasive market failures which arise in the presence of imperfect information and incomplete markets. But if the invisible hand of the market is palsied, the visible hand of government *may* be far worse. . . . We live in an imperfect world. And we must learn to live with those imperfections. Might not limited government intervention – correcting the worse manifestations of market failures, including massive unemployment – after all be the wisest policy to follow? In the end, Keynes, and Keynesian policies, are vindicated.

The Keynesian and neo-Walrasian research programmes proceed from different views of the world: different hard cores and heuristics. The successful research programme will explain (predict) a richer variety of real-world phenomena. Only time will tell which programme is most progressive and succeeds while the other degenerates.

7.7 FURTHER READING

Greenwald and Stiglitz (1987a) summarize the main tenets of the New Keynesian Economics. Stiglitz (1985a) is a good survey article on informational problems and economic analysis, particularly with reference to the 'new theory of the firm'. Stiglitz (1986) surveys the literature on the dependence of quality on price and its implications for macroeconomics. Katz (1986), Stiglitz (1986), and Yellen (1984) summarize wage efficiency theories. Rosen (1985) and Stiglitz (1986) survey implicit contract theory and textbook discussions may be found in Sinclair (1987) and Frank (1986). Okun (1981) and Tobin (1983b) elaborate on implicit contract theories with reference to both prices and wage rates. Greenwald, Stiglitz and Weiss (1984) summarize the arguments relating to capital market imperfections. Solow (1979, 1980) summarizes alternative theories of unemployment and macroeconomics. Klamer (1984) is an interesting set of interviews with economists of various schools.

NOTES

1. Hahn (1984, pp. 192, 292–3) makes this comment and raises the question of what should be the proper underpinning of Keynes's model in order to arrive at a Keynesian position.
2. At the maximum, the derivative of profits with respect to price is zero.

8·THE EFFECTIVENESS OF FISCAL POLICY

> There is no persuasive theoretical case for treating government debt, at the margin, as a net component of perceived household wealth.
>
> Robert J. Barro (1974, p. 1116)

This chapter begins with a reconsideration of the crowding-out debate and then goes on to consider a proposition advanced by the New Classical Economists known as the 'financing equivalence proposition'. The chapter concludes with some comments on discretionary fiscal policy.

8.1 THE CROWDING-OUT DEBATE

Does an increase in government expenditure on goods in the long run completely crowd out an equivalent amount of private expenditure on investment and consumption goods? That is, can long-term unemployment be decreased by government expenditure on goods such as the 'socialization of investment' suggested by Keynes? The debate in Britain over the answer to this question dates back at least to the 1920s when Keynes was disputing the neoclassical view of the economists in the British Treasury who argued that government expenditure was not an effective policy tool for reducing unemployment. This view had been put forth by the British Chancellor of the Exchequer, Winston Churchill, in his 1929 budget speech and cited by Keynes (1972, p. 115):

> It is the orthodox Treasury dogma, steadfastly held, that whatever might be the political or social advantages, very little additional employment and no permanent additional employment, can, in fact, and as a general rule, be created by State borrowing and State expenditure.

This classical view was discussed in section 2.6 where it was shown that, in a model which always returns to full employment after a disturbance as long as price and wage flexibility exist, an increase in government expenditure crowds out an equal amount of private spending on investment and consumption. If the economy is not at the full employment point, it may be because the money wage rate is too high relative to the price of goods and the remedy may be to cut wages and generally restore competitive market conditions.

Keynes argued, however, that one way to compensate for low levels of exogenous private investment expenditure was for government to increase its expenditures on goods. This, with the assistance of the multiplier effect, would drive the economy back towards full employment. The automatic tendency of the system to return to full employment, provided wage and price flexibility exist, was denied by Keynes because of the inherent uncertainty about expectations concerning the profitability of real investment compounded by the psychological nature of liquidity preference and the propensity to consume.

The implications in a simple Keynesian model of three different ways of financing an increase in government expenditure are illustrated in Fig. 8.1:

1. An equivalent increase in taxes by means of a lump-sum tax.
2. Borrowing from private economic agents by selling government bonds to them.
3. Borrowing from the central bank by selling bonds to the central bank and thereby increasing the money supply.

Tax financing

Consider first the case where the government expenditure on goods (g) is financed by an equal increase in real lump sum taxes ($t = T/P$). Under these conditions and assuming that the economy is at less than full employment, the balanced budget multiplier is greater than zero.[1] Figure 8.1a shows the corresponding IS–LM diagram. In this figure IS_1 is the initial IS curve before the fiscal policy changes. The increase in g shifts the IS curve to the right to IS_2, but the increase in t shifts it to the left to IS_3. The small increase in y from y_1 to y_2 results from the balanced-budget multiplier effect which is accompanied by a small increase in r from r_1 to r_2.

Bond financing

An elementary exposition of government expenditure financed by the sale of bonds to the public is shown in Fig. 8.1b. The IS curve shifts to the right from IS_1 to IS_2 as in the tax-financing tax. Real output and real income increase from their initial level y_1 to y_2 (sometimes referred to as 'crowding in') and the resulting increased demand for money drives the interest rate up from r_1 to r_2 and some, but not complete, crowding out of private expenditure occurs as the economy moves up the IS_2 curve to the new equilibrium position. The extent of the crowding out depends on the slope of the LM curve (on the elasticity of the demand for money with respect to the rate of interest) and on the slope of the IS curve (on the elasticity of private spending with respect to the rate of interest).

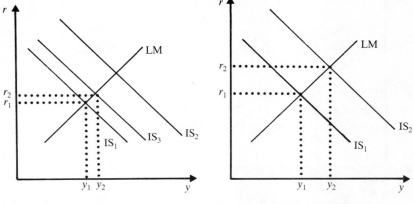

(a) Tax-financed government
    expenditure

(b) Bond-financed government
    expenditure

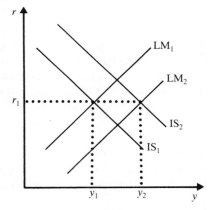

(c) Monetary expansion to finance government expenditure

Fig. 8.1 A Keynesian view of crowding out

An argument against the 'crowding-in' effect is that when bonds are sold to private economic agents the bonds may be perceived by households as an addition to real wealth. This will increase the demand for real money balances. The LM curve will shift to the left to LM_2 and the interest rate may rise to the point where there is complete crowding out, as shown in Fig. 8.2. The final result will depend on the slope of the LM curve and the magnitude of the shift. There may be some offset since the real wealth effect will also shift the IS curve to the right

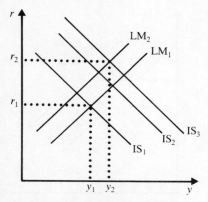

Fig. 8.2 Real wealth effects and crowding out

(the Pigou effect) to IS$_3$, but evidence suggests that this effect will be minor compared with the effect on the LM curve.

Robert Barro (1974) has argued that the bonds held by the private sector should not be regarded as wealth. Indeed, the argument is taken a further step and the 'financing equivalence proposition' is advanced: the effects of an increase in government expenditure are independent of the method of financing so that in all cases the result is the same as where the expenditure is financed by a tax increase. This proposition is considered in the next section.

Monetary expansion
If, instead of selling the bonds to the general public, the bonds are sold to the central bank so that the money supply increases, the LM curve shifts to the right to LM$_2$. Hence, as depicted in Fig. 8.1c, interest rates do not rise and there is no crowding out of private expenditure.

In the case where the expenditure is financed by monetary expansion, it must be recognized that the price level is a variable. In the long run at full employment, P will rise in proportion to the rise in M. Hence, the short-run increase in wealth resulting from the increased holdings of money will be offset by a decrease in the real value of the money supply. Hence, in the long run, the LM curve in Fig. 8.1c will shift back to its original position and the rise in interest rates brought about by the increased demand for money will not be offset by the increase in M. If economic agents form their expectations adaptively, there will be a short-run mitigation of the crowding-out effect, but ultimately the crowding out will occur. When a rational expectations view is taken of monetary expansion, it can be argued that the shift in the LM curve to the left in response to the rise in P will be anticipated immediately and the short-run mitigation of the rise in interest rates will not occur.

There may also be an additional effect on the IS curve. The rise in P will reduce the real value of bonds held by households and firms so that their real wealth will decline. They will tend to increase saving to bring real wealth back to its original level. This will tend to shift the IS curve to the left, reducing further the effect of the increase in government expenditure and increasing the likelihood that complete crowding out will occur.

8.2 THE FINANCING EQUIVALENCE PROPOSITION

The 'financing equivalence proposition' put forth by the New Classical Economists states that the effect of government on real variables is fully measured by the size and content of the real government expenditures and the effect is independent of how these expenditures are financed.[2] This is a revival of a proposition stated originally by David Ricardo and sometimes referred to as the Ricardian Equivalence Theorem.[3]

The crux of the argument is that rational private economic agents will increase their saving to offset completely any government deficit that is financed by borrowing from the private sector or by increasing the money supply. Hence, aggregate demand will be exactly the same as if government had financed the expenditure on goods by raising taxes. With respect to borrowing from the private sector, they argue that a rational individual will recognize that when a government incurs a deficit and issues a bond to finance the deficit, it incurs a future liability to pay interest payments on the bond. The rational individual will also recognize that ultimately the government will aim to balance its budget and will raise taxes to pay the interest on the bonds and to repay the principal when the bond matures. Hence, private economic agents will increase their future tax liabilities and increase their saving so that their asset holdings increase by an amount equal to the value of the bond. Thus, their net worth remains unchanged – the acquisition of the bond does not represent an increase in wealth. The result will be that the IS curve will, because of the increased saving, shift to the left thereby offsetting, in the main, the shift to the right resulting from the increase in government expenditure. There will be no difference, therefore, in the effect from that resulting from tax-financed government expenditure.

This argument is based on a number of assumptions[4]:

1. Individuals are rational and farsighted.
2. Households are linked to past and future generations by bequests and gifts so that their horizon is infinite. Transfers between generations are altruistically motivated.
3. The belief by households that present government deficits imply future taxes is correct.

4. Taxes are in the form of lump-sum taxes, which are non-discriminatory.
5. The availability of deficit financing to the government does not alter the political process.
6. The postponement of the payment of taxes does not redistribute resources within generations.
7. There are no liquidity constraints on economic agents. Capital markets are perfect.
8. Households are homogeneous so that their aggregate behaviour can be represented by that of a single representative household.

These conditions are likely to be violated and Tobin and Buiter (1980, p. 193) conclude that 'realistic departures from [these] assumptions support modern Keynesian views of the short-run and long-run effects of debt finance'. It should be noted, however, that the New Classical Economists would not argue that their financing equivalence proposition should hold in a strict sense. It is a benchmark from which the actual behaviour of the economy can be examined and questions asked as to why actual behaviour may deviate from the norm that rational behaviour would lead one to expect.

If the expenditure is financed by selling bonds to the central bank, the New Classical Economists argue that the rational individual will recognize immediately that the consequences will be a proportionate increase in the price level with no effect on real variables.[5] Households will therefore increase their saving to restore the real anticipated value of their assets. Again the net effect on real variables will be the same as if it had been financed by taxation. There will, of course, be an effect on nominal variables. Thus, the New Classical Economists argue that anticipation of the 'inflation tax' deprives the financing of expenditure by money supply increases of any effects on aggregate demand in the same way that anticipation of explicit taxes offsets the effect of debt financing.

It is arguable (see Tobin and Buiter, 1980, pp. 204–13) that the analogy with debt financing is faulty in several respects:

1. The inflation tax falls on those who hold the money the government has printed to finance the deficit whereas the explicit taxes fall on bond holders only to the extent that those who expect to pay additional taxes voluntarily hold bonds.
2. Any individual can reduce his/her inflation tax by holding less money. It is clearly not a lump-sum tax.
3. A one-shot increase in debt brings about, in the view of the New Classical Economists, expectations of future taxes. A one-shot increase in the money supply leads to an expectation of a proportionate increase in the price level. This is similar to a capital levy in that it reduces the value of previously acquired money as well as the newly issued money. There is

no expectation of higher inflation since there is no expectation of a sustained increase in the rate of growth of the money supply.

8.3 DISCRETIONARY FISCAL POLICY

The neo-Walrasian arguments about the neutrality of financing methods apply to situations where the policy is perceived by private economic agents who respond rationally. When deficit-financed government spending is unanticipated, it will have real effects on aggregate demand in the same way that unanticipated increases in the money supply do.

The crux of the difference between the Keynesians and the neo-Walrasians is again whether government intervention is necessary to move an economy from a position of less than full employment to one that is closer to full employment. Keynesians start with the presumption that the system will, if left alone, remain at less than full employment for a prolonged period of time, given the tendency of wages and/or prices to be set at non-market-clearing levels, unless the exogenous component of aggregate demand is sufficiently high so that effective demand is at the full employment level. Hence, an increase in government expenditure will lead to increased employment although this may be accompanied by an increase in the inflation rate so that there is a genuine trade-off. A side effect of the Keynesian policies may be a nominal government budget deficit which is rising accompanied by an increased inflation rate. The real deficit may, however, remain constant.

Neo-Walrasians reject the Keynesian position and its implications for fiscal policy. They argue that Keynesian policies crowd out private expenditure and cause inflation. The private sector has to understand them and calculate how to bypass their effects. Keynesians agree that demand-management policies are capable of doing harm as well as good. However, they reject the implication of the doctrine that government need not concern itself with the economy's future because the actions of private economic agents will take care of economic growth. To Keynesians, government has a role to play in offsetting the effects of market failures, failures whose existence is essentially denied by the neo-Walrasians.

In the United States in the 1960s and 1970s, Keynesians tended to focus on the 'Okun gap' (named after Arthur Okun) as the critical variable to which demand-management policy should be oriented. The Okun gap is the gap between potential output and actual output, where potential output is the output the economy is capable of producing at the natural rate of unemployment when capital and labour are utilized at standard or normal operating rates. When Okun was Chairman of the Council of Economic Advisers in the 1960s, the objective of demand-management policy was to eliminate the gap by using an expansionary fiscal policy to raise aggregate demand to the level of potential output and an accommodating monetary policy to keep interest rates low. When such a policy is carried on for a long period of time, however, the potential for an inflationary outburst is built up. This was the situation when in the latter part of the 1960s US involvement in Vietnam and the sharp increase in military expenditure ignited an inflationary spiral which ultimately led to double-digit inflation rates. The situation was exacerbated by a number of supply-side shocks affecting the prices of primary products such as crude oil and beef.

In Washington in the early 1980s the emphasis was on 'supply-side economics'. As an alternative to using monetary policy to reduce the inflation rate, it was argued that the level of potential output should be increased, thereby increasing the size of the Okun gap. The principal emphasis was on tax policies designed to increase the supply of labour and capital. A crucial part of the debate was whether such tax policies would increase or decrease tax revenues. The 'supply-siders' have argued on the basis of the 'Laffer curve' (named after Arthur Laffer) that tax revenues will increase. On the basis of convential estimates of the elasticity of tax revenues with respect to tax cuts, it would be expected that tax revenues would decline and the government budget deficit would increase. The latter seems to have been the case although the supply-side experiment is difficult to evaluate because the rapid decrease in the rate of inflation in the 1980s reduced tax revenues and markedly increased the deficit.

8.4 FURTHER READING

Some of the main literature on the crowding-out debate is Blinder and Solow (1973, 1974), Modigliani and Ando (1976), Ando (1974), and Tobin and Buiter (1980). The financing equivalence proposition is discussed by Barro (1974), Tobin (1980, Ch. 3), Tobin and Buiter (1980), and Bernheim (1987). Frenkel and Razin (1987) discuss fiscal policies for an open economy and include an exposition of intertemporal substitution. Aschauer (1988) discusses fiscal policy from the perspective of optimizing agents making decisions in a competitive equilibrium setting. Modigliani (1986) and Stein (1982) discuss demand-management policies and provide econometric evidence.

NOTES

1. The increase in g has a larger effect on y than the negative effect of the increase in taxes because some of the tax revenue represents income that would have been

saved, not spent on consumption goods. The algebra of the balanced budget multiplier is in Appendix 3.1.

2. Sargent (1987a, pp. 41–5) presents an alternative definition of disposable income and uses this to derive algebraically, under specified conditions, the conclusions of the financing equivalence proposition.

3. Tobin and Buiter (1980, p. 192 note e) conclude that Ricardo was aware of the limitations of the proposition and repudiated it. The proposition is similar in some respects to the Miller–Modigliani (1959) theorem for corporate finance.

4. These are summarized critically by Bernheim (1987) and by Tobin and Buiter (1980, pp. 193–9).

5. It should be noted that the argument that there are no effects on real variables of an increase in the money supply is an essential part of the claim. The conditions under which this would be true were discussed in section 2.3.

9·OPEN-ECONOMY MODELS

> A model of the exchange rate is a macro model in which the exchange rate is just another endogenous variable like consumption, inflation, and unemployment.
>
> Patrick Minford (1987, p. 157)

The models of the previous chapters were closed-economy models. The study of the behaviour of a closed economy can be justified on the grounds that, if one wants to focus attention on the necessary conditions for full employment or on the conditions for involuntary unemployment, the extension of the models to include the international flow of goods and capital is not necessary. Moreover, if the foreign exchange rate is perfectly flexible and the degree of substitutability between foreign securities and currencies is low, then the central bank is free to follow a monetary policy that is independent of the policy of that country's trading partners. These were to some extent the conditions that prevailed in the 1930s. Hence, economists tended to regard macroeconomic theory and international trade theory as separate areas of study. Now, however, foreign trade is a source of shocks to aggregate demand, and international capital markets are available to firms for financing their capital expenditures. Moreover, foreign exchange rates tend to be managed rather than allowed to float freely. A modern study of macroeconomics must therefore include a study of open-economy economics and economic policy must take into account the interconnections between internal and external policies.

Some of the models presented in this chapter are neo-Walrasian models in which all markets clear, and one is a Keynesian model. The determination of the foreign exchange rate is discussed in the context of these models. Open-economy versions of the Quantity Theory of Money are presented. The models are all static. In Appendices 9.2 and 9.3, however, some beginnings of a dynamic analysis are presented.

The chapter begins with an outline of the policy regimes that may exist in an open economy since these are relevant to the choice of exogenous variables in an open-economy model.

9.1 POLICY REGIMES FOR AN OPEN ECONOMY

There are three facets of economic policy in an open economy which are inter-connected and use of these policies has a number of components[1]:

1. *Fiscal policy:* The levels of expenditures, revenue, and the method of financing of the government deficit are all interrelated decisions.
2. *Monetary policy:* With respect to the domestic economy, choices have to be made of the target policy (for example, the inflation rate), the variable (money supply or interest rates) to be manipulated to achieve the target, and the mechanism to be used (for example, open-market operations in the domestic bond market).
3. *Exchange-rate policy:* Three choices as to the exchange rate are available to the policy maker in a free market economy:
    (a) A flexible (cleanly floating) rate with no intervention by the central bank in the foreign exchange market. The official reserves of foreign exchange held by the central bank remain constant.
    (b) A fixed (pegged) rate maintained by the central bank through open-market operations in the foreign exchange market. The official reserves of foreign exchange held by the central bank become a variable.
    (c) A managed float in which both the exchange rate and official reserves vary.

Currently many market-economy countries follow an exchange-rate policy in which the rate is pegged in the short run but allowed to find its equilibrium value in the long run. To implement a fixed (pegged) exchange rate system in a free market economy, the central bank must have previously accumulated a large inventory of foreign currency, either by buying it in the open market or by direct purchases or borrowing from the central banks of other countries. The central bank cannot continue, however, to sell foreign currency indefinitely because it will exhaust its foreign currency reserves. When the central bank intervenes in the foreign exchange market, its purchases or sales change the domestic money supply in exactly the same way as do open-market operations in the bond market. Thus, when a pegged exchange rate system is implemented, the central bank gives up control over the money supply unless every time it undertakes a foreign-exchange market transaction it 'sterilizes' the transaction. That is, it undertakes the opposite transaction in the bond market thereby keeping the money supply from changing.

To maintain a pegged rate it is essential that market conditions be created which will produce an equilibrium at that rate. If there is an increased demand for foreign currency and the central bank sells foreign currency and does not sterilize its sales, the resulting reduction in the money supply will create expectations that, other things remaining the same, the price of foreign currency will fall. Thus, there will be a tendency for the forces which were causing the price of foreign currency to rise to be offset. Similarly, when the central bank is buying foreign currency, the resulting rise in the money supply will tend to increase prices in the domestic economy and increase the demand for foreign currency, thus tending to restore equilibrium at the fixed rate. Hence, in the long run, sterilization is not a feasible policy if a fixed exchange rate is being maintained. In the long run, the money supply must be regarded as an endogenous variable under such a policy regime.

Fiscal and monetary policies are interrelated because the financing of the budget deficit may lead to changes in the money supply if the central bank purchases some of the bonds issued to finance the deficit, or to changes in interest rates if the bonds are sold to households or firms. Monetary and exchange-rate policies are interrelated because open-market operations by the central bank in either the bond or foreign exchange markets affect the money supply unless the intervention is sterilized. The government must therefore regard monetary policy, fiscal policy, and exchange-rate policy as interconnected policies which must be coordinated into a single overall strategy. Moreover, it may be that large countries should coordinate their economic strategy with those of their trading partners; otherwise countries may adversely affect each other by their policies and prevent the smooth operation of the world economy.

9.2 SOME BASIC THEORIES

A simple neoclassical model of full employment can illustrate some open-economy propositions.[2] In this simple model there are only two countries: the domestic economy and the rest of the world. Each country has a central bank which issues fiat money. There is an auction market – the foreign exchange market – in which the two currencies may be bought or sold for either spot or forward delivery. The central bank does not intervene in the foreign exchange market.

Law of one price
Assume that all goods are standardized commodities that are bought and sold in auction markets and freely traded between the two countries. Arbitrageurs buy and sell goods when price differences occur in the two countries so that for each commodity and, therefore, for all commodities,

$$P = eP^f \tag{9.1}$$

where P is the average price of goods in the domestic economy in the domestic currency, P^f is the average price of goods in the foreign country in the foreign currency, e is the spot price of a unit of foreign currency in terms of the domestic currency (the spot foreign exchange rate). This equality of prices, which holds under the above assumptions and when prices are denominated in a common currency, is called the 'law of one price'.

Interest-rate parity
Assume that each government issues a bond which can be bought by residents of either country and which is regarded as risk-free. The bonds are regarded by residents of each country as *perfect* substitutes so that economic agents consider only the rate of return when deciding which bond to buy. The proceeds to a domestic household which buys today a one-year foreign bond worth at maturity one unit of foreign currency and then today also sells the foreign currency proceeds in the forward exchange market so that the proceeds will be received in domestic currency and any risk from changes in the exchange rate is eliminated will be, in units of the domestic currency,

$$(1 + R^f)f$$

where R^f is the yield on the foreign bond and f is today's forward price of a unit of foreign currency in terms of the domestic currency.

The cost of buying the foreign bond is the cost of one unit of foreign currency in the spot market plus the forgone interest from not having bought a domestic bond of the same maturity (the opportunity cost):

$$(1 + R)e$$

where R is the yield of the domestic bond.

Arbitrage will ensure that the rate of return on the two bonds will be equal (apart from transactions costs which are ignored here). Hence,

$$(1 + R^f)f = (1 + R)e$$

That is,

$$(1 + R)/(1 + R^f) = f/e \qquad (9.2)$$

This type of interest arbitrage is referred to as 'covered interest arbitrage' since all the risk from exchange rate changes has been eliminated by simultaneously buying foreign currency in the spot market and selling the foreign currency proceeds in the forward market. If the buyer of the foreign bond believes that the spot rate for foreign currency will be higher one year from now than the current forward rate for one-year delivery, then the buyer would not sell the proceeds in the forward market when the bond was bought. The buyer would wait until the bond had matured and then sell the proceeds in the spot market. This would be 'uncovered interest arbitrage'. Again, however, arbitrage would tend to equalize rates of return on the two bonds between covered and uncovered interest arbitrage because a market consensus would tend to be formed about the expected future spot price of foreign currency. This would tend to make

$$f = E(e) \tag{9.3}$$

where $E(e)$ is today's expected (forecast) value of the spot price of foreign currency a year from now. That is, in an efficient market the forward price of foreign currency will equal the market's expectation of the future spot price of a unit of foreign currency.

If equation (9.3) is substituted into equation (9.2) and the logarithms of both sides of the equation are taken, the result is

$$\log(1 + R) - \log(1 + R^f) = \log[E(e)] - \log(e)$$

When R is close to zero (for example, $R = 0.03$), this expression can be approximated by

$$R - R^f = E(\dot{e}/e) = \theta \tag{9.4}$$

where $E(\dot{e}/e)$ is the expected rate of change in the spot price of a unit of foreign currency and is written as θ to shorten the expression. Equation (9.4) is sometimes referred to as the 'Fisher open-economy equation'. It states that the interest rates in the two countries will be equal if the exchange rate is not expected to change. The domestic interest rate will be higher than the foreign interest rate if the spot price of foreign currency is expected to rise (the external value of the domestic currency is expected to depreciate). The domestic interest rate will be lower than the foreign interest rate if the spot price of foreign currency is expected to fall (the external value of a unit of domestic currency is expected to appreciate). Hence, the domestic economy can only maintain an interest rate that is lower than the rate in the rest of the world if market conditions are such that the spot price of foreign currency is expected to fall.

Open-economy Quantity Theory of Money

The determination of the price of foreign currency in this auction-market model can be explained by the Quantity Theory of Money. In each country the price level will be determined as follows:

$$P = M/[m(R, y)] \tag{9.5}$$
$$P^f = M^f/[m^f(R^f, y^f)] \tag{9.6}$$

where M^f is the money supply in the foreign country, m^f is the demand-for-real-money-balances function in the foreign country, and y^f is real output in the foreign country.

Substituting these expressions into equation (9.1) and rearranging the terms,

$$e = [Mm^f(R^f, y^f)]/[M^f m(R, y)] \tag{9.7}$$

Hence, the spot price of foreign currency is determined by the relative quantities of money in the two countries in relation to the relative demands for the two currencies. This result is sometimes referred to as the 'open-economy Quantity Theory of Money'.

From equation (9.7) it can be seen that the market's rational forecast of the future spot price of foreign exchange will be based, other things remaining the same, on the expected money supplies in the two countries. If the money supply in the domestic economy is expected to increase faster than the money supply of the foreign country, relative to the expected demands for the currencies, then the spot price of the foreign currency will be expected to rise.

Real exchange rate

If P^f and P are expressed as index numbers which are equal to unity in some base year, then the 'real exchange rate' is (eP^f/P). Hence, insofar as the nominal exchange rate is changing in response to differential rates of inflation, the change will have no effect on the relative price of goods in the two countries. That is, the real exchange rate will remain unchanged although the nominal exchange rate is changing. The rate of change in the real exchange rate will be the rate of change in the nominal exchange rate minus the difference between the rate of inflation in the domestic economy and in the foreign economy.

9.3 AN ASSET MARKET MODEL

Consider now a model in which the domestic and foreign bonds may *not* be regarded as perfect substitutes for one another and in which separate asset markets are articulated.[3]

9.3.1 Demand and supply of financial assets

Demand for financial assets

To keep the model simple, assume that only households hold financial assets and that there are only three assets: domestic currency (M), bonds issued by the domestic government and denominated in domestic currency (B), and bonds issued by the foreign government and denominated in foreign currency (F). Both bonds have a value of one unit of currency and pay interest at a rate which continuously adjusts in accordance with market demand and supply. It is assumed that foreigners do not hold the domestic bond and domestic households do not hold foreign currency. Total wealth of domestic households in nominal terms and in domestic currency (A) is

$$A = M + B + eF \tag{9.8}$$

Financial capital is assumed to be perfectly mobile between the domestic economy and the rest of the world. Thus, domestic households can very quickly adjust their portfolio of assets to obtain the desired composition. In this model, in contrast to the previous model, households do not consider the domestic bond and the foreign bond to be perfect substitutes for each other. Because the foreign bond is denominated in foreign currency and there is uncertainty about the future exchange rate, there may be a risk premium associated with holding the foreign bond. Moreover, there may also be a nationalistic preference for holding the domestic bond.

The demand functions for the three assets are in nominal (not real) terms and the demand for an asset is assumed to depend only on current yields and total wealth, and *not* on current income. The latter assumption is made to isolate, in the short run, the asset markets from the product market in order to create a self-contained, short-run sub-model. Expectations are assumed to be static so that (1) the expected rate of inflation is zero and there is no distinction between nominal and real interest rates, and (2) the exchange rate is expected to remain at its current level. In the following, the subscript Q after the name of a function refers to the change in the value of that function with respect to a small change in R^f.

$$
\begin{aligned}
B^D &= b(R, R^f, A) & b_R > 0, b_Q \le 0, 0 \le b_A \le 1 & \tag{9.9}\\
(eF)^D &= f(R, R^f, A) & f_R \le 0, f_Q > 0, 0 \le f_A \le 1 & \tag{9.10}\\
M^D &= m(R, R^f, A) & m_R < 0, m_Q \le 0, 0 \le m_A \le 1 & \tag{9.11}
\end{aligned}
$$

From the wealth constraint,

$$M^D + B^D + (eF)^D = A$$

Hence (as in section 2.2.11),

$$
\begin{aligned}
m_R + b_R + f_R &= 0\\
m_Q + b_Q + f_Q &= 0\\
m_A + b_A + f_A &= 1
\end{aligned}
$$

Household wealth will change as a result of saving by households or as a result of capital gains or losses resulting from exchange rate changes since they will affect the domestic currency value of the holdings of the foreign bond. The change in wealth per period of time is the sum of these two sources of change:

$$\dot{A} = \dot{A}^S + \dot{A}^F = S + \dot{e}F$$

where S is household saving in nominal terms. Total wealth is the sum of these changes in wealth from the beginning of time until now and $A = A^S + A^F$.

Supply of bonds

The government budget equation in nominal terms (see section 2.2.8), is

$$G + RB - T + Q = \dot{B}^{\mathrm{T}} \tag{9.12}$$

where Q is transfer payments by the domestic economy to the rest of the world.

The level of the government deficit is assumed to be a policy decision, so that $\dot{B}^{\mathrm{T}}$ is an exogenous variable in the model. Given the exogenously determined level of G, the revenue from the lump-sum tax (T) is set to achieve the desired deficit. Bonds are then sold to finance the deficit.

The bonds issued by the domestic government may be held either by domestic households or the central bank. No domestic bonds are held by foreigners. Hence, the supply of bonds held by households is

$$B = B^{\mathrm{T}} - B^{\mathrm{CB}} \tag{9.13}$$

Domestic households may also hold the foreign bond. The interest rate on the foreign bond is an exogenous variable in the model and the domestic economy is assumed to be very small in relation to the rest of the world so that the supply of the foreign bond is perfectly elastic at the current yield.

Supply of money

The assets of the central bank in an open economy will include both domestic bonds and bonds denominated in foreign currencies together with some foreign currencies. Its balance sheet may therefore be represented by the following identity:

$$B^{\mathrm{CB}} + eK \equiv M + J$$

where K is the central bank's holdings of assets denominated in foreign currency and J is the net worth of the central bank. The net worth of the central bank changes when the foreign exchange rate changes since such changes alter the domestic currency value of the assets denominated in foreign currency. That is, $\dot{J} = \dot{e}K$ and J is the sum of all these changes since the beginning of time. The money supply is therefore

$$M = B^{\mathrm{CB}} + eK - J \tag{9.14}$$

Asset-market clearing conditions

The markets for financial assets will clear when quantity demanded equals quantity supplied. Given the wealth constraint, Walras's Law holds and it is only necessary to include two of the market-clearing conditions in the solution of the model. The market for the foreign bond will, therefore, be omitted and the two market-clearing conditions that will be used are obtained by equating equations (9.9) and (9.13) and equations (9.11) and (9.14):

Domestic bond: $b(R, R^f, A) = B = B^T - B^{CB}$ (9.15)
Money: $m(R, R^f, A) = M = B^{CB} + eK - J$ (9.16)

If the domestic and foreign bonds are assumed to be perfect substitutes, as was assumed in section 9.2, then only equation (9.16) is required.

9.3.2 Short-run effects of disturbances

Assume that the period of time is so short that current income does not affect the demand for financial assets and saving in the current period does not affect A. Hence, in equations (9.15) and (9.16) A can be replaced by A^F. One rationalization of this procedure is that asset markets adjust to a new equilibrium in response to a disturbance very quickly whereas the product market may be slow to adjust. Looking at asset markets in isolation may give some initial insights into the forces determining the foreign exchange rate. The short-run model now consists of the following equations:

$$b(R, R^f, A^F) = B^T - B^{CB}$$ (9.17)
$$m(R, R^f, A^F) = B^{CB} + eK - J$$ (9.18)

B^T, B^{CB} and R^f will be regarded as exogenous variables. To solve two equations, the policy regime must be specified in order to specify which of e or K is an exogenous variable.

Fixed exchange rate
When the exchange rate is pegged at a chosen level, e is an exogenous variable and A^F will be constant if e remains constant. The endogenous variables in the model are R and K. Since K does not appear in equation (9.17), this equation can be solved to determine R, given the values of the exogenous variables. The value of R can then be substituted into equation (9.18) to obtain the value of eK. That is, R is determined in the bond market and K by the demand and supply of money, given the R determined in the bond market. Appendix 9.1 gives the algebra of the comparative statics analysis of this model.

An open-market purchase of the domestic bond will decrease the supply of bonds available to domestic households and the domestic rate of interest will fall until households only wish to hold the smaller quantity of bonds. Purchases of the foreign bond will increase, putting upward pressure on the price of foreign currency. The central bank will intervene and sell foreign exchange to maintain the fixed exchange rate. Hence, the central bank's holdings of foreign currency will decrease.

An increase in the yield on the foreign bond will, assuming substitutability to some extent between the two bonds, increase the demand for it and the rate of interest on the domestic bond will rise so that domestic households will be willing to hold the existing supply of domestic bonds. The increased demand for the foreign bond will cause the central bank to intervene in the foreign exchange market and sell foreign currency from its reserves to maintain the fixed rate.

An increase in the level at which the price of foreign currency is being pegged leads to an increase in the value of domestic holdings of assets denominated in foreign currency. The value of household wealth in domestic currency therefore increases and this increases demand for all assets, including the domestic bond. Hence, the price of bonds is driven up thereby decreasing the rate of interest until households are again willing to hold the available supply. The rise in the price of foreign currency reduces the extent to which the central bank has to intervene in the foreign exchange market to maintain the pegged rate. The level of foreign currency assets held by the central bank increases, however, relative to the previous level.

Flexible exchange rate
When the central bank is not intervening in the foreign exchange market and the exchange rate is floating cleanly, the exchange rate is an endogenous variable and there is no change in the holdings of foreign exchange reserves by the central bank. A^F will now vary when e varies so that a change in e affects both equations (9.17) and (9.18). The two equations must now be solved simultaneously.

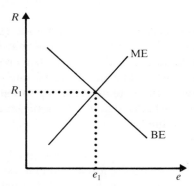

Fig. 9.1 Short-run asset market equilibrium

Figure 9.1 depicts the solution. The BE curve represents the combinations of R and e which will equate the demand for the domestic bond with the supply of the bond. Since a rise in the price of a unit of foreign currency will increase the value, in domestic currency, of the holdings of households of the foreign bond, total wealth will increase. This will increase the demand for all assets, including the domestic bond. A decrease in R will, therefore, be required to produce an offsetting decrease in the demand for the domestic bond and restore equilibrium in the market for the domestic bond. Hence, the BE curve will slope downward to the right. (See Appendix 9.1 for the algebra.) The ME curve shows the combinations of e and R which will equate the demand for money with its supply. Since a rise in the price of a unit of foreign currency will increase the demand for domestic goods and therefore for domestic money, a rise in R is required to remove the excess demand for money. Hence, the ME curve has a positive slope. The equilibrium values of R and e will be at the point of intersection of the two curves.

The R determined by the intersection of the BE and ME curves must be, in a complete model, the same R as is determined by the intersection of the IS–LM curves (see Fig. 3.2). The explanation is in section 2.2.10 where the 'loanable funds' interpretation of product market equilibrium is given. The BE and ME curves are the open-economy representation of the market for loanable funds.

Open-market purchases of the domestic bond by the central bank increase the money supply and shift the ME curve to the right. The rate of interest falls and households are now willing to hold a smaller quantity of the domestic bond. The foreign bond becomes more attractive and the increased demand for foreign currency with which to purchase it leads to a rise in the price of foreign currency. The value of households' holdings of the foreign bond increases and so does their total wealth. There is an induced increase in the demand for money which restores balance between the demand for it and the increased supply of it.

A rise in the yield on the foreign bond also increases the demand for foreign currency and leads to a rise in the price of foreign currency. If the degree of substitutability between the foreign and domestic bonds is high, there is a decrease in the demand for the domestic bond so that the domestic rate of interest rises to restore equilibrium. Otherwise, the increase in the opportunity cost of holding money leads to an increase in the demand for the domestic bond so that the interest rate falls to restore equilibrium.

Special cases of asset substitutability
One limiting case is where households do not regard the foreign bond to be a substitute for holding domestic bonds. In this case under either a fixed or flexible exchange rate regime, a change in R^f has no effect on R since the demand for the domestic bond is completely insensitive to the yield on the foreign bond. Under a fixed exchange rate regime there will also be no effect on the holdings of official reserves by the central bank since there will be no need for the central bank to intervene in the foreign exchange market when the foreign interest rate changes. Similarly, under a flexible exchange rate regime there will be no effect

on the exchange rate. Hence, in this special case, monetary policy can be conducted by the central bank as if the economy were closed.

The other limiting case is where households regard the two bonds as perfect substitutes so that the decision as to which bond to hold in their portfolios is made solely on the basis of the yield on the bond. If interest rates are the same in both countries, households are indifferent as to which bond they hold. Then, under either exchange rate regime, a change in the yield on the foreign bond induces an equal change in the yield on the domestic bond so that interest rates continue, in the absence of any expectation of a change in the exchange rate, to be equal. Since capital is perfectly mobile, arbitrage will immediately restore interest-rate parity if a difference in yields should occur.

In the case of perfect substitutability, when the central bank increases the money supply by buying bonds in the open market, households, in order to restore portfolio balance, will immediately buy foreign bonds to replace the domestic bonds they have sold to the central bank. Hence, there will be an increased demand for foreign currency. Under a fixed exchange rate regime, the central bank will have to sell foreign currency from its reserves, thereby decreasing the money supply by an amount identical to the amount by which the money supply had increased as a result of its operations in the bond market. Hence, in this case the central bank cannot change the money supply and it cannot influence domestic interest rates.

When the exchange rate is flexible, the increased demand of households for the foreign bond will cause the price of foreign currency to rise and the value, in domestic currency, of household holdings of foreign bonds rises to restore portfolio balance. Again, there will be no interest rate effects. The increase in the money supply will cause the price of domestic goods to rise until parity between prices in the two countries is restored. There will be no effect on the values of real variables.

9.4 THE BALANCE OF INTERNATIONAL PAYMENTS

The current-account balance of international payments is defined as

$$X + R^f(eF) - V - Q \tag{9.19}$$

where X is the nominal value of exports of goods and services, V is the nominal value of imports of goods and services, and Q is transfer payments by the domestic economy to the rest of the world. To keep the model simple, it will be assumed that $R^f(eF) = Q$ so that the current-account balance is simply $X - V$. If $X > V$, then financing for the export surplus must be provided to the rest of the world either by buying foreign currency or buying foreign bonds. That is,

$X - V = e\dot{K} + e\dot{F}$, where the right-hand side is the capital account of the balance of international payments.

When the exchange rate is fixed, the 'balance of international payments' may be defined as the change in the central bank's holdings of foreign currency-denominated assets required to maintain the pegged rate:

$$e\dot{K} = X - V - e\dot{F} \tag{9.20}$$

9.5 SAVING AND INTERNATIONAL CAPITAL FLOWS

There are three identities relevant to the saving of domestic households that must hold at each point of time.

1. From national income accounting:

    net investment $\equiv$ household saving + government surplus + corporate undistributed profits + deficit on current account of international payments

In the model all corporate profits are assumed to be distributed to households so that, transposing terms, the identity may be rewritten as:

$$S - I \equiv \dot{B}^{\mathrm{T}} + X - V$$

If $S = I$, so that domestic saving is only sufficient to provide the resources for domestic investment in real capital, then $\dot{B}^{\mathrm{T}} \equiv V - X$. That is, the amount of the government deficit exactly equals the current-account deficit in the balance of international payments. It is the rest of the world that is providing the resources to enable the government to buy more goods than it can obtain command over from tax revenues.

2. From the balance of international payments:

    current-account surplus $\equiv$ purchases of the foreign bond + additions to the central bank's holdings of foreign exchange

$$X - V \equiv e\dot{F} + e\dot{K}$$

Hence, when $I = 0$, $S \equiv \dot{B}^{\mathrm{T}} + e\dot{F} + e\dot{K}$

That is, if there is no real investment and no equities for households to invest in, all saving goes into financing the government deficit, purchases of the foreign bond, or foreign exchange reserves held by the central bank. In a flexible exchange rate regime $\dot{K} = 0$.

3. From the balance sheet of the central bank:

    holdings of domestic bonds plus assets denominated in foreign currency $\equiv$ supply of domestic money + net worth of central bank

$$B^{CB} + eK \equiv M + J$$
$$B^T = B + B^{CB}, B^{CB} = M + J - eK, \text{and } \dot{J} = \dot{e}K,$$
$$\dot{B}^T = \dot{B} + \dot{M} + \dot{e}K - (\dot{e}K + e\dot{K}) = \dot{B} + \dot{M} - e\dot{K}$$
$$\therefore S \equiv \dot{B} + \dot{M} + e\dot{F}$$

That is, the increase in household saving is distributed over the three financial assets available to households.

9.6 THE QUANTITY THEORY OF MONEY REVISITED

The asset market model is an alternative to the model of section 9.2 for deriving the open-economy version of the Quantity Theory of Money. There are two versions depending upon whether or not the exchange rate is flexible.

Flexible exchange rate
When the two bonds are perfect substitutes, the domestic and foreign interest rates must be the same. Hence, when there is a flexible exchange rate regime, equation (9.17) is not required to determine the domestic rate of interest. Given R, equation (9.18) in itself determines the price of foreign currency. That is, under these assumptions, the exchange rate is the price which adjusts to equate the demand for money to the supply of money. This is referred to as the 'Monetarist theory of the determination of the foreign exchange rate' and is the open-economy version of the Quantity Theory of Money which was derived in section 9.2.

Consider what happens if domestic households increase their demand for money balances. They offer for sale some of their holdings of domestic and foreign bonds. As residents of the foreign country buy back some of their bonds, the supply of foreign currency increases and the price of a unit of foreign currency falls. The decrease, in domestic currency, of the value of the remaining holdings of foreign bonds by domestic households reduces their wealth and, therefore, their demand for money. The change in the exchange rate restores equilibrium between the demand and supply of money.

Fixed exchange rate
Under a fixed exchange rate regime, equation (9.17) determines the domestic interest rate, given the foreign interest rate. Equation (9.18) then determines, given the interest rates, the change in the central bank's holdings of foreign exchange – the balance of international payments. Equation (9.18) is, however, the market-clearing equation for the demand and supply of domestic money. Hence, the balance of international payments is determined by the condition for equilibrium between the demand and supply of money. This is the 'Monetarist theory of the balance of international payments'.

Consider again what happens if households increase their demand for domestic money balances. They offer for sale some of their holdings of domestic and foreign bonds and the supply of foreign currency increases as foreigners buy some of the bonds. The central bank intervenes in the foreign exchange market to buy the excess supply of foreign currency, thereby increasing the supply of domestic money and satisfying the increased demand of households for domestic money. There has been, however, an increase in the central bank's holdings of foreign exchange.

9.6.1 Dichotomy between real and financial sectors

The dichotomy between the determination of the values of real and nominal variables which exists in the static neoclassical model of Chapter 2, given the assumptions made to make the dichotomy hold, also holds in an open economy under a similar set of conditions. That is, if the change in the exchange rate resulting from a change in the money supply has an equiproportionate effect on the price level and on the price of a unit of foreign currency, the relative price of the imported good and the domestically produced good will remain unchanged so there will be no effect on the demand for goods. If the real government budget constraint is also defined so that changes in the domestic price level do not affect product market equilibrium, then the determination of the values of real variables will be independent of the money supply.

9.7 A KEYNESIAN MACROECONOMIC MODEL

To present a model which explains the long-run stationary-state determination of the foreign exchange rate without imposing flexible prices in all markets, Keynes's model from Chapter 3 will be adapted to an open economy and appended to the asset market model.[4] The assumption of static expectations is retained.

9.7.1 The product market

There are now two goods in the model: a domestically produced good which may either be used domestically or exported to foreign countries, and a good which may be imported from the rest of the world. To keep the model simple, it is assumed that real investment (i) equals zero. Hence, the capital stock (k) is constant. The money wage rate (W), government real expenditure on goods (g), and real tax revenue ($t = T/P$) are exogenously determined.

The three demand functions for goods are

$$c = c(P, eP^f, z) \qquad c_P < 0, c_e > 0, c_q > 0, c_z > 0 \qquad (9.21)$$

where c is real consumption of the *domestically* produced good (excluding consumption of the imported good), z is real disposable income, and c_q gives the effect on c of a change in P^f; and

$$x = x(P, eP^f, z^f) \qquad x_P < 0, x_e > 0, x_q > 0, x_z > 0 \qquad (9.22)$$
$$v = v(P, eP^f, z) \qquad v_P > 0, v_e < 0, v_q < 0, v_z > 0 \qquad (9.23)$$

where x and v are, respectively, real exports and imports of goods.

The aggregate supply function is the Keynesian aggregate supply function (see section 3.6). Hence, quantity supplied is an increasing function of the price level:

$$y = h(P) \qquad h_P > 0 \qquad (9.24)$$

The market-clearing condition for the product market is

$$c + g + x = h(P) \qquad (9.25)$$

The government budget constraint is

$$G + RB - T + Q = \dot{B}^T \qquad (9.26)$$

where, as explained in section 9.4, $Q = R^f(eF)$.

Continuing the assumption that firms distribute all their net income to households who are the only equity holders, the nominal disposable income of households is

$$Z = Y + RB + R^f(eF) - T = Y - G + \dot{B}^T \qquad (9.27)$$

where $Z = Pz$, $Y = Py$ and $G = Pg$. In real terms this becomes

$$z = y - g + (\dot{B}^T/P) = h(P) - g + (\dot{B}^T/P)$$

Household saving in nominal currency units (S) equals $Z - (C + V)$, where C is nominal consumption of the domestically produced good ($= Pc$), and V is nominal imports ($= eP^f v$):

$$S = S(R, R^f, Z, A) \qquad (9.28)$$

9.7.2 Stationary-state equilibrium

One definition of long-run equilibrium is that of a stationary state; that is, when there is no tendency for any flow variables to change and all stocks are constant. In a stationary state $i = s = 0$ and $\dot{B}^T = 0$. Hence, $z = h(P) - g$. In the long run, the government budget must be balanced so that B^T is constant. Hence, B^T

(instead of $\dot{B}^{T}$) will now be regarded as being exogenously determined. In a stationary state, the holdings of the foreign bond by both households and the central bank must also be constant so that there are no international capital flows. Hence $\dot{F} = 0$, $\dot{K} = 0$, and $X = V$.

The six equations required to solve the complete model for a stationary state are:

Asset market:
$$b(R, R^f, A) = B^T - B^{CB} \tag{9.29}$$
$$m(R, R^f, A) = B^{CB} + eK - J \tag{9.30}$$

Product market:
$$S(R, R^f, Z, A) = 0 \tag{9.31}$$
$$Z = Pz \tag{9.32}$$
$$z = h(P) - g \tag{9.33}$$
$$c(P, eP^f, z) + x(P, eP^f, z^f) + g = h(P) \tag{9.34}$$

Exogenous variables: B^T, B^{CB}, g, R^f, P^f, z^f
Endogenous variables: A, R, Z, z, P and either e or K depending on the exchange rate regime.
Note that J is a function of e and K (see section 9.3.1) and is, therefore, not a separate variable.

Flexible exchange rate
Under a flexible exchange rate regime, e is an endogenous variable and K is exogenous. As is spelled out in Appendix 9.1, the asset market equations jointly determine the long-run equilibrium values of R and A. Given that in a stationary state saving must equal zero, and given the solution values of R and A, the saving equation then determines the level of Z. The next two equations may then be solved simultaneously to obtain the equilibrium values of P and z. The last equation is then solved for e, given the values of the other variables determined by the first five equations. Thus, the exchange rate is determined by the complete model with feedback from the product market to the asset market. Hence, the exchange rate depends on the values of all the exogenous variables and on the parameters of all the behavioural equations, including the export and import functions. The value of e will depend, in large part, on the elasticities of the demand for the imported good and of the demand for the domestically produced consumption good and of the exported good with respect to the price of domestically produced good and with respect to the price of the foreign good. Other parameters such as the elasticity of the supply of the domestically produced good with respect to its price will also play an important role in determining the level of the exchange rate.

Fixed exchange rate

Under a fixed exchange rate regime, K is an endogenous variable and e is exogenous. Unless there is a change in the pegged exchange rate, there will be no capital gains or losses on the holding of the foreign bond. Household wealth (A) will change therefore only as a result of saving (S). But the conditions for a long-run stationary state require that $\dot{A} = 0$ and $S = 0$. The rate of interest (R) is, therefore, determined in the bond market (as in the short-run asset-market model of section 9.3), subject to the constraints that in the long run total wealth is constant and saving is zero. Nominal saving (S) is determined by the product-market relationships which determine personal disposable income (Z) and household expenditures ($C + V$) (as is explained in Appendix 9.1). The holdings of assets denominated in foreign currency of the central bank then adjust to equate the demand and supply of domestic money. Thus, the solution of the complete model is consistent with the Monetarist approach to the balance of international payments. The stationary-state levels of prices and expenditures on goods are determined in the product market, given that the rate of interest (R) has adjusted to satisfy the stationary-state constraints.

If the government has chosen a fixed exchange rate regime, the rate at which the monetary authorities should choose to peg the rate is the long-run equilibrium exchange rate. In practice, the central bank will let disturbances move the exchange rate around this equilibrium level within a band, intervening in the foreign exchange market when the rate begins to approach the limits of the band. When the long-run equilibrium rate changes, the government should change the level at which the rate is being pegged. In many situations it is difficult, of course, for the government to determine what the actual long-run equilibrium exchange rate is.[5] It should also be noted that when a country has many trading partners, it is the 'effective exchange rate' (a weighted average of exchange rates with all its trading partners, where the weights are total trade with each country), not the bilateral rate between it and its principal trading partner, that is relevant for overall economic performance.[6]

9.7.3 Purchasing power parity

In an economy in which not all goods are standardized and freely traded internationally, the law of one price may not apply to all goods. There may, however, be a tendency for the prices of nontraded goods to be produced at the same unit costs as those of traded goods because of the tendency of wage rates and the cost of capital to be equalized. If this is the case, there may be a tendency for price levels across countries to be equalized when expressed in a common currency. This tendency is referred to as 'purchasing power parity'.[7]

9.7.4 Dichotomy between real and financial sectors

In the Keynesian model the dichotomy between real and financial sectors does not hold because changes in the money supply affect the product market through interest rate effects and domestic prices are determined as a markup on exogenously determined money wage rates and will not move in proportion to changes in the price of foreign currency.

9.7.5 IS–LM solution of the Keynesian model

An open-economy version of the IS–LM diagram in (R, Y) space can depict the stock and flow equilibrium conditions which are related to equilibrium for goods (IS curve), money (LM curve), domestic bonds (BB curve), and foreign exchange (XV curve), as shown in Fig. 9.2. The equilibrium combination of R and Y (R_1, Y_1) must lie on all four curves and does so if they all intersect at a common point. In the equations below, all variables are expressed in *nominal* terms for this purpose. The bond market and money equations can be thought of as being in (R, Y) space if one thinks of A as being a function of S, which in turn is a function of Z, which in turn is a function of Y. Since W is treated as an exogenous variable, regard P as exogenous and held constant during the analysis.

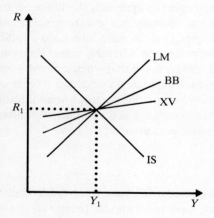

Fig. 9.2 Open-economy IS–LM model

The IS curve is then defined by the equation

$$I = S(R, R^f, Y) - \dot{B}^T + V(P, eP^f, Y) - X(P, eP^f, Y^f) \tag{9.35}$$

An increase in Y will increase imports. To maintain equilibrium in the product market, the saving of domestic households must fall. A decline in the rate of interest will accomplish this. Hence, a rise in Y must be associated with a fall in R for there to be product market equilibrium. The IS curve therefore has a negative slope. The position of the IS curve will depend on the price of imported goods relative to the price of domestically produced goods. An increase in e or P^f, P remaining constant, will decrease the demand for imported goods and increase the demand for domestically produced goods, thereby shifting the IS curve to the right. Conversely, a fall in e or P^f will shift the IS curve to the left. (The algebra is in Appendix 9.1.)

The LM curve is defined by the equation

$$m(R, R^f, Y) = M \tag{9.36}$$

An increase in Y increases the demand for money. To restore equilibrium, given the supply of money, an offsetting force must come into play which will decrease the demand for money. An increase in R will increase the opportunity cost of holding money and accomplish this. Hence, a rise in Y must be associated with a rise in R for there to be equilibrium between the demand for money balances and the supply of money. The LM curve therefore has a positive slope.

The BB curve is defined by the equation

$$b(R, R^f, Y) = B \tag{9.37}$$

An increase in Y, other things remaining the same, will decrease the demand for the domestic bond (see section 2.2.11). Hence, R must rise to offset this and restore equilibrium. The BB curve therefore also has a positive slope.

The XV curve is defined by the equation

$$X(P, eP^f, Y^f) - V(P, eP^f, Y) = e\dot{F} + e\dot{K} \tag{9.38}$$

An increase in Y will increase the imports of goods by domestic households. To restore equilibrium, the right-hand side of the equation must decline. In the absence of central bank intervention in the foreign exchange market, K will remain unchanged. An increase in R, assuming R^f is determined on world markets and remains unchanged, will reduce, however, the demand for the foreign bond and decrease $\dot{F}$. The XV curve will therefore also have a positive slope.

The relative slopes of the LM, BB, and XV curves will depend on the elasticities of the demand for the financial assets with respect to the rate of interest on the domestic bond. If the domestic bond and the foreign bond are perfect substitutes, the BB curve will be identical with the XV curve and the BB curve can be omitted from the analysis. If the domestic economy is very small relative to the size of the rest of the world so that the domestic economy is a price-taker in financial markets, the domestic rate of interest will equal the world rate of interest. The XV curve will then be horizontal at R^f.

Assume that the BB curve is redundant and that the small open-economy case applies so that the XV curve is horizontal. The initial equilibrium position is shown in Fig. 9.3 at point 1. Assume that because of a crop failure in the rest of the world, there is an increased demand for the exports of the domestic economy. The IS curve shifts to the right and the new IS curve intersects the LM curve at point 2. The domestic interest rate tends to rise to R_2 reflecting the increased demand for money resulting from the higher level of income arising from the increased exports. The higher domestic interest rate leads to a decrease in the demand for the foreign bond. What happens next depends on the exchange rate regime.

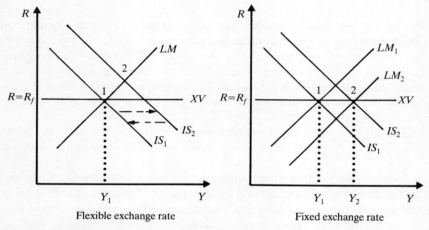

Fixed exchange rate

Flexible exchange rate

Fig. 9.3 Small open-economy IS–LM model

Flexible exchange rate
Under the flexible exchange rate regime, the decrease in the demand for the foreign bond decreases the demand for foreign exchange and the price of foreign currency falls. This decreases the relative price of imports, in domestic currency, and the IS curve shifts to the left (Fig. 9.3a). Since the foreign and domestic bonds are perfect substitutes, the price of foreign currency will fall until the IS curve has returned to its original position and equilibrium is restored at the world interest rate, which is assumed not to have changed from its original level. (If the world interest rate had risen, the XV curve would shift upward and the IS curve would not shift all the way back to its original position.) The net effect on the domestic economy is that total output remains unchanged, but a larger portion of output is exported. Total consumption remains unchanged but the consumption of the domestically produced good has declined while the consumption of the imported good has increased by an

equal amount. There has been a permanent reduction in the price of foreign currency but only a temporary change in the domestic interest rate which is quickly reversed.

Fixed exchange rate

Under a fixed exchange rate regime, the central bank will intervene in the foreign exchange market and buy foreign currency, thereby increasing the money supply. The LM curve will shift to the right, as is shown in Figure 9.3b. The money supply increase may be augmented by the purchase of domestic bonds until the LM curve shifts sufficiently to the right to make the point of intersection with the new IS curve take place at point 3 on the XV curve. If the economy was at full employment prior to the increase in exports, the increase in Y will be entirely a result of the increase in P brought about by the increase in M. Otherwise, both real output and product prices will rise.

9.8 EXPECTATIONS AND EXCHANGE RATE DETERMINATION

So far in this chapter it has usually been assumed that expectations are static and there has been no distinction between nominal and real interest rates. The demand for financial assets should, however, be based on expected rates of return over the length of time it is planned to hold the asset. Households do distinguish between nominal and real magnitudes. In making their forecasts of the real rate of return on financial assets, they adjust the nominal yield for the expected rate of inflation of consumer goods (π) – computed as a weighted average of the expected rates of change in imported goods and domestically produced goods – and the expected rate of change of the price of a unit of foreign currency (θ). The expected real rates of return on the domestic and foreign bonds will then be $r = R - \pi$ and $r^f = R^f + \theta - \pi$, respectively.

The model described by equations (9.29)–(9.34) can now be written with expected values inserted into the appropriate equations:

$$c(P, eP^f, z) + x(P, eP^f, z^f) + g = h(P) \tag{9.34}$$
$$z = h(P) - g \tag{9.33}$$
$$Z = Pz \tag{9.32}$$
$$b(R - \pi, R^f + \theta - \pi, A) \quad = B^T - B^{CB} \tag{9.39}$$
$$m(R - \pi, R^f + \theta - \pi, A) \quad = B^{CB} + eK - J \tag{9.40}$$
$$S(R - \pi, R^f + \theta - \pi, Z, A) = 0 \tag{9.41}$$

The equations have been ordered so that the product-market clearing condition comes first because, in the long run, the exchange rate is determined primarily by the parameters of the product-market behavioural equations. It is from the product-market equations that households form their long-term expectation about the rate of change of the foreign exchange rate. This long-run expectation (θ) enters into the demand-for-financial-assets functions. Hence, as soon as expectations are no longer static, assets markets are no longer isolated, even in the very short run, from the product market.

Consider the effect of an increase in the demand for exports. Households with rational expectations will anticipate that the long-run effect will be for the price of a unit of foreign currency to fall. They will realize that this will lower the expected real yield on their holdings of the foreign bond and they will begin selling the bond. The increased supply of foreign currency will cause its price to fall in order to clear the foreign exchange market. Hence, the increased demand for exports will cause a change in the exchange rate to occur almost immediately.

An increase in the nominal rate of return on the foreign bond, an increase in the government deficit, or open-market purchases of the domestic bond will all lead to an immediate rise in the price of a unit of foreign currency since this is what is required for stationary-state equilibrium. The expectation of a rise in the price of foreign currency will increase the real expected yield to domestic households on the foreign bond. The demand for the foreign bond immediately increases and the price of foreign currency immediately rises to clear the foreign exchange market.

A dynamic phenomenon known as 'overshooting' occurs in some situations when a shock occurs.[8] One factor which may cause this is prices which are sticky in the short run. In such a situation the speed of adjustment may be very fast in asset markets but very slow in the product market. Suppose, for example, that the money supply of the domestic economy increases so that, given the stickiness of prices, the real money stock also increases, leading to an excess supply of money balances. Households will increase their demand for bonds, including the foreign bond. Interest rates will fall. To maintain interest-rate parity and asset market equilibrium, there must be an expectation that the price of a unit of foreign currency will fall. To bring this about, the price of a unit of foreign currency must rise immediately and rise more than in proportion to the increase in the money stock so that it rises above its new long-run value and thereby creates an expectation that will fall in the future. The amount of the rise will depend on the interest-elasticity of the demand for money. In the long run, goods prices begin to rise because of the increased price of imports and the real money stock begins to decline. The price of a unit of foreign currency then falls to its new long-run value so that the overshooting is corrected.

9.9　FORECASTING EXCHANGE RATES

For short time periods (horizons of less than 18 months), it has been asserted on the basis of statistical analysis that the best description of the movement of the nominal spot foreign exchange rate is that it behaves as if generated by a random walk process; that is, the change in the exchange rate is a white noise process.[9] Hence, the best short-term forecast of the nominal spot exchange rate is today's spot rate. The forward rate is often regarded as the best predictor of the spot rate, but, if the spot rate follows a random walk, its predictor will also have that property. Although less convincing, the evidence also suggests that the real exchange rate follows a random walk. One explanation of the random walk hypothesis for exchange rates is that, although the rate will be tending towards its long-run equilibrium value, 'new' (unpredictable) events will be continually changing the equilibrium value. Since these new events are by definition random (unpredictable), the movement of the long-run rate will be as if generated by a random walk process.

The random walk hypothesis is sometimes regarded as an argument against constructing structural (neoclassical or Keynesian) models of exchange rate behaviour. One must distinguish, however, between *unconditional* and *conditional* forecasts; that is, between answers to questions such as 'What will be next month's spot exchange rate?' and 'What will be the effect on next month's spot exchange rate if the central bank undertakes open-market operations in the bond market, starting today, which bring about a sustained increase in the rate of interest?' The answer to the first question could be that today's one-month forward rate is the best forecast. The answer to the second question requires, however, a complete macroeconomic model which articulates the responses of the asset and product markets, including their linkages.

9.10 FURTHER READING

Krueger (1983) is a good introduction to the theory of the determination of exchange rates. Williamson (1985) explains the international monetary system. McKinnon (1979) discusses the use of money in international exchange with particular reference to spot and forward markets. Allen and Kenen (1980, 1983) present a series of models on the determination and econometric evidence relevant to them. Dornbusch (1980) integrates some open-economy models with macroeconomics. Frenkel (1983), Bhandari and Putnam (1983), and Jones and Kenen (1985) are collections of papers, many of which deal with exchange rate determination. Arndt and Richardson (1987) is a set of essays dealing with the linkages between the real and financial sectors of an open economy. Floyd (1985) is a neoclassical presentation of the monetary theory of the world economy with an historical perspective. Prachowny (1984, 1986) presents macroeconomic and monetary theories of small open economies.

APPENDIX 9.1 COMPARATIVE STATICS OF THE OPEN-ECONOMY MODEL

Short-run asset market effects

The asset-market clearing conditions are:

Domestic bond: $b(R, R^f, A^F) = B = B^T B^{CB}$ (9.17)

Money: $m(R, R^f, A^F) = M = B^{CB} + eK - J$ (9.18)

where $A^F = \int_0^T (\dot{e}F)dt$, $J = \int_0^T (\dot{e}K)dt$, t is time, $dA^F = Fde$, and $dJ = Kde$.

Take the total differentials of the two equations:

$$b_R dR + b_Q dR^f + b_A Fde = dB^T - dB^{CB}$$ (9.42)

$$m_R dR + m_Q dR^f + m_A Fde = dB^{CB} + (edK + Kde) - Kde$$

$$m_R dR + m_Q dR^f + m_A Fde = dB^{CB} + edK$$ (9.43)

where the subscript Q is short for R^f. To simplify the analysis, hold B^T constant and set $dB^T = 0$. dR^f and dB^{CB} are also exogenous variables but they will be retained so that the effect of a change in either of them on the endogenous variables can be examined.

Fixed exchange rate
Under a fixed exchange rate regime, de is an exogenous variable. The endogenous variables in the model are dR and dK. Since dK does not appear in equation (9.42), this equation can be solved to determine dR, given the values of the exogenous variables. dK is then determined by the demand and supply of money, given the dR determined in the bond market:

$$dR = 1/b_R(-dB^{CB} - b_Q dR^f - b_A Fde)$$ (9.44)

The value of dR can then be substituted into equation (9.43) to obtain

$$edK = m_R/b_R(-dB^{CB} - b_Q dR^f - b_A Fde) - dB^{CB} + m_R dR^f + m_A Fde$$
$$= -1/b_R(b_R + m_R)dB^{CB} + (m_Q - m_R b_Q/b_R)dR^f + (m_A - b_A m_R/b_R)Fde$$ (9.45)

From section 9.3.1, $b_R + m_R = -f_R$

Hence, $\partial R/\partial B^{CB} < 0$, $\qquad \partial K/\partial B^{CB} < 0$

$\qquad \partial R/\partial R^f > 0$, $\qquad \partial K/\partial R^f < 0$

$\qquad \partial R/\partial e < 0$, $\qquad \partial K/\partial e > 0$

Flexible exchange rate
de is now an exogenous variable and $dK = 0$. Since de appears in both equations (9.42) and (9.43), the two equations must now be solved simultaneously. The following solution can be obtained using Cramer's rule:

$$dR = 1/H\{(-m_A - b_A)dB^{CB} + (-b_Q m_A + m_Q b_A)dR^f\} \tag{9.46}$$
$$de = 1/FH\{(b_r + m_R)dB^{CB} + (-b_R m_Q + m_R b_Q)dR^f\} \tag{9.47}$$

where $H = (b_R m_A - b_A m_R) > 0$
Since $b_R + m_R = -f_R$, it can be seen that

$$\partial R/\partial B^{CB} < 0, \qquad \partial e/\partial B^{CB} > 0$$
$$\partial e/\partial R^f > 0$$

If $|b_Q m_A| > |m_Q b_A|$, $\partial R/\partial R^f > 0$. Otherwise, $\partial R/\partial R^f < 0$.

The slopes of the BE and ME curves can be derived from equations (9.42) and (9.43):

BE: $\partial R/\partial e = (-b_A F)/b_R < 0$
ME: $\partial R/\partial e = (-m_A F)/m_R > 0$

Special cases of asset substitutability
One limiting case is where households do not regard the foreign bond to be a substitute for holding domestic bonds, so that $b_Q = f_R = 0$ (which implies that $m_Q = 0$). In this case under either a fixed or flexible exchange rate regime, $\partial R/\partial R^f = 0$.

The other limiting case is where households regard the two bonds as perfect substitutes, so that $|b_Q| = |f_R| \longrightarrow \infty$.

Under a fixed exchange rate regime

$$\partial R/\partial R^f = -b_Q/b_R = -b_Q/(-f_R - m_R) \longrightarrow 1$$

Under a flexible exchange rate regime

$$\partial R/\partial R^f = (-b_Q m_A + m_Q b_A)/(b_R m_A - b_A m_R)$$
$$= (-b_Q m_A + m_Q b_A)/[(-f_R - m_R)m_A - b_A m_R] \longrightarrow 1$$

Solving the Keynesian model

Consider the model represented by equations (9.29)–(9.34) and take the total differentials. To simplify the algebra, hold B^T, P^f and z^f constant; that is, set $dB^T = dP^f = dz^f = 0$. Transpose terms to obtain the equations below.

Flexible exchange rate
de is endogenous and d$k = 0$, dR^f, dB^{CB} and dg are exogenous.

$$b_R dR + b_A dA = -b_Q dR^f - dB^{CB} \tag{9.48}$$
$$m_R dR + m_A dA = -m_Q dR^f + db^{CB} \tag{9.49}$$
$$S_z dZ = -S_R dR - S_A dA - S_Q dR^f \tag{9.50}$$
$$P dz + z dP = dZ \tag{9.51}$$
$$h_P dP - dz = dg \tag{9.52}$$
$$(c_e + x_e)P^f de = (h_P - c_P + x_P)dP - c_z dz - dg \tag{9.53}$$

The first two equations are a recursive block which can be solved for dA and dR for given values of dR^f and dB^{CB}. The solution values for these two variables can then be fed into the third equation to solve for dZ. The solution value of dZ and the given value of dg can then be used to solve simultaneously the next two equations and obtain solution values for dz and dP. Feeding all these solution values and the given value of dg into the last equation produces a solution value for de.

Fixed exchange rate
dK is endogenous and $de = 0$; dR^f, dB^{CB} and dg are exogenous.
The equations can be rewritten to reflect this and rearranged as follows:

$$c_z dz + (e_P + x_P - h_P)dP = -dg \qquad (9.54)$$
$$dz - h_P dP = -dg \qquad (9.55)$$
$$dZ = Pdz + zdP \qquad (9.56)$$
$$S_R dR + S_A dA = -S_z dZ - S_Q dR^f \qquad (9.57)$$
$$b_R dR + b_A dA = -b_Q dR^f - dB^{CB} \qquad (9.58)$$
$$edK = -m_R dR - m_A dA - m_Q dR^f + db^{CB} \qquad (9.59)$$

The first two equations can be solved simultaneously to obtain solution values for dz and dP. Given the value of dg, the third equation then provides a solution value for dZ. Given the value of dZ and the values of dR^f and dB^{CB}, the fourth and fifth equations determine dR and dA. The sixth equation then determines dK.

Slopes of the IS, LM, BB and XV curves

Consider equation (9.35), hold $\dot{B}^T$, P^f, Z^f, and K constant so that their differentials equal zero. Then,

$$dI = S_R dR + S_Y dY + V_P dP + V_e de + V_y dY - X_P dP - X_e de$$
IS: $\partial R/\partial Y = -(S_Y + V_Y)/S_R < 0$

Consider equation (9.36):

$$m_R dR + m_Q dR^f + m_Y dY = dM$$
LM: $\partial R/\partial Y = -m_Y/m_R > 0$

Consider equation (9.37):
$$b_R dR + b_Q dR^f + b_Y dY = dB$$
BB: $\partial R/\partial Y = -b_Y b_R > 0$ \qquad $[b_Y < 0$ from equation (2.14)$]$

If $|m_Y/m_R| > |b_Y/b_R|$, then the LM curve is steeper than the BB curve. Consider equation (9.38) and note that $eF = f(R, R^f, A)$. The right-hand side of the equation is then a function of $f(R, R^f, A) = h(R, R^f, A)$, where $h_R < 0$.

$$X_P dP + X_e P^f de - V_e P^f de - V_P dP - V_Y dY = h_R dR + h_Q dR^f + h_A dA$$
XV: $\partial R/\partial Y = -V_Y/h_R > 0$

Since h_R is a function of f_R, if $|f_R| \longrightarrow \infty$, $\partial R/\partial Y \longrightarrow \infty$. That is, the XV curve becomes horizontal.

APPENDIX 9.2   SUPPLY AND DEMAND OF FOREIGN CURRENCY

The traditional explanation of the determination of the exchange rate has been in terms of the total demand and supply of foreign exchange resulting from current- and capital-account transactions.[10] The modern approach focuses attention on asset markets. The two approaches can be reconciled as follows.[11] To simplify the explanation, the assumption that foreigners do not hold domestic assets will be continued.

The demand for foreign currency is $F^D - F$, where F^D is the total demand for the foreign bond, and F is the current holdings of the foreign bond. Under a fixed exchange rate regime, $F^D - F = \dot{K}$, the change in the central bank's holdings of assets denominated in foreign currency. Under a flexible exchange rate regime, $F^D - F = 0$ since the foreign exchange rate adjusts to clear the foreign exchange market. Let e_1 be the exchange rate at which $F^D - F = 0$. At e_1, since there is a balance between the demand for foreign exchange and the existing holdings by domestic households, there are no purchases of the foreign bond and the demand for foreign exchange is zero. If the yield on the foreign bond (R^f) increases, F^D will increase and the price of foreign currency will rise, increasing the value, in domestic currency, of the existing holdings of the foreign bond and equilibrium will be restored at a higher exchange rate, e_2.

The interrelation between the current and capital accounts can be seen as follows. When the exchange rate is flexible, $X - V = e\dot{F}$ and the value of the holdings of the foreign bond, in domestic currency, changes when the current account balance is not zero. The market equilibrium is reached at e_2 where $X - V = 0$ and $e\dot{F} = 0$ and F is constant.

If the demand function for the foreign bond is respecified so that

$$(eF)^D/A = f(R, R^f)$$

where $f(\ )$ is now the proportion of total wealth held in the form of foreign bonds, then, in the special case where foreigners do not hold the domestic bond, the following expression can be derived (Kouri, 1983, pp. 126–9) for the rate of change in the foreign exchange rate:

$$\dot{F}^D = (fA/e)(-\dot{e}/e) = X - V$$

Hence, $\dot{e}/e = (V - X)/F$. That is, in order for the foreign exchange market to remain in equilibrium after a disturbance, the exchange rate must change over time in such a way that the net supply of foreign exchange from the current-account surplus equals the net demand for foreign exchange arising from the desire to add to the net holdings of the foreign bond. The demand for the foreign bond is, however, a function of the level of the foreign exchange rate and, therefore, the capital outflow (the purchases of the foreign bond) is a function of the rate of change of the foreign exchange rate. Hence, the rate at which the price of foreign currency increases is equal to the ratio of the current-account deficit to the value of international investment – measured in this case by the value of the holdings of the foreign bond, valued in foreign currency. (More generally, total international investment will be the sum of domestic holdings of foreign assets and foreign holdings of domestic assets.)

The dynamics of the foreign exchange market are consistent with the real-world behaviour of countries with current-account deficits. For such countries, the price of foreign currency rises (other things remaining the same), while for countries with current-account surpluses, the price of foreign currency falls.

APPENDIX 9.3 DYNAMICS OF AN ADJUSTMENT TO INCREASED SAVING

The demand-for-financial-asset functions from section 9.3.1 and the identities from section 9.5 can be used to explain some of the dynamics of the adjustment to equilibrium following, for example, a disturbance that leads domestic households to increase their saving.[12] To simplify the analysis, the government budget deficit and real investment will both be assumed to be zero.

Fixed exchange rate

When their saving increases, households will attempt to increase their holdings of the three financial assets. The supply of the domestic bond is constant since the government budget is balanced and the central bank is assumed not to be engaging in open-market operations in the bond market. The interest rate on the domestic bond must, therefore, fall to restore equilibrium in the bond market. The market-clearing condition for the domestic bond market is

$$b(R, R^f, A) = B$$

Hence, $b_R \dot{R} + b_Q \dot{R}^f + b_A \dot{A} = \dot{B}$. Since R^f is exogenous, $\dot{R}^f = 0$. Since the exchange rate is fixed, there are no capital gains from holding the foreign bond so all the change in wealth comes about from saving. Thus, $\dot{A} = S$. Hence,

$$\dot{R} = -(b_A/b_R)S \tag{9.60}$$

The change in R affects the demand for money and the foreign bond. The market-clearing condition for money is:

$$m(R, R^f, A) = M$$

Hence,

$$m_R \dot{R} + m_A \dot{A} = \{-m_R(b_A/b_R) + m_A\}S = \dot{M} = e\dot{K} \tag{9.61}$$

That is, the central bank intervention in the foreign exchange market changes the money supply by an amount that is equal to the bank's change in its holdings of foreign currency (valued in domestic currency).

The market-clearing condition for the market for the foreign bond is:

$$f(R, R^f, A) = eF$$

Hence,

$$f_R \dot{R} + f_A \dot{A} = \{-f_R(b_A/b_R) + f_A\}S = e\dot{F} \tag{9.62}$$

The increase in households' holdings of the foreign bond is the counterpart of the surplus on the current account of the balance of payments.

The market behaviour described by these equations is as follows. When the government budget is balanced, there is no real investment, and positive household saving is occurring, there will be a surplus on the current account of the balance of payments since $S = X - V$. The central bank will be buying up the excess supply of foreign exchange, thereby increasing the money supply. The increased demand for the foreign bond resulting from the saving will lead to a capital outflow, partially balancing the current-account surplus. Any balance will be met by the central bank increasing its holdings of assets denominated in foreign currency. Thus, balance will be maintained in the balance of payments at every point of time and the current-accounts surplus will always equal the amount of household saving, given the assumptions of zero government deficit and zero real investment. Over time, the decline in R and the increase in A associated with the increase in saving will lead to saving being reduced to zero and stationary-state equilibrium again being reached.

Flexible exchange rate

Under a flexible exchange rate regime there is no intervention in the foreign exchange market by the central bank and no open-market operations in the bond market; hence, the supply of money does not change. The adjustment mechanism which worked for a fixed exchange rate will no longer apply because R must fall in order to restore equilibrium in the bond market, but to reduce the demand for money R must rise. Hence, there must be a variable other than R which adjusts in order to restore equilibrium. That variable is the exchange rate. The explanation is that because households are saving there will be a surplus in the current account of the balance of international payments. At the exchange rate prevailing at the time of the increase in saving, the amount of surplus will exceed the increase in the demand for the foreign bond which results from the increased saving:

$$(X - V) - e\dot{F} = S - e\dot{F} = \dot{A}^S - e\dot{F}$$

The price of a unit of foreign currency will therefore fall to clear the foreign exchange market and it will do so at the rate

$$(\dot{e}/e) = -(1/eF)\dot{A}^S \tag{9.63}$$

This the rate which satisfies the following three conditions:

1. In the long run for stationary-state equilibrium,

$$\dot{A} = \dot{A}^S + \dot{A}^F = -(\dot{e}/e)eF + (\dot{e}/e)eF = 0$$

2. When both wealth and the interest rate are constant, the demand for domestic assets will be constant.
3. When both wealth and the interest rate are constant, the demand for the foreign bond, expressed in domestic currency, will be constant. But since the price of a unit of foreign currency is falling, households will be experiencing capital losses on their holdings of the foreign bond. They will offset these losses by buying more of the foreign bond at a rate equal to the amount of their saving. Indeed, there is no other asset the holding of which can be increased in order to accommodate their saving since the supply of both the domestic bond and money are constant and real investment is zero.

As the price of a unit of foreign currency falls, the current account surplus falls until it ultimately disappears. At the same time the motive for households to accumulate the foreign bond disappears. Hence, saving ceases and long-term equilibrium is restored at a lower price of foreign currency.

NOTES

1. See R.C. Bryant (1980) for a detailed discussion upon which this outline is based.
2. This model is adapted from McKinnon (1981) who explains the implications of the increased openness of world economies from the 1940s to the 1980s.
3. This section is based on Allen and Kenen (1980, 1983).
4. The presentation follows that of Allen and Kenen (1980, Chs 2–3). Allen and Kenen develop a model in which the distinction is made between domestically produced traded goods and non-traded goods. That distinction is not made here.
5. Williamson (1985, 1987) terms this the 'fundamental equilibrium exchange rate

(FEER)' and has estimated FEERs for some countries.

6. To avoid a problem with different currency units, the effective exchange rate is calculated using indices of exchange rate, where each exchange rate is 1.0 in the base period.

7. Arndt and Richardson (1987, pp. 7–14) discuss the relationship of the law of one price to purchasing power parity.

8. See Dornbusch (1980, pp. 207–9), or De Grauwe (1983, pp. 179–81), for further explanation of overshooting.

9. See the study by Frankel and Meese (1987, especially p. 122). Minford (1987, p. 158), points out that, since every shock will impinge upon the nominal exchange rate, it will have a high variance and an ARIMA(1,1,1) model may fit equally as well as an ARIMA(0,1,0) model – the random walk model.

10. See, for example, J.A. Sawyer (1975, pp. 282–7) for the traditional approach.

11. Kouri (1983) presents an exposition of the relation between these two approaches which is the basis for this section.

12. See Allen and Kenen (1980, pp. 156–74) for a more detailed analysis of the dynamics of adjustment to a disturbance.

10·ECONOMIC POLICY IN AN OPEN ECONOMY

Sustained shifts in the federal government's deficit have powerful effects on the value of the dollar.

Martin Feldstein (1986, p. 389)

This chapter deals with a few topics related to economic policy in an open economy. First it presents an analysis of the effects of a government budget deficit on the current account of the balance of international payments and the exchange rate. This is followed by a discussion of the world money supply and its implications for internal monetary policy. The chapter concludes with a discussion of the economics of intervention in the foreign exchange market by the central bank. When should intervention be sterilized and when should it not be sterilized?

10.1 BUDGET DEFICITS AND EXCHANGE RATE MOVEMENTS

The United States dollar appreciated markedly in value against the West German mark and the Japanese yen over the period 1980 to 1984 and then depreciated after 1985. Four alternative explanations for the appreciation of the dollar during the earlier period have been set out.[1] Applied in reverse, these explanations should also explain the subsequent depreciation of the dollar against these currencies.

1. Martin Feldstein (1986, p. 356) argues strongly that 'the dollar's rise could be traced primarily to the increase in current and expected structural deficits in the federal budget and to the shift to an anti-inflationary monetary policy'. The increase in the US government budget deficit since 1982 was financed mainly by selling bonds to the private sector. If the additional bonds held by households are viewed as an increase in their wealth, then they increase their demand for all financial assets, including money. This leads to higher interest rates and some crowding out of pri-

vate expenditure.[2] Given that the excess of domestic saving over net investment in new capital in the United States was not sufficient to finance the deficit, a rise in the interest rate was required to attract foreign funds and to run a current-account deficit. To achieve portfolio equilibrium it would be necessary for the price of foreign currency to fall enough so that its expected future rise equals the differential between the yield on dollar-denominated securities and foreign-currency denominated securities. Another aspect of the same phenomenon[3] is that the increase in government expenditure, especially in an economy close to full employment, would increase the demand for domestically produced goods relative to imported goods. This would increase the demand for money and put upward pressure on interest rates and thereby increase the inflow of foreign currency. The lower price of foreign currency would make imports less expensive and help reduce the excess demand for domestically produced goods. This would also contribute to the current-account deficit.

2. The tax changes and the reduction in the rate of inflation led to an increased rate of after-tax return on new investment by business in capital goods. This induced a comparable rise in the yield in bonds to restore portfolio equilibrium. The combined effect was to raise rates of return in the US relative to the rest of the world and led to an appreciation of the value of the US dollar.

3. Foreigners believed that the Reagan Government in the United States had to provide a 'safe haven' for investments in the United States, given the environment in other parts of the world.

4. The appreciation of the dollar reflected only the effect of the slowing down of the rate of growth of the money supply; that is, monetary policy in the United States had been too tight.

The effects of the interest payments that must be made to foreigners should be taken into account. These will create a demand for foreign currency and tend to increase, rather than reduce, the price of foreign currency. This effect will be strengthened if the increased spending in the United States implied by the budget deficit leads to a significant increase in expenditure on imported goods. Another factor leading towards a depreciation, rather than an appreciation, of the value of the US dollar would exist if Americans feel that there is an increase in risk in holding these bonds because of the threat of inflation, and switch to holding a larger portion of foreign-currency denominated securities in their portfolios.

As a budget deficit is reduced, if the first explanation is accepted, the appreciation of the dollar should be reversed so that the price of German marks and Japanese yen in terms of the US dollar will rise. This depreciation of US currency will be strengthened by the continuing effects of the interest payments on the outstanding debt and any shifts in US demand towards imported goods.

If the government is running a deficit which is not being financed by domestic saving, it must be financed from abroad (there must be a current-account deficit). In such a case, foreigners must be purchasing domestic bonds and the expected yield on the domestic bond must be such to attract foreign investors. If the expectations of foreign investors are such that this is not occurring, either the price of foreign currency will continue to rise (leading to upward pressures on the domestic price level), the domestic real interest rate must rise creating adverse conditions for the domestic demand for goods, or the government must reduce its expenditures and/or increase taxes to reduce the budget deficit.

10.2 EXCHANGE RATES AND POLITICAL OBJECTIVES

There is a substantial literature on the relation between business cycles and political elections. It is possible that management of the exchange rate may help a government achieve political goals.[4] If a government follows a policy of maintaining its exchange rate at an overvalued level (the price of foreign currency too low), it lowers the price of imported goods and thereby reduces the inflation rate and raises real incomes. Hence, it is popular with the voters. Over time, however, the substitution of imports for domestically produced goods reduces domestic output and employment and a loss of competitiveness in world markets results.

When a large country with a flexible exchange rate tightens monetary policy, this has an immediate disinflationary effect because of the appreciation of the value of its currency. Such a policy is equivalent to exporting inflation. Unless countries coordinate their monetary policies, competitive exchange rate policies may be engaged in, which are both disruptive of world trade patterns and political stability, as well as causing major impacts on world financial markets.

10.3 WORLD MONEY SUPPLY AND PRICE LEVEL
   STABILITY

The analysis of a closed economy was based on the assumption that national autonomy in monetary policy was possible if countries adopted flexible exchange rates and if the securities and currencies of the various countries are not close substitutes. A model of a closed economy was therefore appropriate for the study of the effects of monetary policy upon macroeconomic aggregates. Indeed, this was the principal argument that was used to persuade the free-market economies of the Western world to switch from a system of flexible exchange rates in 1973. In 1971 the convertibility of the US dollar into gold on demand by the central banks of members of the International Monetary Fund had ended and, with it, came the end of the system of pegged exchange rates which had existed since the implementation of the Bretton Woods agreement following the Second World War.[5]

The currencies of the key industrial economies whose currencies are convertible into one another in the market place (principally Western Germany, Japan, the United Kingdom, and the United States) may be, however, highly substitutable in the demand functions of residents of these countries. Anticipated exchange rate movements may lead to the substitution of one currency for another. A crude index of 'world' money supply for the industrial countries that have convertible currencies has been constructed and the conclusion drawn that for the United States, this measure explained the inflation of the 1970s much better than any measure of the domestic American money supply.[6] This has significant implications for the monetary policy of these countries, implications which tended to be ignored prior to the 1980s. One aspect of this currency substitution is that the direct linkage between the rate of growth of national currencies and national inflation rates that was expressed in equations (9.5) and (9.6) no longer exists.

The model of section 9.2 can be extended to study the implications of the world demand and supply of money. The simplifying assumption that the world consists of two countries will be continued. Let the domestic economy be called America and let the rest of the world be called Gerpan (a name chosen to remind the reader that the principal countries in the rest of the world for the purpose of this analysis are Western Germany and Japan). Define the world's nominal stock of money (M^w), measured in units of America's currency (the dollar), to be

$$M^w = M + eM^f \tag{10.1}$$

where M is the number of units of America's currency

M^f is the number of units of Gerpan's currency (the yenmark)

e is the spot price of a unit of Gerpan currency in American currency

The exchange rate (e) is assumed to be pegged at a rate chosen by government policy and maintained by intervention in the foreign exchange market by the Gerpan central bank. (This implies that the international currency system is an 'American dollar standard'.) This pegged rate may however be changed from time to time by a government policy decision. The expected rate of change in the exchange rate (θ) is an exogenous variable in the model. It is assumed that, after θ is taken into account, investors are indifferent between investments in the short-term bonds of the two countries. The world yield on these bonds (r^w) is the opportunity cost of holding money. The world demand-for-money function, which is assumed to be independent of θ, is

$$(M^w/P^w)^D = m^w(r^w, y^w) \tag{10.2}$$

where $y^w = y + y^f$ and P^w is the world price level.

If y^w and P^w are taken as given in the very short run, equation (10.2) then indicates how r^w must vary in response to any change in M^w.

Let α be the ratio of dollar-denominated bonds to the world total of bonds outstanding and let α be used as a measure of America's financial weight. Assume that the yields on the bonds in the two countries are

$$r = r^w + (1-\alpha)\theta \tag{10.3}$$
$$r^f = r^w - \alpha\theta \tag{10.4}$$

If capital is perfectly mobile, equation (9.4) will hold so that $r - r^f = \theta$ and the world interest rate will be

$$r^w = \alpha r + (1-\alpha)r^f \tag{10.5}$$

Consistent with the above assumptions, demand functions for the national currencies can be defined. Let β be the dollar share of the world money and let β be a function of the expected change in the exchange rate, θ, and relative incomes:

$$\beta = \beta(\theta, y/y^f)$$

Then,

$$M^D = \beta(M^w)^D \tag{10.6}$$

and

$$e(M^f)^D = (1-\beta)(M^w)^D \tag{10.7}$$

That is, the demands for national currencies are arrived at in two stages. The first stage (equation (10.2)) determines the total world demand for money; the second (equations (10.6) and (10.7)) divides the total demand between the two currencies. If the price of yenmarks is expected to rise, then M^D declines and $(M^f)^D$ increases accordingly so that the total world demand for money remains constant for a given world interest rate. Hence, the effect on β of a change in e may be regarded as a measure of the pure 'currency substitution' between dollars and yenmarks. On the other hand, α does not vary with β because interest rates on bonds adjust to compensate for expected changes in the exchange rate.

There are two ways in which changes in β may affect the national demand for currencies. If there is an anticipation that the American dollar will decrease in value (the price of yenmarks will rise), corporations, and especially commercial banks, with large cash balances will shift some of their holdings from dollars to yenmarks. This effect may, however, not be large.

The second way may be that, if capital is perfectly mobile, there will be a tendency in the bond market for investors to switch from dollar-denominated bonds to yenmark bonds. This will have an immediate effect on interest rates with r rising and r^f falling so that, at this stage, capital may not flow since the profit from arbitrage because of the expected change in the exchange rate is offset by the change in interest rates. The interest rate change leads, however, to a shift by Americans from holding American money to holding American bonds and a shift by foreigners from holding yenmark bonds to holding yenmarks since the opportunity cost of holding money has, for them, fallen. But this shift affects interest rates so that r falls and r^f rises. The equilibrium between r and $r^f + \theta$ is disturbed and interest arbitrage now becomes profitable and capital flows out of America into Gerpan until equilibrium is restored:

$$r = r^f + \theta.$$

The role of the central banks of the two countries in influencing the world money supply can now be examined. The balance sheet of the Gerpan central bank, which is the one that intervenes in the foreign exchange market under an American dollar standard, is

$$M^f \equiv (B^{CB})^f + (K^M)^f/e + (K^B)^f/e \tag{10.8}$$

where $(B^{CB})^f$ is its holdings of Gerpan bonds
$\quad(K^M)^f$ is its holdings of American dollars as exchange reserves
$\quad(K^B)^f$ is its holdings of American bonds as exchange reserves
(Since the exchange rate is fixed, $J = 0$.)
The balance sheet of the American central bank is

$$M \equiv B^{CB} \tag{10.9}$$

Hence, the world's money supply is

$$M^w = M + eM^f = B^{CB} + e(B^{CB})^f + (K^B)^f \tag{10.10}$$

An important influence on the world money supply is the decision of the Gerpan central bank as to how it will hold its American dollar reserves. If when the Gerpan central bank intervenes in the foreign exchange market it purchases American bonds, then (according to equation (10.10) the world's money supply increases, other things remaining the same. If, however, the Gerpan central bank holds American money, there is no change in the world's money supply since the increase in M^f offsets the reduction in public holdings of M.

Should the Gerpan central bank sterilize its intervention in the foreign exchange market? The answer is no, because the intervention is aimed at stabilizing the exchange rate at its pegged level. If there is a tendency for the price of yenmarks to fall, then what is required to restore equilibrium in the foreign exchange market at the pegged rate is either an increase in the rate of interest to attract capital into Gerpan or a decrease in the price of goods of Gerpan to reduce imports and/or increase exports. In the short run to keep the exchange rate at the pegged level, the Gerpan central bank will sell dollars, thereby reducing the Gerpan money supply. This will have the desired effects on the Gerpan interest rate and the Gerpan price level. Sterilization would prevent the Gerpan money supply from changing and this would prevent the adjustment mechanism from working. Hence, the Gerpan money supply becomes an endogenous variable. Moreover, nonsterilization means that flights from one currency to another will not affect the total world money supply.

If the Gerpan money supply is endogenous, what is the role for monetary policy in Gerpan and America? If the hypothesis is accepted that it is the *world* money supply and demand that are the relevant variables, then it is the influence of each country on the world money supply that is the indicator of its discretionary monetary policy. The world money supply, as equation (10.10) shows, depends on the domestic components of the monetary base: $(B^{CB})^f$ and B^{CB}. To maintain a constant price level and thereby avoid inflation, the world money supply should grow at the same rate as the world demand for money (see equation (10.2)). America and Gerpan should therefore cooperate so that there is a coordinated expansion by each central bank of its domestic asset base that matches each country's share in the world money supply to satisfy the world demand for money at a stable price level. Nonsterilization of foreign exchange market intervention by the central banks means that currency substitution by economic agents will not affect the world money supply.

The alternative is a cleanly floating exchange rate system in which central banks do not intervene in the foreign exchange market and the exchange rate moves freely in response to disturbances. Such a policy implies, however, that the demand for each national currency is stable. As McKinnon (1982, p. 332) points out, governments in open economies find that they cannot risk prolonged upward or downward movements in the external prices of their currency because of (1) the possibility of a cumulative currency substitution, or (2) the effects on the domestic economy of major exchange-rate movements. For a country with a fiat currency, the direct stabilization of its international purchasing power in the short run may be viewed as an important step in stabilizing its domestic purchasing power in the long run.

10.4 INTERVENTION IN THE FOREIGN EXCHANGE MARKET

10.4.1 Sterilized v. nonsterilized intervention

To see the difference in the effects of sterilized and nonsterilized intervention in the foreign exchange market by the central bank and to examine optimal policy for such intervention, the model described by equations (9.17) and (9.18) can be used.[7] To simplify the analysis, assume that the foreign interest rate remains constant. Let the domestic interest rate and the foreign exchange rate be endogenous variables and the central bank's purchases of bonds and foreign exchange be exogenous variables. The total stock of bonds outstanding remains unchanged so that B^T is constant.

Nonsterilized purchases of foreign exchange by the central bank lead to an increase in the money supply and result in the short run in a decrease in the domestic interest rate and an increase in the price of a unit of foreign currency (see Appendix 10.1 for the algebra). If the intervention is sterilized, then the money supply remains constant and the domestic interest rate does not fall. Thus, the increase in the price of a unit of foreign currency is smaller when intervention is sterilized than when it is not sterilized. If economic policy requires an increase in the exchange rate to offset a shock, it may be, therefore, that nonsterilized intervention achieves the result with a smaller amount of intervention in the foreign exchange market, provided the effect of the induced change in the money supply is not adverse.

It should be noted that if the domestic and foreign bonds are regarded by households as perfect substitutes, sterilized intervention will not be possible. If the central bank tries to sell domestic bonds, households will reduce their demand for foreign bonds and cause the price of a unit of foreign currency to fall. This will nullify the effect on the exchange rate of the central bank's intervention in the foreign exchange market. Hence, nonsterilized intervention must then be used. The increase in the money supply brought about by the central bank's purchases of foreign exchange will be necessary to achieve a rise in the price of a unit of foreign currency.

Consider now the optimal policy to be followed, given the model, of an exogenously generated increase in the demand of households for financial assets. Total wealth will be assumed not to have changed, so that an increase in demand for a particular asset must be accompanied by an equivalent decrease in the total demand for the other assets. Two cases are considered in which there is an increase in the demand for (1) domestic money and (2) the domestic bond. It is assumed that there is an offsetting decrease in the demand for the foreign bond.

As demonstrated in Appendix 10.1, an exogenous addition to the demand for the domestic bond will decrease the domestic rate of interest and lower the price of a unit of foreign currency, while an exogenous increase in the demand for money will raise the domestic interest rate and lower the price of a unit of foreign currency. Consider now the appropriate policy to stabilize the exchange rate when there is an increase in the demand for domestic money and a decrease in the demand for the foreign bond. Since an increase in the demand for money will lead, in the short run, to a decrease in the price of a unit of foreign currency, the appropriate policy to stabilize the exchange rate will be the one that has the larger exchange-rate effect. Thus, nonsterilized purchases of foreign exchange by the central bank may be the preferable policy to offset the shock. An important consideration is that nonsterilized intervention increases the money supply and thus accommodates the increased demand for money. Moreover, the increase in the money supply will, in the short run, tend to reduce the interest rate, thereby offsetting the rise in the interest rate which otherwise would have resulted from the increase in the demand for money.

In contrast, consider an increase in the demand for the domestic bond and a decrease in the demand for the foreign bond. The decrease in the demand for the foreign bond leads to a fall in the price of a unit of foreign currency. It might appear that nonsterilized intervention is appropriate since the exchange-rate effect is larger than that of sterilized intervention. To restore equilibrium, however, the increased demand for the foreign bond must be accommodated by central bank sales of domestic bonds in the open market at the same time that it is purchasing foreign currency. The result is sterilized intervention. Since the increased demand for the foreign bond will be satisfied, there is no long-term effect on the interest rate.

10.4.2 Stationary-state equilibrium

The counterparts of the IS–LM curves for stationary-state equilibrium are curves in (R, A) space which describe the conditions which will simultaneously produce equilibrium in the bond market and equate the demand and supply of money. In addition, the conditions for zero saving must be satisfied. Equations (9.29)–(9.31) describe these conditions. To simplify the analysis, assume that R^f and B^T are constant.

$$b(R, R^f, A) = B^T - B^{CB} \tag{9.29}$$
$$m(R, R^f, A) = B^{CB} + eK - J \tag{9.30}$$
$$s(R, R^f, Z, A) = 0 \tag{9.31}$$

Denote the combinations of (R, A) which will produce equilibrium in the domestic bond market as the DD curve. Similarly, MM and SS curves may be defined for equilibrium between the demand and supply of money and the requirement that saving be zero. The slopes of these curves are derived in Appendix 10.1. The slope of the DD curve is negative, while the slopes of the MM and SS curves are positive. Figure 10.1 shows these curves.

Figure 10.2 shows the effects of nonsterilized and sterilized intervention on these curves. Point 1 is the initial equilibrium and point 2 is the final equilibrium. The immediate effects of an intervention in the foreign exchange market in the form of purchases of foreign exchange, as shown in Fig. 10.2a, are an

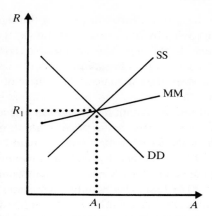

Fig. 10.1 Stationary-state equilibrium

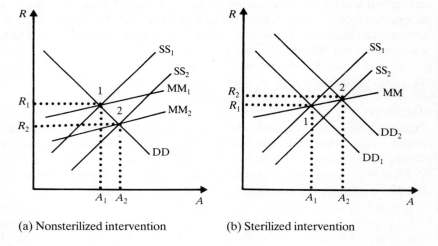

(a) Nonsterilized intervention   (b) Sterilized intervention

Fig. 10.2 Sterilized and nonsterilized intervention

increase in the price of a unit of foreign currency and an increase in the money supply. The MM curve shifts downward to the right from MM_1 to MM_2 because a decrease in the rate of interest is now required to increase the demand for money by a corresponding amount and to restore equilibrium. Because of the increase in e, eF increases leading to an increase in A. Hence, the demand for the domestic bond increases. A fall in R reduces the demand for the domestic bond and there is a movement down the DD curve to point 2, which is the new equilibrium point since there are no further shifts in the MM or DD curves. For there to be general equilibrium, the SS curve must shift down to pass through point 2. The two factors that lead to dissaving by households, relative to the saving at point 1, are the increase in A and the fall in R. Thus, households consume more and income rises until saving again equals zero at the higher level of wealth. There is a permanent increase in disposable income and the price of a unit of foreign currency.

Figure 10.2b shows the effects of sterilized intervention. The impact effects of the purchase of foreign exchange are an increase in the price of a unit of foreign currency and an increase in the quantity of domestic bonds held by households. The DD curve shifts from DD_1 to DD_2 because an increase in the rate of interest is now required to bring the demand for bonds into equilibrium with the increased supply. Total wealth (A) increases as a result of the increase in eF and this leads to an increased demand for money. There is a movement along the MM curve to point 2 and the rise in the rate of interest offsets the increase in the demand for money attributable to the increase in wealth, and equilibrium is restored. There are no further shifts in the DD or MM curves so that point 2 is the new long-run equilibrium position. The SS curve shifts downward to the right to SS_2. There is dissaving relative to the original equilibrium position since the effect of the increase in wealth dominates the effect of the increase in the rate of interest. Consumption and income rise until saving again equals zero at the new level of wealth. Disposable income and the price of a unit of foreign currency are both permanently higher in the new equilibrium position.

Consider now the effect of a shift of household demand from the foreign bond to the domestic bond. The central bank must intervene and buy foreign exchange to maintain the exchange rate at its pegged level. The effects depend on whether or not the intervention is sterilized. With nonsterilized intervention, the money supply increases and the MM curve shifts downward to the right as in Fig. 10.3. The increased demand for the domestic bond shifts the DD curve downward to the left. The new equilibrium will be at point 2 with the same level of A since there has only been a shift in the composition of assets and no change in the exchange rate. Again the SS curve must shift downward to the right to pass through point 2. Consumption and income rise to restore saving to zero at the lower level of the interest rate. In the case of sterilized intervention, the DD curve shifts upwards to the right, thereby offsetting the original downward shift so that the DD, MM, and SS curves all are in the original position in long-run equilibrium. That is, the increased demand for the domestic bond has been satisfied by increasing the supply of the domestic bond and equilibrium is restored with no side effects. Sterilized intervention is clearly preferable in this case.

Consider now the effect of a shift in household demand from the foreign bond to domestic money. The central bank must buy foreign currency to main-

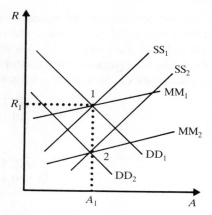

Fig. 10.3 Shift from foreign to domestic bond

tain the pegged exchange rate. In this case nonsterilized intervention is preferable because the increased demand for money is thereby satisfied by the induced increase in the money supply resulting from the central bank's purchase of foreign exchange. There are no side effects.

10.5 FURTHER READING

R.C. Bryant (1980) and Dornbusch and Fischer (1986) are general discussions of economic policy in an open economy. Kenen (1982) presents an analysis of central bank intervention. Feldstein (1986) discusses governments budget deficits and exchange rate movements. McKinnon (1982) presents a model of the demand and supply of money in the world economy and its implications for domestic monetary policy. Frenkel and Razin (1987) discuss fiscal policy in an open economy.

APPENDIX 10.1 INTERVENTION IN THE FOREIGN EXCHANGE MARKET

Sterilized v. nonsterilized intervention

The model is equations (9.42) and (9.43):

$$b_R dR + b_Q dR^f + b_A F de = dB^T - dB^{CB}$$
$$m_R dR + m_Q dR^f + m_A F de = dB^{CB} + e dK$$

To simplify the analysis, assume that the foreign interest rate remains constant so that $dR^f = 0$. Let the domestic interest rate and the foreign exchange rate be endogenous variables and the central bank's purchases of bonds and foreign exchange to be exogenous variables. The total stock of bonds outstanding remains unchanged so that $dB^T = 0$. The equations can then be rewritten:

$$b_R dR + b_A Fde = -dB^{CB} \qquad (10.11)$$
$$m_R dR + m_A Fde = dB^{CB} + edK \qquad (10.12)$$

Then,

$$dR = 1/H\{(-m_A - b_A)dB^{CB} - b_A edK\} \qquad (10.13)$$
$$de = 1/FH\{(b_R + m_R)dB^{CB} + b_R edK\} \qquad (10.14)$$

where $H = (b_R m_A - b_A m_R) > 0$

Nonsterilized intervention in the foreign exchange market means that $dB^{CB} = 0$. Hence,

$$\partial R/\partial K = (e/H)(-b_A) < 0, \qquad \partial e/\partial K = (e/FH)b_R > 0$$

If the intervention is sterilized, then $dB^{CB} = -edK$

$$\partial e/\partial B^{CB} = (1/FH)(b_R + m_R)$$

Since $b_R + m_R = -f_R$, $\partial e/\partial B^{CB} > 0$

The net effect of sterilized intervention is

$$\partial e/\partial K - \partial e/\partial B^{CB} = (1/FH)(eb_R + f_R)$$

If $eb_R > |f_R|$, $de > 0$.

Increased demand for a financial asset

The model is augmented to include 'shift variables' to represent exogenous changes in demand. Let $d\bar{B}$ and $d\bar{M}$ be exogenous additions to the demand for the domestic bond and domestic money, respectively. The equations of the model are now

$$b_R dR + b_A Fde + d\bar{B} = -dB^{CB} \qquad (10.15)$$
$$m_R dR + m_A Fde + d\bar{M} = dB^{CB} + edK \qquad (10.16)$$

The effects of an increase in the demand for the domestic bond or for money are:

$$\partial r/\partial \bar{B} = -m_A/FH < 0, \; \partial e/\partial \bar{B} = m_R/H < 0$$
$$\partial R/\partial \bar{M} = b_A/FH > 0, \; \partial e/\partial \bar{M} = -b_R/H < 0$$

Slopes of the DD, MM and SS curves

For a stationary-state equilibrium, the equations defining the DD, MM and SS curves are:

$$b(R, R^f, A) = B^T - B^{CB} \tag{9.29}$$
$$m(R, R^f, A) = B^{CB} + eK - J \tag{9.30}$$
$$s(R, R^f, Z, A) = 0 \tag{9.31}$$

Assume that B^T is constant so that $dB^T = 0$. The total differentials of the three equations are then:

$$b_R dR + b_Q dR^f + b_A dA = -dB^{CB} \tag{10.17}$$
$$m_R dR + m_Q dR^f + m_A dA = dB^{CB} + edK \tag{10.18}$$
$$S_R dR + S_Q dR^f + S_Z dZ + S_A dA = 0 \tag{10.19}$$

The slopes of the DD, MM and SS curves are:

DD: $\partial R/\partial A = -(b_A/b_R) < 0$
MM: $\partial R/\partial A = -(m_A/m_R) > 0$
SS: $\partial R/\partial A = -(s_A/s_R) > 0$

If $|s_A/s_R| > |m_A/m_R|$, the SS curve will be steeper than the MM curve.

NOTES

1. See Feldstein (1986) for an elaboration of the argument on which this section is based.
2. The effect of the deficit on interest rates was reinforced by the deflationary policy followed from 1979 onward by the US central bank's reduction of the rate of growth of the money supply which caused an increase in real interest rates.
3. As pointed out by Hutchison and Pigott (1987, p. 140).
4. Dornbusch (1987, pp. 14–15) discusses this point.
5. See Friedman (1953, pp. 157–203) or Johnson (1972b, pp. 198–222) for an advocacy of flexible exchange rates.
6. McKinnon (1982) has made this analysis and the model in this section is taken from McKinnon's analysis, which builds on an earlier study by Swoboda (1978).
7. See Kenen (1982) for an analysis upon which this section is based.

REFERENCES AND SELECT BIBLIOGRAPHY

Akerlof, G., and J. Yellen (1985), 'A near rational model of the business cycle with wage and price inertia,' *Quarterly Journal of Economics*, **100**, Supplement, 832–8.

Alogoskoufis, G.S. (1987), 'Aggregate employment and intertemporal substitution,' *Economic Journal*, **97**, 403–15.

Allen, P.A., and P.B. Kenen (1980), *Asset Markets, Exchange Rates, and Economic Integration: A Synthesis*. New York: Cambridge University Press.

Allen, P.A., and P.B. Kenen (1983), *Asset Markets and Exchange Rates: Modelling an Open Economy*. New York: Cambridge University Press. A shorter version of Allen and Kenen (1980) which omits the chapters on economic integration.

Allen, R.G.D. (1959), *Mathematical Economics*. London: Macmillan.

Andersen, T.M. (1987), 'Effective demand, differential information and the multiplier,' *Economic Journal*, **97**, 353–71.

Ando, A.K. (1974), 'Some aspects of stabilization policies, the monetarist controversy, and the MPS model' in L.R. Klein and Edwin Burmeister (eds), *Econometric Performance: Comparative Simulation Studies of the U.S. Economy*. Philadelphia: University of Pennsylvania Press.

Arndt, S.W., and J.D. Richardson (eds) (1987), *Real-Financial Linkages among Open Economies*. Cambridge, MA: The MIT Press.

Arrow, K.J. (1978), 'The future and the present in economic life,' *Economic Inquiry*, **16**, 157–69.

Aschauer, D.A. (1988), 'The equilibrium approach to fiscal policy,' *Journal of Money, Credit and Banking*, **20**, 41–62.

Atkinson, A.B. (1969), 'The time scale of economic models; how long is the long run?' *Review of Economic Studies*, **36**, 136–52

Azariadis, C. (1975), 'Implicit contracts and underemployment equilibria,' *Journal of Political Economy*, **83**, 1183–202.

Azariadis, C. (1979), 'Implicit contracts and related topics: a survey' in Z. Hornstein *et al.* (eds), *The Economics of the Labour Market*. London: Her Majesty's Stationery Office.

Azariadis, C., and J.E. Stiglitz (1983), 'Implicit contracts and fixed price equilibria,' *Quarterly Journal of Economics*, **98**, Supplement, 1–22.

Baily, M.N. (1974), 'Wages and employment under certain demands,' *Review of Economic Studies*, **41**, 37–50.

Barro, R.J. (1974), 'Are government bonds net worth?' *Journal of Political Economy*, **82**, 1095–117. Reprinted in Barro (1981, pp. 243–65).

Barro, R.J. (1979), 'Second thoughts on Keynesian Economics,' *American Economic Review*, Papers and Proceedings, **69**, 54–68.

Barro, R.J. (1981), *Money, Expectations and Business Cycles: Essays in Macroeconomics*. New York: Academic Press.

Barro, R.J. (1986), 'Comment' in *NBER Macroeconomics Annual 1986*. Cambridge, MA: The MIT Press, pp. 135–9.

Barro, R.J., and S. Fischer (1976), 'Recent developments in monetary theory,' *Journal of Monetary Economics*, **6**, 257–67.

Barro, R.J., and D.B. Gordon (1983), 'A positive theory of monetary policy in a natural rate model,' *Journal of Political Economy*, **91**, 589–610.

Begg, D.K.H. (1982), *The Rational Expectations Revolution in Macroeconomics*. Baltimore: The Johns Hopkins University Press.

Bell, D., and I. Kristol (1981), *The Crisis in Economic Theory*. New York: Basic Books.

Benassy, J.-P. (1982), *The Economics of Market Disequilibrium*. New York: Academic Press.

Benassy, J.-P. (1986), *Macroeconomics: An Introduction to the Non-Walrasian Approach*. New York: Academic Press.

Bernheim, B.D. (1987), 'Ricardian equivalence: an evaluation of theory and evidence' in *NBER Macroeconomics Annual 1987*. Cambridge, MA: The MIT Press, pp. 263–304.

Bhandari, J.S., and B.H. Putnam (eds) (1983), *Economic Interdependence and Flexible Exchange Rates*. Cambridge, MA: The MIT Press.

Blanchard, O.J. (1988), 'Why does money affect output? a survey' in Friedman and Hahn (1988).

Blaug, M. (1976), 'Kuhn versus Lakatos *or* Paradigms versus research programmes in the history of economics' in Latsis (1976a, pp. 149–80).

Blaug, M. (1980), *The Methodology of Economics*. Cambridge: Cambridge University Press.

Blaug, M. (1985), *Economic Theory in Retrospect*. Fourth edition. Cambridge: Cambridge University Press.

Blinder, A.S. (1979), *Economic Policy and the Great Stagflation*. New York: Academic Press.

Blinder, A.S. (1980), 'Inventories in the Keynesian macro model,' *Kyklos*, **33**, 585–614.

Blinder, A.S. (1982), 'Inventories and sticky prices: more on the microfoundations of macroeconomics,' *American Economic Review*, **72**, 334–48.

Blinder, A.S. (1987a), 'Keynes, Lucas and scientific progress,' *American Economic Review*, Papers and Proceedings, **77**, 130–6.

Blinder, A.S. (1987b), 'Credit rationing and effective supply failures,' *Economic Journal*, **97**, 327–52.

Blinder, A.S., and S. Fischer (1981), 'Inventories, rational expectations, and the business cycle,' *Journal of Monetary Economics*, **8**, 277–304.

Blinder, A.S., and R.M. Solow (1973), 'Does fiscal policy matter?' *Journal of Public Economics*, **2**, 319–37.

Blinder, A.S., and R.M. Solow (1974), 'Analytical foundations of fiscal policy' in A.S. Blinder *et al.*, *The Economics of Public Finance*. Washington: The Brookings Institution, pp. 3–115.

Blinder, A.S., and J.E. Stiglitz (1983), 'Money credit constraints and economic activity,' *American Economic Review*, **73**, 297–302.

Boland, L.A. (1985), 'The foundation of Keynes' methodology: *The General Theory*', in Lawson and Pesaran (1985, pp. 181–94).

Branson, W.H., and D.W. Henderson (1985), 'The specification and influence of asset markets' in Jones and Kenen (1985, Ch. 15).

Brems, H. (1986), *Pioneering Economic Theory, 1630–1980*. Baltimore: The Johns Hopkins University Press.

Brock, W.A. (1975), 'A simple perfect foresight monetary model,' *Journal of Monetary Economics*, **1**, 133–50.

Bryant, J. (1983), 'A simple rational expectations Keynes-type model,' *Quarterly Journal of Economics*, **98**, 525–8.

Bryant, R.C. (1980), *Money and Monetary Policy in Interdependent Nations*. Washington: The Brookings Institution.

Butkiewicz, J.L., et al. (eds) (1986), *Keynes' Economic Legacy*. New York: Praeger.

Cagan, P. (1956), 'The monetary dynamics of hyperinflation' in Friedman (1956, pp. 25–117).

Cagan, P. (1979), *Persistent Inflation: Historical and Policy Essays*. New York: Columbia University Press.

Caravale, G. (1987), 'The Neo-Keynesian school: some internal controversies,' *Atlantic Economic Journal*, **15**, 1–15.

Carlton, D.W. (1986), 'The rigidity of prices,' *American Economic Review*, **76**, 637–58.

Carlton, D.W. (1987), 'The theory and the facts of how markets clear: is industrial organization valuable for understanding macroeconomics?' in R. Schmalensee and R. Willig (eds), *Handbook of Industrial Organization*. Amsterdam: North-Holland.

Casson, M. (1981), *Unemployment: A Disequilibrium Approach*. Oxford: Martin Robertson.

Chiang, A.C. (1984), *Fundamental Mathematics of Economics*. Fourth edition. New York: McGraw-Hill.

Chick, V. (1973), *The Theory of Monetary Policy*. London: Gray-Mills Publishing Ltd.

Chick, V. (1983), *Macroeconomics after Keynes: A Reconsideration of the General Theory*. Oxford: Philip Allan.

Chick, V. (1985), 'Time and the wage-unit in the method of *The General Theory*: history and equilibrium' in Lawson and Pesaran (1985, pp. 195–208).

Clower, R.W.: see Walker (1984).

Coats, A.W. (1976), 'Economics and psychology: the death and resurrection of a research programme' in Latsis (1976a, pp. 43–64).

Coddington, A. (1976), 'Keynesian economics: the search for first principles,' *Journal of Economic Literature*, **14**, 1258–73.

Coddington, A. (1982), 'Deficient foresight: a troublesome theme in Keynesian economics,' *American Economic Review*, **72**, 480–7.

Coddington, A. (1983), *Keynesian Economics: The Search for First Principles*. London: Allen & Unwin.

Coutts, K., W. Godley and W. Nordhaus (1978), *Industrial Pricing in the United Kingdom*. Cambridge: Cambridge University Press.

Cuddington, J.T., P.-O. Johansson and K.-G. Lofgren (1984), *Disequilibrium Macroeconomics in Open Economies*. Oxford: Basil Blackwell.

Cukierman, A. (1984), *Inflation, Stagflation, and Imperfect Information*. New York: Cambridge University Press.

Cuthbertson, K., and M.P. Taylor (1987), *Macroeconomic Systems*. Oxford: Basil Blackwell.

Darby, M.R. (1976), *Macro-economics: The Theory of Income, Employment, and the Price Level*. New York: McGraw-Hill.

Darity, W.W., Jr., and A.F. Cottrell (1987), 'Meade's *General Theory* model: a geometric reprise,' *Journal of Money, Credit and Banking*, **19**, 210–21.

Davidson, P. (1981), 'Post Keynesian Economics' in Bell and Kristol (1981, pp. 151–73).

Deane, P. (1978), *The Evolution of Economic Ideas*. Cambridge: Cambridge University Press.

Desai, M. (1981), *Testing Monetarism*. London: Frances Pinter Publishers.

Dillard, D. (1948), *The Economics of John Maynard Keynes*. New York: Prentice-Hall.

Dixit, A.K. (1976), *Optimization in Economic Theory*. Oxford: Oxford University Press.

Dornbusch, R. (1980), *Open Economy Macroeconomics*. New York: Basic Books.

Dornbusch, R. (1983), 'Exchange rate economics: Where do we stand?' in Bhandari and Putnam (1983, pp. 45–83).

Dornbusch, R. (1987), 'Exchange rate economics 1986,' *Economic Journal*, **97**, 1–18.

Dornbusch, R., and S. Fischer (1986), 'The open economy: implications for monetary and fiscal policy' in R.J. Gordon (ed.), *The American Business Cycle: Continuity and Change*. Chicago: University of Chicago Press, 1986, pp. 459–516.

Dow, A., and S. Dow (1985), 'Animal spirits and rationality' in Lawson and Pesaran (1985, pp. 46–65).

Dow, S.C. (1985), *Macroeconomic Thought: A Methodological Approach*. Oxford: Basil Blackwell.

Dow, S.C., and P.E. Earl (1982), *Money Matters: A Keynesian Approach to Monetary Economics*. Oxford: Martin Robertson.

Drazen, A. (1980), 'Recent developments in macroeconomic disequilibrium theory,' *Econometrica*, **48**, 283–306.

Dunlop, J.T. (1938), 'The movement of real and money wage rates,' *Economic Journal*, **48**, 413–34.

Eichenbaum, M., and K.J. Singleton (1986), 'Do equilibrium real business cycle theories explain postwar U.S. business cycles?' in *NBER Macroeconomics Annual 1986*. Cambridge, MA: The MIT Press, pp. 91–135.

Feiwel, G.R. (1975), *The Intellectual Capital of Michal Kalecki: A Study in Economic Theory and Policy*. Knoxville, TN: University of Tennessee Press.

Felderer, B., and S. Homburg (1987), *Macroeconomics and New Macroeconomics*. New York: Springer-Verlag.

Feldstein, M.S. (1986), 'The budget deficit and the dollar' in *NBER Macroeconomics Annual 1986*. Cambridge, MA: The MIT Press, pp. 355–92.

Fender, J. (1981), *Understanding Keynes: An Analysis of the 'General Theory'*. Brighton, Sussex: Wheatsheaf Books.

Fine, B., and A. Murfin (1984), *Macroeconomics and Monopoly Capitalism*. Brighton, Sussex: Wheatsheaf Books.

Fischer, S. (1977), 'Long-term contracts, rational expectations, and the optimal money supply rule,' *Journal of Political Economy*, **85**, 191–206.

Fischer, S. (ed.) (1980), *Rational Expectations and Economic Policy*. Chicago: University of Chicago Press.

Fischer, S. (1988), 'Recent developments in macroeconomics,' *Economic Journal*, **98**, 294–339.

Fitoussi, J.-P. (ed.) (1983), *Modern Macroeconomic Theory*. Oxford: Basil Blackwell.

Fletcher, G.A. (1987), *The Keynesian Revolution and its Critics*. London and Basingstoke: Macmillan.

Floyd, J.E. (1985), *World Monetary Equilibrium: International Monetary Theory in an Historical Institutional Context*. Oxford: Philip Allan.

Frank, J. (1986), *The New Keynesian Economics: Unemployment, Search and Contracting*. Brighton, Sussex: Wheatsheaf Books.

Frankel, J.A. (1979), 'On the mark: a theory of floating exchange rates based on real interest differentials,' *American Economic Review*, **69**, 610–22.

Frankel, J.A. (1983), 'Monetary and portfolio-balance models of exchange rate determination' in Bhandari and Putnam (1983, pp. 84–115).

Frankel, J.A., and R. Meese (1987), 'Are exchange rates excessively variable?' in *NBER Macroeconomics Annual 1987*. Cambridge, MA: The MIT Press, pp. 117–53.

Frenkel, J.A. (ed.) (1983), *Exchange Rates and International Macroeconomics*. Chicago: University of Chicago Press.

Frenkel, J.A., and M.L. Mussa (1985), 'Asset markets, exchange rates, and the balance of payments' in Jones and Kenen (1985, Ch. 14).

Frenkel, J.A., and A. Razin (1987), *Fiscal Policies and the World Economy*. Cambridge, MA: The MIT Press.

Friedman, B.M., and F.H. Hahn (eds) (1988), *Handbook of Monetary Economics*. Amsterdam: North-Holland.

Friedman, M. (1949), 'The Marshallian demand curve,' *Journal of Political Economy*, **57**, 463–95; reprinted in Friedman (1953, pp. 47–99).

Friedman, M. (1953), *Essays in Positive Economics*. Chicago: University of Chicago Press.

Friedman, M. (ed.) (1956), *Studies in the Quantity Theory of Money*. Chicago: University of Chicago Press.

Friedman, M. (1957), *A Theory of the Consumption Function*. Princeton: Princeton University Press.

Friedman, M. (1968), 'The role of monetary policy,' *American Economic Review*, **58**, 1–17.

Friedman, M. (1971), *A Theoretical Framework for Monetary Analysis*. New York: National Bureau of Economic Research. A Symposium on Friedman's *Theoretical Framework* is in the *Journal of Political Economy*, **80** (1972), 837–950.

Friedman, M. (1977), 'Nobel lecture: inflation and unemployment,' *Journal of Political Economy*, **85**, 451–72.

Frisch, H. (1983), *Theories of Inflation*. Cambridge: Cambridge University Press.

Frisch, R. (1933), 'Propagation problems and impulse problems in dynamic economics' in *Economic Essays in Honour of Gustav Cassel*. London, pp. 171–205.

Frydman, R. (1981), 'Sluggish price adjustments and the effectiveness of monetary policy under rational expectations,' *Journal of Money, Credit and Banking*, **13**, 94–102.

Frydman, R., and E.S. Phelps (1983), *Individual Forecasting and Aggregate Outcomes: 'Rational Expectations' Examined*. Cambridge: Cambridge University Press.

Geanakoplos, J.D., and H.M. Polemarchakis (1986), 'Walrasian indeterminacy and Keynesian macroeconomics,' *Review of Economic Studies*, **53**, 755–80.

Gilbert, J.C. (1982), *Keynes's Impact on Monetary Economics*. London: Butterworth.

Glaister, S. (1978), *Mathematical Methods for Economists*. Revised edition. Oxford: Basil Blackwell.

Gordon, D.F. (1974), 'A neo-classical theory of Keynesian unemployment,' *Economic Inquiry*, **12**, 431–59.

Gordon, R.J. (1981), 'Output fluctuations and gradual price adjustment,' *Journal of Economic Literature*, **19**, 493–530.

Gordon, R.J. (1983), 'A century of evidence on wage and price stickiness in the United States, the United Kingdom, and Japan' in Tobin (1983b).

Gram, H., and V. Walsh (1983), 'Joan Robinson's economics in retrospect,' *Journal of Economic Literature*, **21**, 518–50.

Grandmont, J.-M. (1985), 'On endogenous competitive business cycles,' *Econometrica*, **53**, 995–1046.

Grauwe, P. De (1983), *Macroeconomic Theory for the Open Economy*. Aldershot, Hampshire: Gower Publishing Company.

Greenwald, B., and J.E. Stiglitz (1986a), 'Externalities in economies with imperfect information and incomplete markets,' *Quarterly Journal of Economics*, **101**, 227–646.

Greenwald, B., and J.E. Stiglitz (1986b), 'Money, imperfect information, and economic fluctuations' in *Symposium on Monetary Theory*. Taiwan: The Institute of Economics, Academia Sinica.

Greenwald, B. and J.E. Stiglitz (1986c), 'Information, finance constraints and business fluctuations' in *Symposium on Monetary Theory*. Taiwan: The Institute of Economics, Academia Sinica.

Greenwald, B. and J.E. Stiglitz (1987a), 'Keynesian, New Keynesian and New Classical Economics,' *Oxford Economic Papers*, **39**, 119–32.

Greenwald, B. and J.E. Stiglitz (1987b), 'Imperfect information, credit markets and unemployment,' *European Economic Review*, **31**, 444–56.

Greenwald, B., J.E. Stiglitz, and A.M. Weiss (1984), 'Informational imperfections and macroeconomic fluctuations,' *American Economic Review*, Papers and Proceedings, **74**, 194–99.

Haberler, G. (1937), *Prosperity and Depression*. Geneva: League of Nations.

Hacking, I. (ed.) (1981a), *Scientific Revolutions*. Oxford: Oxford University Press.

Hacking, I. (1981b), 'Lakatos's philosophy of science' in Hacking (1981a, pp. 128–43).

Hahn, F.H. (1973), *On the Notion of Equilibrium in Economics*. Cambridge: Cambridge University Press.

Hahn, F.H. (1977), 'Keynesian economics and general equilibrium theory: reflections on some current debates' in Harcourt (1977, pp. 25–40).

Hahn, F.H. (1978), 'On non-Walrasian equilibrium,' *Review of Economic Studies*, **45**, 1–17.

Hahn, F.H. (1983a), *Money and Inflation*. Cambridge, MA: The MIT Press.

Hahn, F.H. (1983b), 'Comment' in Frydman and Phelps (1983, pp. 223–30).

Hahn, F.H. (1984), *Equilibrium and Macroeconomics*. Oxford: Basil Blackwell.

Hahn, F.H. (1985), *Money, Growth and Stability*. Oxford: Basil Blackwell.

Hahn, F.H. (1987), 'On involuntary unemployment,' *Economic Journal*, **97**, Supplement, 1–16.

Hall, R.E. (1986), 'Market structure and macroeconomic fluctuations,' *Brookings Papers on Economic Activity*, 1986, no. 2, 285–338.

Hall, R.L., and C.J. Hitch (1939), 'Price theory and business behaviour,' *Oxford Economic Papers*, 12–45.

Ham, J. (1986), 'Testing whether unemployment represents intertemporal labour supply substitution,' *Review of Economic Studies*, **53**, 559–78.

Hamilton, J.D. (1983), 'Oil and the macroeconomy since World War II,' *Journal of Political Economy*, **91**, 228–48.

Hansen, A.H. (1953), *A Guide to Keynes*. New York: McGraw-Hill.

Harcourt, G.C. (ed.) (1977), *The Microeconomic Foundations of Macroeconomics*. London and Basingstoke: Macmillan.

Harcourt, G.C. (ed.) (1985), *Keynes and his Contemporaries*. London and Basingstoke: Macmillan.

Harris, S.E. (1947), *The New Economics: Keynes' Influence on Theory and Public Policy*. New York: Alfred Knopf.

Harris, S.E. (1955), *John Maynard Keynes: Economist and Policy Maker*. New York: Scribners.

Harrod, R.F. (1951), *The Life of John Maynard Keynes*. London: Macmillan.

Hegeland, H. (1951), *The Quantity Theory of Money*. Goteborg: Elanders Boktryckeri Aktiebolag.

Hempel, C.G (1965), *Aspects of Scientific Explanation and Other Essays in the Philosophy of Science*. New York: The Free Press.

Hicks, (Sir) J. (1937), 'Mr. Keynes and the Classics; a suggested interpretation,' *Econometrica*, **5**, 147–59; reprinted in American Economic Association, *Readings in the Theory of Income Distribution*. Philadelphia: Blakiston, 1946, pp. 461–76.

Hicks, (Sir) J. (1946) *Value and Capital*. Second edition. Oxford: Oxford University Press.

Hicks, (Sir) J. (1950), *A Contribution to the Theory of the Trade Cycle*. Oxford: Oxford University Press.

Hicks, (Sir) J. (1959), *A Revision of Demand Theory*. Reprinted with corrections. Oxford: Oxford University Press.

Hicks, (Sir) J. (1965), *Capital and Growth*. Oxford: Oxford University Press.

Hicks, (Sir) J. (1974) *The Crisis in Keynesian Economics*. Oxford: Basil Blackwell.

Hicks, (Sir) J. (1976), '"Revolutions" in economics' in Latsis (1976a, pp. 207–18).

Hicks, (Sir) J. (1979), *Causality in Economics*. Oxford: Basil Blackwell.

Hicks, (Sir) J. (1985), *Methods of Dynamic Economics*. Oxford: Oxford University Press.

Hillier, B. (1986), *Macroeconomic Models, Debates and Developments*. Oxford: Basil Blackwell.

Hodgson, G. (1985), 'Persuasion, expectations and the limits to Keynes' in Lawson and Pesaran (1985, pp. 10–45).

Howitt, P. (1986), 'Innis lecture: the Keynesian recovery,' *Canadian Journal of Economics*, **19**, 626–41.

Hutchison, M.M., and C.A. Pigott (1987), 'Real and financial linkages in the macroeconomic response to budget deficits: an empirical investigation' in Arndt and Richardson (1987, pp. 139–66).

Hutchison, T.W. (1976), 'On the history and philosophy of science and economics' in Latsis (1976a, pp. 181–206).

Hutchison, T.W. (1977a), *Keynes v. the 'Keynesians'. . .?* London: The Institute for Economic Affairs.

Hutchison, T.W. (1977b), *Knowledge and Ignorance in Economics*. Oxford: Basil Blackwell.

Hutchison, T.W. (1978), *On Revolutions and Progress in Economic Knowledge*. Cambridge: Cambridge University Press.

Hutchison, T.W. (1981), *The Politics and Philosophy of Economics: Marxians, Keynesians and Austrians*. Cambridge: Cambridge University Press.

Jevons, W.S. (1892), *The Principles of Science: A Treatise on Logic and Scientific Method*. Second edition with corrections. London: Macmillan.

Jevons, W.S. (1970), *The Theory of Political Economy*, edited by R.D.C. Black. Hardmondsworth, England: Penguin Books.

Johnson, E.S., and H.G. Johnson (eds) (1978), *The Shadow of Keynes*. Oxford: Basil Blackwell.

Johnson, H.G. (1962), *Money, Trade and Economic Growth*. London: Allen & Unwin.

Johnson, H.G. (1972a), *Macroeconomics and Monetary Theory*. Chicago: Aldine Publishing Co.

Johnson, H.G. (1972b), *Further Essays in Monetary Economics*. London: Allen and Unwin.

Johnson, H.G. (1975), *On Economics and Society*. Chicago: University of Chicago Press.

Jones, R.W., and P.B. Kenen (eds) (1985), *Handbook of International Economics*, vol. 2. Amsterdam: North-Holland.

Kahn, R.F. (Lord) (1931), 'The relation of home investment to unemployment,' *Economic Journal*, **41**, 173–98.

Kahn, R.F. (Lord) (1978), 'Some aspects of the development of Keynes's thought,' *Journal of Economic Literature*, **16**, 545–59.

Kahn, R.F. (Lord) (1984), *The Making of Keynes's General Theory*. Cambridge: Cambridge University Press.

Kaldor, N. (Lord) (1972), 'The irrelevance of equilibrium economics,' *Economic Journal*, **82**, 1237–55.

Kaldor, N. (Lord) (1983), 'Keynesian economics after fifty years' in Worswick and Trevithick (1983, pp. 1–28).

Kalecki, M. (1935), 'A macrodynamic theory of business cycles,' *Econometrica*, **3**, 327–44.

Kalecki, M. (1938), 'The determinants of distribution of the national income,' *Econometrica*, **6**, 97–112.

Kantor, B. (1979), 'Rational expectations and economic thought,' *Journal of Economic Literature*, **17**, 1422–41.

Katz, L.F. (1986), 'Efficiency wage theories: a partial evaluation' in *NBER Macroeconomics Annual 1986*. Cambridge, MA: The MIT Press, pp. 235–75.

Kenen, P.B. (1982), 'Effects of intervention and sterilization in the short run and the long run' in R.N. Cooper *et al.* (eds), *The International Monetary System under Flexible Exchange Rates*. Cambridge, MA: Ballinger Publishing Co.

Kenen, P.B. (1985), 'Macroeconomic theory and policy: How the closed economy was opened' in Jones and Kenen (1985, Ch. 13).

Keynes, J.M. (Lord) (1921), *A Treatise on Probability*; reprinted in *The Collected Writings of John Maynard Keynes*, vol. VIII. London and Basingstoke: Macmillan, and New York: Cambridge University Press (1973).

Keynes, J.M. (Lord) (1923), *A Tract on Monetary Reform*; reprinted in the *The Collected Writings of John Maynard Keynes*, vol. IV. London and Basingstoke: Macmillan, and New York: Cambridge University Press (1973).

Keynes, J.M. (Lord) (1926), 'The end of *laissez-faire*'; reprinted in *The Collected Writings of John Maynard Keynes*, vol. IX. London and Basingstoke: Macmillan, and New York: Cambridge University Press (1972), pp. 272–94.

Keynes, J.M. (Lord) (1929), 'Can Lloyd George Do It?'; reprinted in *The Collected Writings of John Maynard Keynes*, vol. IX. London and Basingstoke: Macmillan, and New York: Cambridge University Press (1972), pp. 86–125.

Keynes, J.M. (Lord) (1930), *A Treatise on Money*. London and Basingstoke: Macmillan; reprinted in *The Collected Writings of John Maynard Keynes*, vols V and VI. London and Basingstoke: Macmillan, and New York: Cambridge University Press (1973).

Keynes, J.M. (Lord) (1936), *General Theory of Employment, Interest and Money*. London and Basingstoke: Macmillan; reprinted in *The Collected Writings of John Maynard Keynes*, vol. VII. London and Basingstoke: Macmillan, and New York: Cambridge University Press (1973).

Keynes, J.M. (Lord) (1937a), 'The general theory of employment,' *Quarterly Journal of Economics*, **51**, 209–23; reprinted in *The Collected Writings of John Maynard Keynes*, vol. XIV. London and Basingstoke: Macmillan, and New York: Cambridge University Press (1973), pp. 109–23.

Keynes, J.M. (Lord) (1937b), Keynes's 1937 lecture notes; reprinted in *The Collected Writings of John Maynard Keynes*, vol. XIV. London and Basingstoke: Macmillan, and New York: Cambridge University Press (1973), pp. 179–83.

Keynes, J.M. (Lord) (1937c), Letter to R.F. Kahn, 20 October 1937; reprinted in *The*

Collected Writings of John Maynard Keynes, vol. XIV. London and Basingstoke: Macmillan, and New York: Cambridge University Press (1973), p. 259.

Keynes, J.M. (Lord) (1938), Letters on economic models to Roy Harrod, 4 and 16 July 1938; reprinted in *The Collected Writings of John Maynard Keynes*, vol. XIV. London and Basingstoke: Macmillan, and New York: Cambridge University Press (1973), pp. 295–301.

Keynes, J.M. (Lord) (1939a), Preface to the French edition of *The General Theory*; reprinted in *The Collected Writings of John Maynard Keynes*, vol. VII. London and Basingstoke: Macmillan, and New York: Cambridge University Press (1973), pp. xxxi–xxxv.

Keynes, J.M. (Lord) (1939b), 'Relative movements in real wages and output,' *Economic Journal*, **49**, 34–51; reprinted in *The Collected Writings of John Maynard Keynes*, vol. VII. London and Basingstoke: Macmillan, and New York: Cambridge University Press (1973), pp. 394–412.

Keynes, J.M. (Lord) (1944), Letter on the Pigou effect to Michal Kalecki, 8 March 1944; reproduced in Patinkin (1982, p. 103).

Keynes, J.M. (Lord) (1972), *Essays in Persuasion*, vol. IX of *The Collected Writings of John Maynard Keynes*. London and Basingstoke: Macmillan, and New York: Cambridge University Press.

King, R.G., and C.I. Plosser (1984), 'Money, credit, and prices in a real business cycle,' *American Economic Review*, **74**, 363–80.

Klamer, A. (1984), *The New Classical Macroeconomics: Conversations with the New Classical Economists and their Opponents*. Brighton: Sussex: Wheatsheaf Books.

Klein, L.R. (1966), *The Keynesian Revolution*. Second edition. New York: Macmillan.

Knight, F.H. (1921), *Risk, Uncertainty and Profit*. Boston: Houghton and Mifflin.

Kogiku, K.G. (1968), *An Introduction to Macroeconomic Models*. New York: McGraw-Hill.

Kouri, P.J.K. (1983), 'Balance of payments and the foreign exchange market: a dynamic partial equilibrium model' in Bhandari and Putnam (1983, pp. 116–56).

Kregel, J.A. (1976), 'Economic methodology in the face of uncertainty: the modelling methods of Keynes and the Post-Keynesians,' *Economic Journal*, **86**, 209–25.

Kregel, J.A. (1983), 'The microfoundations of the "generalization" of *The General Theory* and "bastard Keynesism": Keynes's theory of employment in the long and the short period,' *Cambridge Journal of Economics*, **7**, 343–61.

Krueger, A.O. (1983), *Exchange-Rate Determination*. Cambridge: Cambridge University Press.

Kuh, E. (1967), 'A productivity theory of wage levels – an alternative to the Phillips curve,' *Review of Economic Studies*, **34**, 333–60.

Kuhn, T.S. (1970), *The Structure of Scientific Revolution*. Second edition. Chicago: University of Chicago Press.

Kydland, F.E., and E.C. Prescott (1982), 'Time to build and aggregate fluctuations,' *Econometrica*, **50**, 1345–70.

Laidler, D. (1981), 'Monetarism: an interpretation and assessment,' *Economic Journal*, **91**, 1–28.

Lakatos, I. (1970), 'Falsification and the methodology of scientific research programmes' in I. Lakatos and A. Musgrave, *Criticism and the Growth of Knowledge*. Cambridge: Cambridge University Press, pp. 91–196; reprinted in Lakatos (1978a, pp. 8–101).

Lakatos, I. (1978a), *The Methodology of Scientific Research Programmes*, edited by J. Worrall and G. Currie. Cambridge: Cambridge University Press.

Lakatos, I. (1978b), *Mathematics, Science and Epistemology*, edited by J. Worrall and G. Currie. Cambridge University Press.

Lange, O. (1942), 'Say's Law: a restatement and criticism' in Lange *et al.* (eds) (1942), *Studies in Mathematical Economics and Econometrics*. Chicago: University of Chicago Press, pp. 49–68.

Lange, O. (1944), *Price Flexibility and Employment*. Bloomington, IN: Principia Press.

Latsis, S.J. (ed. (1976a), *Method and Appraisal in Economics*. Cambridge: Cambridge University Press.

Latsis, S.J. (1976b), 'A research programme in economics' in Latsis (1976a, pp. 1–42).

Lavington, F. (1922), *The Trade Cycle*. London: P.S. King & Son.

Lawson, T. (1985a), 'Keynes, prediction, and econometrics' in Lawson and Pesaran (1985, pp. 116–33).

Lawson, T. (1985b), 'Uncertainty and economic analysis,' *Economic Journal*, 95, 909–27.

Lawson, T., and H. Pesaran (eds) (1985), *Keynes' Economics: Methodological Issues*. Beckenham, Kent: Croom Helm.

Leijonhufvud, A. (1968), *On Keynesian Economics and the Economics of Keynes*. London: Oxford University Press.

Leijonhufvud, A. (1976), 'Schools, "revolutions" and research programmes in economics' in Latsis (1976a, pp. 65–108).

Leijonhufvud, A. (1981), *Information and Coordination: Essays in Macroeconomic Theory*. New York: Oxford University Press.

Leijonhufvud, A. (1983), 'Keynesianism, monetarism, and rational expectations: some reflections and conjectures' in Frydman and Phelps (1983, pp. 203–23).

Lindley, D.V. (1987), 'The probability approach to the treatment of uncertainty in artificial intelligence and expert systems,' *Statistical Science*, 2, 17–24.

Lipsey, R. (1960), 'The relation between unemployment and the rate of change of money wage rates in the United Kingdom, 1862–1957: a further analysis,' *Economica*, NS 27, 1–31.

Lipsey, R. (1981), 'The understanding and control of inflation: is there a crisis in macroeconomics?' *Canadian Journal of Economics*, 14, 545–77.

Long, J.B., Jr., and C.I. Plosser, 'Real business cycles,' *Journal of Political Economy*, 91, 39–69.

Lovell, M.C. (1986), 'Tests of the rational expectations hypothesis,' *American Economic Review*, 76, 110–24.

Lucas, R.J., Jr. (1981), *Studies in Business-Cycle Theory*. Cambridge, MA: The MIT Press.

Lucas, R.J., Jr. (1987), *Models of Business Cycles*. Oxford: Basil Blackwell.

Lucas, R.J., Jr., and T.J. Sargent (1981), 'After Keynesian macroeconomics' in Lucas and Sargent (eds) (1981), *Rational Expectations and Econometric Practice*. Minneapolis: University of Minnesota Press, pp. 295–320.

Lucas, R.J., Jr. and N.L. Stokey (1983), 'Optimal fiscal and monetary policy in an economy without capital,' *Journal of Monetary Economics*, 10, 335–60.

Lucas, R.J., Jr. and N.L. Stokey (1987), 'Money and interest in a cash-in-advance society,' *Econometrica*, 55, 491–514.

McCallum, B.T. (1979), 'The current state of the policy-ineffectiveness debate,' *American Economic Review*, 69, 240–5.

McCallum, B.T. (1980a), 'The significance of rational expectations theory,' *Challenge*, Jan.–Feb., pp. 37–43.

McCallum, B.T. (1980b), 'Rational expectations and macroeconomic stabilization policy: an overview,' *Journal of Money, Credit and Banking*, 12, 716–46.

McCallum, B.T. (1983), 'The liquidity trap and the Pigou effect: a dynamic analysis with rational expectations,' *Economica*, **50**, 395–405.

McCallum, B.T. (1986), 'On "real" and "sticky-price" theories of the business cycle,' *Journal of Money, Credit and Banking*, **18**, 397–414.

McCallum, B.T. (1987), 'The development of Keynesian macroeconomics,' *American Economic Review*, Papers and Proceedings, **77**, 125–29.

McCallum, B.T. (1988), 'Inflation: theory and evidence' in Friedman and Hahn (1988).

Macdonald, R. (1988), *Floating Exchange Rates: Theories and Evidence*. London: Unwin Hyman.

McKinnon, R.I. (1979), *Money in International Exchange: The Convertible Currency System*. New York: Oxford University Press.

McKinnon, R.I. (1981), 'The exchange rate and macroeconomic policy: changing postwar perceptions,' *Journal of Economic Literature*, **19**, 531–58.

McKinnon, R.I. (1982), 'Currency substitution and instability in the world dollar standard,' *American Economic Review*, **72**, 320–33.

Malinvaud, E. (1984), *Mass Unemployment*. Oxford: Basil Blackwell.

Malinvaud, E. (1985), *The Theory of Unemployment Reconsidered*. Second edition. Oxford: Basil Blackwell.

Malkiel, B.G. (1981), *A Random Walk Down Wall Street*. Second edition. New York: W.W. Norton and Company.

Mankiw, N.G. (1985), 'Small menu costs and large business cycles: a macroeconomic model of monopoly,' *Quarterly Journal of Economics*, **100**, 225–53.

Mankiw, N.G. (1987), 'Comment' in *NBER Macroeconomics Annual 1987*. Cambridge, MA: The MIT Press, pp. 105–10.

Mankiw, N.G., J. Rotemberg and L. Summers (1985), 'Intertemporal substitution in macroeconomics,' *Quarterly Journal of Economics*, **100**, 529–39.

Marshall, A. (1920), *Principles of Economics*. Eighth edition. London and Basingstoke: Macmillan.

Marshall, A. (1926), *Official Papers*. London and Basingstoke: Macmillan.

Mayer, T., *et al.* (1978), *The Structure of Monetarism*. New York: Norton.

Meade, J.E. (1937), 'A simplified model of Mr. Keynes' system,' *Review of Economic Studies*, **4**, 98–107; reprinted in Harris (1947, pp. 606–18).

Meade, J.E. (1965), *The Stationary State*. London: Allen and Unwin.

Meltzer, A.H. (1981), 'On Keynes's *General Theory*: a different perspective,' *Journal of Economic Literature*, **19**, 34–64.

Meltzer, A.H. (1983), 'On Keynes and Monetarism,' in Worswick and Trevithick (1983, pp. 49–72).

Milgate, M. (1982), *Capital and Employment: A Study of Keynesian Economics*. New York: Academic Press.

Miller, M.H., and F. Modigliani (1959), 'The cost of capital, corporation finance, and the theory of investment,' *American Economic Review*, **49**, 655–69.

Minford, P. (1987), 'Comment' in *NBER Macroeconomics Annual 1987*. Cambridge, MA: The MIT Press, pp. 157–60.

Minford, P., and D. Peel (1983), *Rational Expectations and the New Macroeconomics*. Oxford: Martin Robertson.

Minsky, H.P. (1975), *John Maynard Keynes*. New York: Columbia University Press.

Mints, L.W. (1950), *Monetary Policy for a Competitive Society*. New York: McGraw-Hill.

Mises, L. von (1978), *The Ultimate Foundation of Economic Science*. Second edition. Kansas City: Shed Andrews and McMeel, Inc.

Modigliani, F. (1944), 'Liquidity preference and the theory of interest and money,' *Econometrica*, **12**, 45–88; reprinted in American Economic Association (1951), *Readings in Monetary Theory*. Philadelphia: Blakiston, pp. 186–240.

Modigliani, F. (1986), *The Debate over Stabilization Policy*. Cambridge: Cambridge University Press.

Modigliani, F., and A. Ando (1976), 'Impacts of fiscal actions on aggregate income and the monetarist controversy' in Stein (1976a, pp. 17–42).

Moggridge, D.E. (1976), *Keynes*. Glasgow: Collins/Fontana.

Montiel, P. (1986), 'Long-run equilibrium in a Keynesian model of a small open economy,' *International Monetary Fund Staff Papers*, **33**, 28–59.

Morishima, M. (1977), *Walras' Economics: A Pure Theory of Capital and Money*. Cambridge: Cambridge University Press.

Morishima, M. (1984), *The Economics of Industrial Society*. Cambridge: Cambridge University Press.

Moss, S. (1984), *Markets and Macroeconomics*. Oxford: Basil Blackwell.

Muellbauer, J., and R. Portes (1978), 'Macroeconomic models with quantity rationing,' *Economic Journal*, **88**, 788–821.

Muth, J.F. (1961), 'Rational expectations and the theory of price movements,' *Econometrica*, **29**, 1–23.

Neary, J.P., and J.E. Stiglitz (1983), 'Towards a reconstruction of Keynesian economics: expectations and constrained equilibria,' *Quarterly Journal of Economics*, **98**, Supplement, 199–228.

Neary, J.P., and J.E. Stiglitz (1987), 'Wage rigidity, implicit contracts, unemployment and economic efficiency,' *Economic Journal*, **97**, 416–30.

Negishi, T., *Microeconomic Foundations of Keynesian Economics*. Amsterdam: North-Holland.

Nelson, C.R., and C.I. Plosser (1982), 'Trends and random walks in macroeconomic time series,' *Journal of Monetary Economics*, **10**, 139–62.

Newbury, D.M., and J.E. Stiglitz (1987), 'Wage rigidity, implicit contracts and economic efficiency,' *Economic Journal*, **97**, 416–30.

Niehans, J. (1978), *The Theory of Money*. Baltimore: The Johns Hopkins University Press.

Niehans, J. (1987), 'Classical monetary theory, new and old,' *Journal of Money, Credit and Banking*, **19**, 409–24.

Nordhaus, W.D. (1972), 'Recent developments in price dynamics' in Board of Governors of the Federal Reserve System, *The Econometrics of Price Determination*. Washington, DC.

O'Driscoll, G.P. (1977), *Economics as a Coordination Problem: The Contributions of Friedrich A. Hayek*. Kansas City: Shed Andrews and McMeel, Inc.

Okun, A.M. (1981), *Prices and Quantities: A Macroeconomic Analysis*. Washington: The Brookings Institution.

Parkin, M. (1986), 'The output–inflation tradeoff when prices are costly to change,' *Journal of Political Economy*, **94**, 200–24.

Pasinetti, L.L (1983), 'Comment' in Worswick and Trevithick (1983, pp. 205–11).

Patinkin, D. (1948), 'Price flexibility and full employment,' *American Economic Review*, **38**, 543–64; reprinted with modifications in American Economic Association (1951), *Readings in Monetary Theory*. Philadelphia: Blakiston, pp. 252–83.

Patinkin, D. (1965), *Money, Interest, and Prices*. Second edition. New York: Harper and Row.

Patinkin, D. (1976), *Keynes' Monetary Thought: A Study of its Development*. Durham, NC: Duke University Press.

Patinkin, D. (1981), *Essays On and In the Chicago Tradition*. Durham, NC: Duke University Press.

Patinkin, D. (1982), *Anticipations of the General Theory? and Other Essays on Keynes*. Chicago: University of Chicago Press.

Patinkin, D., and J.C. Leith (eds) (1977), *Keynes, Cambridge and the General Theory*. London and Basingstoke: Macmillan.

Pesaran, H., and R. Smith (1985), 'Keynes on econometrics' in Lawson and Pesaran (1985, pp. 134–50).

Phelps, E. (1967), 'Phillips curves, expectations of inflation, and optimal unemployment over time,' *Economica*, NS **34**, 254–81.

Phelps, E., *et al.* (1970), *Microeconomic Foundations of Employment and Inflation Theory*. New York: W.W. Norton and Company.

Phillips, A.W. (1958), 'The relation between unemployment and the rate of change of money wage rates in the United Kingdom, 1861–1957,' *Economica*, NS **25**, 99–113.

Pigou, A.C. (1913), *Unemployment*. London: Williams and Norgate.

Pigou, A.C. (1917), 'The value of money,' *Quarterly Journal of Economics*, **32**, 38–65.

Pigou, A.C. (1929), *Industrial Fluctuations*. Second edition. London and Basingstoke: Macmillan.

Pigou, A.C. (1933), *The Theory of Unemployment*. London and Basingstoke: Macmillan.

Pigou, A.C. (1935), *Economics in Practice: Six Lectures on Current Issues*. London and Basingstoke: Macmillan.

Pigou, A.C. (1943), 'The classical stationary state,' *Economic Journal*, **53**, 343–51.

Pigou, A.C. (1945), *Lapses from Full Employment*. London and Basingstoke: Macmillan.

Pigou, A.C. (1947), 'Economic progress in a stable environment,' *Economica*, NS **14**, 180–8.

Pigou, A.C. (1949), *Employment and Equilibrium: A Theoretical Discussion*. Second edition. London and Basingstoke: Macmillan.

Pigou, A.C. (1950), *Keynes's General Theory: A Retrospective View*. London and Basingstoke: Macmillan.

Pigou, A.C. (1953), *Alfred Marshall and Current Thought*. London and Basingstoke: Macmillan.

Popper, (Sir) K. (1965), *Conjectures and Refutations: The Growth of Scientific Knowledge*. Second edition. New York: Basic Books.

Popper, (Sir) K. (1968), *The Logic of Scientific Discovery*. Second edition. New York: Harper Torchbooks.

Prachowny, M.F.J. (1984), *Macroeconomic Analysis for Small Open Economies*. Oxford: Clarendon Press.

Prachowny, M.F.J. (1986), *Money in the Macroeconomy*. New York: Cambridge University Press.

Presley, J.R. (1979), *Robertsonian Economics*. London and Basingstoke: Macmillan.

Reder, M.W. (1982), 'Chicago economics: permanence and change,' *Journal of Economic Literature*, **20**, 1–38.

Ricardo, D. (1951), *On the Principles of Political Economy and Taxation*, edited by P. Sraffa and M.H. Dobb. Cambridge: Cambridge University Press.

Robinson, J. (1933), *The Economics of Imperfect Competition*. London and Basingstoke: Macmillan.

Robinson, J. (1979), 'Garegnani on effective demand,' *Cambridge Journal of Economics*, **3**, 179–80.

Rosen, S. (1985), 'Implicit contracts: a survey,' *Journal of Economic Literature*, **23**, 1144–75.

Rotemberg, J. (1982), 'Monopolistic price adjustment and aggregate demand,' *Review of Economic Studies*, **44**, 517–31.

Rotemberg, J. (1987), 'The new Keynesian microfoundations,' in *NBER Macroeconomics Annual 1987*. Cambridge, MA: The MIT Press, pp. 69–105.

Rowe, N. (1987), 'An extreme Keynesian macro-economic model with formal microeconomic foundations,' *Canadian Journal of Economics*, **20**, 306–20.

Samuelson, P.A. (1947), *Foundations of Economic Analysis*. Cambridge, MA: Harvard University Press.

Santomero, A.M., and J.J. Seater (1978), 'The inflation–unemployment trade-off: a critique of the literature,' *Journal of Economic Literature*, **16**, 499–544.

Sargent, T.J. (1986), *Rational Expectations and Inflation*. New York: Harper & Row.

Sargent, T.J. (1987a), *Macroeconomic Theory*. Second edition. New York: Academic Press.

Sargent, T.J. (1987b), *Dynamic Macroeconomic Theory*. Cambridge, MA: Harvard University Press.

Sargent, T.J., and C.A. Sims (1977), 'Business cycle modeling without pretending to have too much a priori economic theory' in Federal Reserve Bank of Minneapolis, *New Methods of Business Cycle Research: Proceedings from a Conference*. Minneapolis: Federal Reserve Bank of Minneapolis, pp. 45–109.

Sawyer, J.A. (1975), *Macroeconomics: Theory and Policy in the Canadian Economy*. Toronto: Macmillan of Canada.

Sawyer, M.C. (1982), *Macro-Economics in Question: The Keynesian–Monetarist Orthodoxies and the Kaleckian Alternative*. Brighton, Sussex: Wheatsheaf Books.

Say, J.-B. (1964), *A Treatise on Political Economy or the Production, Distribution and Consumption of Wealth*. Translated by C.R. Prinsep. Reprinted, New York: A.M. Kelley.

Scherer, F.M. (1970), *Industrial Pricing: Theory and Evidence*. Chicago: Rand-McNally and Co.

Schumpeter, J.A. (1954), *History of Economic Analysis*. New York: Oxford University Press.

Shackle, G.L.S. (1973), 'Keynes and today's establishment in economic theory,' *Journal of Economic Literature*, **11**, 516–19.

Shackle, G.L.S. (1974), *Keynesian Kaleidics*. Edinburgh: Edinburgh University Press.

Shapiro, C., and J.E. Stiglitz (1984), 'Equilibrium unemployment as a worker discipline device,' *American Economic Review*, **74**, 433–44.

Shapiro, N. (1978), 'Keynes and equilibrium economics,' *Australian Economic Papers*, **17**, 207–23.

Sheffrin, S.M. (1983), *Rational Expectations*. Cambridge: Cambridge University Press.

Shiller, R.J. (1980), 'Can the Fed control real interest rates' in Fischer (1980, pp. 117–67).

Simon, H.A. (1956), 'Dynamic programming under uncertainty with a quadratic criterion function,' *Econometrica*, **24**, 534–44.

Sims, C. (1980), 'Macroeconomics and reality,' *Econometrica*, **48**, 1–48.

Sinclair, P. (1987), *Unemployment: Economic Theory and Evidence*. Oxford: Basil Blackwell.

Slutzky, E. (1937), 'The summation of random causes as the source of cyclical processes,' *Econometrica*, , **5**, 105–46.

Smith, A. (1937), *An Inquiry into the Nature and Causes of the Wealth of Nations*, edited by E. Cannan. New York: The Modern Library.

Smithies, A. (1947), 'Effective demand and employment' in Harris (1947, pp. 558–71).

Solow, R.M. (1979), 'Alternative approaches to macroeconomic theory: a partial view,' *Canadian Journal of Economics*. **12**, 339–54.

Solow, R.M. (1980), 'On theories of unemployment,' *American Economic Review*. **70**, 1–10.

Sowell, T. (1972), *Say's Law: An Historical Analysis*. Princeton: Princeton University Press.

Sowell, T. (1974), *Classical Economics Reconsidered*. Princeton: Princeton University Press.

Spiegel, H.W. (1983), *The Growth of Economic Thought*. Revised edition. Durham, NC: Duke University Press.

Stein, J.L. (ed.) (1976a), *Monetarism*. Amsterdam: North-Holland.

Stein, J.L. (1976b), 'Inside the monetarist black box' in Stein (1976a, pp. 183–232).

Stein, J.L. (1982), *Monetarist, Keynesian and New Classical Economics*. Oxford: Basil Blackwell.

Stigler, G.J. (1957), 'Perfect competition, historically contemplated,' *Journal of Political Economy*, **65**; reprinted in Stigler (1965), *Essays in the History of Economics*. Chicago: University of Chicago Press, pp. 234–67.

Stiglitz, J.E. (1984), 'Price rigidities and market structure,' *American Economic Review*, Papers and Proceedings, **74**, 350–6.

Stiglitz, J.E. (1985a), 'Information and economic analysis: a perspective,' *Economic Journal*, **95**, Supplement, 21–41.

Stiglitz, J.E. (1985b), 'Credit markets and the control of capital,' *Journal of Money, Credit and Banking*, **17**, 133–52.

Stiglitz, J.E. (1986), 'Theories of wage rigidity,' in Butkiewicz *et al*. (1986, pp. 153–206).

Stiglitz, J.E. (1987), 'The causes and consequences of the dependence of quality on price,' *Journal of Economic Literature*, **25**, 1–48.

Stiglitz, J.E., and A.M. Weiss (1981), 'Credit rationing in markets with imperfect information,' *American Economic Review*, **71**, 393–410.

Stiglitz, J.E., and A.M. Weiss (1987), 'Macro-economic equilibrium and credit rationing,' National Bureau of Economic Research Working Paper No. 2164. Cambridge, MA.

Stockman, A.C. (1987), 'Some interactions between goods markets and asset markets in open economies' in Arndt and Richardson (1987, pp. 33–44).

Suppes, P. (1984), *Probabilistic Metaphysics*. Oxford: Basil Blackwell.

Swoboda, A. (1978), 'Gold, dollars, EuroDollars, and the world money stock under fixed exchange rates,' *American Economic Review*, **68**, 625–42.

Tarshis, L. (1939), 'Changes in real and money wages,' *Economic Journal*, **49**, 150–4.

Taylor, J.B. (1980), 'Aggregate dynamics and staggered contracts,' *Journal of Political Economy*, **88**, 1–23.

Taylor, J.B. (1982), 'The role of expectations in the choice of monetary policy, in *Monetary Policy Issues in the 1980s*. A symposium sponsored by the Federal Reserve Bank of Kansas City.

Thirlwall, A.P. (1982), *Keynes as a Policy Adviser*. London and Basingstoke: Macmillan.

Timbrell, M. (1985), *Mathematics for Economists*. Oxford: Basil Blackwell.

Timlin, M.F. (1942), *Keynesian Economics*. Toronto: University of Toronto Press.

Tobin, J. (1947), 'Money wage rates and employment' in Harris (1947, pp. 572–87).

Tobin, J. (1977), 'How dead is Keynes?' *Economic Inquiry*, **16**, 459–68.

Tobin, J. (1980), *Asset Accumulation and Economic Activity*. Chicago: University of Chicago Press.

Tobin, J. (1981), 'The Monetarist counter-revolution today – an appraisal,' *Economic Journal*, **91**, 29–42.

Tobin, J. (1982), *Essays in Economics: Theory and Policy*. Cambridge, MA: The MIT Press.

Tobin, J. (1983a), 'Comment' in Worswick and Trevithick (1983, pp. 28–37).

Tobin, J. (ed.) (1983b), *Macroeconomics, Prices and Quantities*. Washington: The Brookings Institution.

Tobin, J., and W.C. Brainard (1977), 'Asset markets and the cost of capital'; reprinted in Tobin (1982, pp. 46–73).

Tobin, J., and W. Buiter (1976), 'Long-run effects of fiscal and monetary policy on aggregate demand' in Stein (1976a, pp. 273–319).

Tobin, J., and W. Buiter (1980), 'Fiscal and monetary policies, capital formation, and economic activity'; reprinted in Tobin (1982, pp. 181–259).

Turnovsky, S.J. (1977), *Macroeconomic Analysis and Stabilization Policy*. New York: Cambridge University Press.

Vicarelli, F. (1985), *Keynes' Relevance Today*. Philadelphia: University of Pennsylvania Press.

Walker, D.A. (ed.) (1984), *Money and Markets: Essays by Robert W. Clower*. New York: Cambridge University Press.

Walras, L. (1954), *Elements of Pure Economics*. Translated by W. Jaffe. London: Allen and Unwin.

Weintraub, E.R. (1975), '"Uncertainty" and the Keynesian Revolution,' *History of Political Economy*, **7**, 530–48.

Weintraub, E.R. (1979), *Microfoundations*. New York: Cambridge University Press.

Weintraub, E.R. (1982), *Mathematics for Economists: An Integrated Approach*. New York: Cambridge University Press.

Weintraub, E.R. (1985), *General Equilibrium Analysis: Studies in Appraisal*. New York: Cambridge University Press.

Weitzman, M.L. (1982), 'Increasing returns and foundations of unemployment theory,' *Economic Journal*, **92**, 787–804.

West, K.D. (1988), 'On the interpretation of new random-walk behavior in GNP,' *American Economic Review*, **78**, 202–9.

Wicksell, K. (1936), *Interest and Prices*. Translated by R.F. Kahn. London and Basingstoke: Macmillan.

Williamson, J. (1985), *The Exchange Rate System*. Second edition. Washington: Institute for International Economics.

Williamson, J. (1987), 'A FEER for the Canadian Dollar' in P. Wonnacott (1987), *The United States and Canada: The Quest for Free Trade*. Washington: Institute for International Economics.

Wood, J.C. (1983), *John Maynard Keynes: Critical Assessments*, vols I–IV. Beckenham, Kent: Croom Helm.

Worswick, D., and J. Trevithick (eds) (1983), *Keynes and the Modern World*. Cambridge: Cambridge University Press.

Wren-Lewis, S. (1985), 'Expectations in Keynesian econometric models' in Lawson and Pesaran (1985, pp. 66–79).

Yellen, J.L. (1984), 'Efficiency wage models of unemployment,' *American Economic Review*, Papers and Proceedings, **74**, 200–5.

Zarnowitz, V. (1985), 'Recent work on business cycles in historical perspective: a review of theories and evidence,' *Journal of Economic Literature*, **23**, 523–80.

Zellner, A. (1984), *Basic Issues in Econometrics*. Chicago: University of Chicago Press.

AUTHOR INDEX*

*(Excluding names in 'References and
Select Bibliography')

SUBJECT INDEX